THE NEW
MORNINGSIDE PAPERS

PETER GZOWSKI

M&S

McClelland and Stewart
The Canadian Publishers
481 University Avenue
Toronto, Ontario
M5G 2E9

Canadian Cataloguing in Publication Data

Gzowski, Peter
  The new Morningside papers

Commentary on and correspondence to the CBC radio program Morningside.
Includes index.
ISBN 0-7710-3745-7

1. Morningside (Radio program). I. Morningside (Radio program). II. Title.

PN1991.3.C3G97 1987   791.44'72   C87-094234-4

Illustrations by James Wardell
Book design by Linda Gustafson
Printed and bound in Canada by Webcom Ltd

Contents

A clue to figuring out who wrote what

The system we designed for the original *Morningside Papers* has been refined a bit for this second collection, but the principles behind it remain the same. Once again, in other words, we have tried to make a book to peruse, to dip in and out of, to use as the literary equivalent of the radio program on which it's based, rather than one to read right through, like a novel – although, of course, there is nothing to prevent you from doing that if you wish. To make browsing easier (who wants to do serious detective work in the bathroom?), there are a couple of important symbols. A ✎ means the words that follow are by me, the host, either a piece I've written or an editorial guide – as, for instance, in the collection of light verse that's called "What Starts with A and Ends With a Double-Dactyl?" A ✉ announces the beginning of a letter from somebody else. Signatures are at the end of each letter. There are some variations, as, for instance, when a chapter is all the work of one person. But I think they're self-explanatory. Anyway, as I said the first time, don't worry; it's simpler than it sounds.

A note to (and about) my fellow authors

Some of the most pleasant moments in the preparation of these volumes occur when I open the replies to my requests for permission to print what appears in them. As with the first edition, though, there are a few people who, in spite of my best efforts, I have been unable to reach. I have once again taken the liberty of including their work anyway. I would rather, as I said the first time, risk their annoyance at that than their disappointment at having been left out.

And a bouquet of dedication

This one's for Gill, who hears the replays every night.

Introduction

Glen Allen, a shy and courtly writer who has worked at almost as many places as I have over the years, and who spent the second of the two seasons this book represents as a *Morningside* producer, has a gift for metaphors from the kingdom of nature. He once described his own peripatetic career, for instance, as that of a "hum-ming-bird sipping from different orchards." And one day towards the end of his tenure as a producer, when he was trying to put his finger on the aspect of *Morningside* that had most impressed him as a journalist, he turned again to God's creatures for an anal-ogy. "At *Morningside*," he said, "the little fish get eaten by the bigger fish that get eaten by the . . . you know what I mean. What starts as a minnow often ends up as a whale. I've never seen any-thing like it."

Neither have I, and, Glen Allen's single season at the program being my fifth as its host, I've experienced the phenomenon he was describing a lot longer than he has.

Morningside, as most Canadians know by now – about a million of them listen every week and many more seem to keep in touch – is a daily three hours of what radio programmers call a magazine format, which runs from approximately 9:00 A.M. (*very* approxi-mately in Newfoundland) to noon every weekday on the CBC's AM English network. Along with the much zippier and more topical *As It Happens* and the more documentary and tightly edited *Sunday Morning*, it forms the heart of what many people claim (albeit with-out always knowing the details of the competition) is the finest radio service in the world. *Morningside* is unique. It is not, that is to say, a Canadian interpretation of someone else's idea, as, for instance, the estimable *fifth estate* is simply an edition of *60 Minutes* with all the *eh*s left in, or *Maclean's*, as it is currently constituted, is simply *Newsweek* with Allan Fotheringham on the back page. It's just something a bunch of Canadians have figured out how to do for other Canadians. Or, better, are still figuring out, for, like all living organisms, *Morningside* is constantly changing and renewing itself, learning from its misadventures, expanding – occasionally to the point of exhausting them – from its successes. In the five years I've been its host, for example (the actor Don Harron preceded me for five years, setting a very different tone), we have invented the three-person weekly panel of political punditry, seen it picked up by everyone else from *Canada AM* to the supper-hour show in Halifax, and after our original wise men were skimmed off to join the government or the diplomatic corps or to return to active politics, have been struggling to keep it alive. (*Canada AM*'s, I happened to notice after our season ended, is working not too badly.) We have instituted, alone in the media, I think, such devices as the two-person regional report – sort of stereophonic letters from home – and weekly panel discussions of such diverse subjects as business, the arts, and the work place. Under the guidance of our literary producer, Hal Wake, we have become, I think it is agreed, the single most important forum for the discussion and promulgation of Canadian writing. We have established beach-heads on the topic we have labelled War and Peace – there is a chapter in this book about how we did that, by the producer who ran it, Richard Handler – and, led by yet another producer, Talin Vartanian, on the continuing existence of intolerable poverty in this comfortable land.

Not all our experiments, as I say, have been successful. A regular discussion of women's concerns collapsed after a few months from our failure to find a focus; we have not yet found a way satisfactorily to reflect Canada's mixture of racial origins and mother tongues; our coverage of native affairs, a breach we tried to step into after the CBC jettisoned its weekly *Our Native Land*, has been too sporadic. But we are working on those shortcomings, and others. That's part of our personality. And at the heart of that personality, I think, is the characteristic Glen Allen was trying to define with his analogy from the ocean.

In radio terms, that phenomenon means this: an idea, or perhaps just a fact, gets thrown out on *Morningside*, sometimes deliberately, sometimes not. The minnow. Then someone – a bigger fish – responds to it, and more and larger fish join the chase until . . . . Well, a lot of the whales (and some of the minnows) are in this collection of letters: the duke and the fork, as we came to call the correspondence that makes up the first chapter here, in which one naïve question put to a panel of dignitaries grew into a full-fledged search of the personal and historical archives of Canada (who *did* say "keep your fork, Duke, there's pie"?); the series of gripping, personal stories about adoption, which went from one reference on a drama to a couple of letters to three interviews to still more letters and even more interviews (and concluded – if this *was* the conclusion – with a studio link between Ottawa and Sudbury, where a mother talked to the daughter she had given up twenty-two years previously but decided to seek out because of what she'd heard on *Morningside*); the compilation of light verse (the only such anthology I'm aware of, as I say in introducing it, with a plot), which began with an attempt to recreate a rhyming Canadian alphabet and ended with double dactyls in the inter-office mail; and much else, including a series of reports, in the chapter I've called "The Morningside Bestiary," about various fauna that fall from the sky (that started with frogs, as I remember), and, of course and perhaps most notably, the torrent of one-page short stories – there are *three* chapters of them here – that fell from our own skies simply because I read one that had come in the mail one morning and wondered aloud if anyone else wanted to try the same device.

If I can squeeze one more kettleful from Glen's analogy, in fact (and, yes, I know whales are mammals) this whole book is something of a bigger fish, chasing the minnow we published in 1985, *The Morningside Papers*, or, as I'd have called it if I'd known then what I know now, *The Morningside Papers I*. That book elicited mail on its own – the Memorable Meals I've included here, for instance, were written, as you'll see when I introduce them, by people who knew *only* the book and still haven't heard CBC radio. But more than that, its publication changed the program that had engendered it.

The first book, as I trust most readers of this one will recall, was made of three years of mail and musings. I had returned to daily CBC radio in the autumn of 1982. Very shortly after, and with the collaboration of Eve McBride, who had signed on to help me cope with the steadily increasing flow of mail, I began saving some of the letters that seemed particularly moving or, as I said then, just fun to read again, with an eye to putting together a collection for posterity. At the end of the third season we felt ready, and the result was the blue volume with my picture and some of the more imaginative spellings of my name on the cover, which became, to everyone's delight – or if not everyone's, mine and my fellow authors' – one of the best-sellers of that literary season. But the *subsequent* result – and one that no one had foreseen (Glen Allen and his ichthyological explanation not yet being handy) – was that the mail to *Morningside* grew even heavier. If it had consisted, as I wrote in the introduction to the original *Papers*, of "ten or twenty and sometimes thirty or more a day [of] arguments, thank-yous, grievances, corrections, praise, criticism, challenges, jokes, travel notes clippings, invitations and often just hello, how are you doing?," it rose over the two seasons that followed the book's publication to as much as twice that – twenty and forty and sometimes a hundred pieces a day. My own schedule was changed by it. In the first seasons after my return to the daily routine of radio, as I noted in a phrase that people still delight in introducing me with, I had been setting my alarm for 4:44 A.M. ("I rather like the symmetry on my digital clock," I wrote cheerily.) After *The Morningside Papers* became part of the landscape, I found that to be able to continue my habit of reading the mail as the first of my morning chores and still be ready for the opening notes of the theme, at 9:05 Atlantic time (oops, I almost forgot: 9:35 in Newfoundland), I had to set my clock for 4:14, which is neither as symmetrical on the dial nor as easy to be cheery about.

The rise was not instantaneous, and much, I'm sure, could be attributed to another aspect of the little-fish-big-fish theory: the more you get, and the higher it assays for radio, the more you read on the air, and the more you read on the air . . . and so on. But the first book *did* have an effect, if for no other reason than that it signalled how much the mail mattered to us, that *Morningside* was indeed a place that cared about broadcasting the opinions of people who took the trouble to write, a kind of village bulletin board for the nation. In any case, by the end of two seasons after the publication of a book that had taken three to prepare, the files I had been keeping for a sequel were brimming, and you are, gentle reader, holding the result in your hand – bigger than the first book (and because of that, I'm afraid, slightly more expensive), red instead of blue, minus the misspelled names on the cover but plus, I hope, even more of the pleasures, challenges and amusements, not to mention the evidence of flowering literary skills, that were offered the first time round.

In the chapter by Richard Handler that I've called "The Making of War and Peace," Richard claims that I take the mail more seri-ously than I take my producers. Although I'd like to think he's overstating his case, I know what lies behind his thought. "My" producers – if there is any ownership involved in our relationship it is surely they who are stuck with me more than I with them – are, not to put too fine a point on it, wonderful. They work incre-dibly long hours at incredibly difficult tasks. They think up the ideas that fill three hours of radio a day, five days a week, forty weeks a year. They seek out and make preliminary contact with potential guests. They pre-interview all of them, trying to make my apparently spontaneous radio chats as unsurprising to me at least as a crown attorney's cross-examination should be to her. (Lawyers are *told* never to ask a question they don't know the answer to; I am *equipped* not to do so.) They weed out the cranks, the vainglorious, and the hopelessly earnest, and replace them with people from their apparently inexhaustible supply of the delightfully eccentric, the fluidly articulate, and the intellectually expressive. They arrange studios, taxis, fees – no one at *Morningside* is ever paid enough – and phone and radio links, and orchestrate a daily parade of guests and panels that must run smoothly from the open-ing theme to the closing drama. Then, when it's over, I get the honorary degrees, the ACTRA awards – well, not the ACTRA awards, which seem destined for other mantelpieces – and the Order of Canada and they, the producers, get to go to meetings.

And I never am able to thank them properly.

I wish I could. *Morningside*, as I tried to make clear in the introduction I wrote in 1985, is far more a group effort than anyone but the people who work on it will ever know. But on the air, except for the credits I read once a week – which, typically, I suppose, I follow by reading each week another list, the one we call "listener credits" – their contributions to the program are almost never acknowledged.

In this book, wherever possible, I've mentioned the producer or producers who shaped the story or series out of which particular groups of letters arose. A lot of chapters, though, were the result of combined efforts, or sometimes just serendipity. As a result, I've treated as a group the people who did the work in the first place, as well as the incomparable technical and clerical staff that supports us all. As a group then, I hope they will accept the thanks I offer here. It is their work that has made the past five years of my life the most rewarding of my checkered career, and it is their program it has been, and will be for a while yet, I hope, my privilege to host.

Their names, by the way, appear at the end of this collection. I meant to run them at the end of the original *Morningside Papers*, and the somewhat shorter list of that time – there have been more people added since as some of the originals moved on – was all ready to go. But at the last minute, it got squeezed out.

Richard Handler could have guessed by what.

That said about the program, which is where it all starts, there are a few people I want to single out about the book, which is why we are here.

One is Glen Allen, the journalistic humming-bird who alighted in our midst in the fall of 1986. Astute readers of the first *Papers* may remember his name. For one thing, that collection included a series of pieces about getting off the booze he'd written for and read on *Morningside*. Those accounts were numbered from days 3 to 29 of his newfound sobriety. There's another one in the new *Papers*, coupled with the spiritual story of Herb Nabigon, who also happens to be a friend of Glen's, and who brought us the story he told on the air, I think, largely because of that. Glen's own piece, which he wrote before he joined us, is numbered day 000.

He's winning.

The other reason you may remember his name is that in the introduction to the first book I said that although Glen is the son of a man who was very important to my early days as a journalist, the great editor Ralph Allen, he and I had not yet met. That's been changed now, obviously; the already satisfying experience of coming in to work for in the season of 1986–1987 – I really do have one of the best jobs in the world – was made even more satisfying for me by the pleasure of his company. As well, Glen brought to our unit not only his own background in print, but a passion, which he shared with me, for making radio out of the mail, and over the year he was with us I'm sure there were hundreds of people whose first response to what they'd written to me was a phone call from a soft-spoken, gentle writer, who talked to them as long as they wanted to about what they were trying to say, and about how to make it better. In the same way, he worked with me on almost every page of this book, and if there is a slightly different feel to it than the first one – a little more literate, perhaps, and even wider ranging (not to mention just occasionally whackier and more daring) – his touch has shown through. The "Bestiary," as you may have guessed, is almost entirely his.

And then there's Lynda. When the increased mail became too much for Eve McBride to continue to handle and still have time to pursue her own career as a writer, Eve decided to take the plunge as a novelist and columnist for the *Toronto Star*, and Gloria Bishop, the executive producer, came up, as she has come up with so many other solutions to my needs over the years, with Lynda Hanrahan, a bright young Queen's University graduate who had been working at CBC Enterprises. Lynda is everything I'm not: organized, unfailingly polite, endlessly energetic. On paper, she is my executive assistant, but in real life she is my travel agent, corresponding secretary, business manager, friend and, when the occasion calls for it, my conscience. In the two years she's been around, she has blossomed as an editor, too, and it is she who now prepares most of the mail the effervescent Shelagh Rogers reads with me on the radio. Contrary to the opinions some of us have of the younger generation, Lynda is not above the grit work, and when one of the typists I'd hired to help the editorial team finish this manuscript somehow managed to make my Macintosh word processor frown and surrender, Lynda, who is the age of one of my children, cheerfully took over and retyped the final chapters. God bless her.

Other people helped, too. Edna Barker, who also happens to be one of *Morningside*'s more passionate listeners, was so crucial in copy-editing the first *Papers* that this time round I've involved her from the beginning, and she, too, with Glen and Lynda and sometimes Gillian Howard, to whom I've dedicated this book for other reasons, became involved in the long and (usually) happy battles over favourite letters, pet hates, and attempts to balance that editing these collections have become. On top of all that, Eve McBride came out of her literary retreat once again to take bundles of letters home and bring them back spruced up for print. And over the last few weeks, Judith Thompson (who is not the person who made my computer scowl) took time off from finishing her Ph.D. to join the typing brigades.

They are the real heroes, they and my fellow authors. As with the first *Papers*, nearly all the people whose work appears here are amateurs in the true sense: they write for the love of it (see the letter from Margaret Fraser that ends the book, for example), or because they have something to say and *Morningside* is the place they want to say it. I think that word – amateurs – applies to the people I want to mention now, too. But it is worth noting not only that the novelist Timothy Findley graces this anthology with his memorial to Margaret Laurence, that the authors Sandra Birdsell and Lesley Choyce have contributed their thoughts on why they

14

live where they live, and that the children's writer Jean Little has shared her private passion for talking books, but that at least three others who join me here present work that, although it was first written for radio, will also be the basis for future books of their own. My friend and colleague Stuart McLean is one; both Stuart and I are convinced that a collection of the pieces that have become so special to *Morningside*'s Mondays would sell millions in print, and I offer the chapter of his written reports, which also contains my thoughts about him, as a sampler for alert publishers. So, too, with Vivienne Anderson, whose letters comprise most of the chapter I've called "Weaver's Hill and Longshot," and with Chris Czajkowski, whose pieces appear as "Chris's Life." Both Vivienne and Chris intend to publish longer versions of the journals they keep of their fascinating lives at some future date, and it pleases me to include their preliminary sketches here. I know also that Dorothy Beavington, Amber Hayward, and Lynda Weston, who appear variously in these pages, have other works under way, and I suspect there may be more. If so, I'm delighted. Maybe *The Morningside Papers*, new this season, still newer and even more expanded in seasons to come, ought to be a regular event, a grown-up Canadian version of the British children's annuals I remember from my childhood, and a place for aspiring authors to test the feel of print.

In the meantime, studious readers of the first volume will find some familiar names in the second. Mark Leier, who contributed a Memorable Meal to the original *Papers*, writes on a very different subject here, and Anne Cameron is back (yes, she, too, is a published author), and Catharine Hay and Penny Simpson and some others. And Krista Munroe, who wrote what I will now confess was my single favourite letter in the original *Papers*, has added to the story she began there with a letter. I have included her letter with Vivienne Anderson's essays.

In the years since all this began, I have met in person some of the people who share these pages and chatted with others on the phone or in radio studios. But all of them, I feel, have become my friends. If *Morningside*'s listeners have taken pleasure from their

ability to be heard, so has its host found inspiration, encourage-
ment, and guidance in what they've written. I thank them for that,
and for the opportunity to make these books.

As for me, I settled as many of the editorial arguments as I could,
and got up in the mornings to start sending out the minnows again.

At 4:14.

I wonder what lies in wait now.

Peter Gzowski,
June, 1987

KEEP YOUR FORK, DUKE- OR SOMETHING

I had often wondered where I first heard the punch line of the story that started all this, and when *Morningside* assembled a panel of lieutenant-governors, in April 1986, it seemed a handy opportunity to find out where it originated.

The story is the one about a royal, or at least viceroyal, personage on tour in Canada. He is at a banquet in a small town, and after the main course a waiter (or perhaps waitress) sidles up to him and whispers in his ear: "Keep your fork, Duke, there's pie coming." The lieutenant-governors were the Hon. Lincoln Alexander of Ontario, the Hon. Pearl McGonigal of Manitoba, and the Hon. George Stanley of New Brunswick. Ostensibly, they were in our studio – Paul McLaughlin, our producer, had a vice-devil of a time co-ordinating space in their busy schedules – to talk about their jobs: what exactly does a lieutenant-governor do? But I grabbed the chance to ask them if they happened personally to know where, or when, the incident had first occurred. Their honourable memories turned out to be as vague as my own, although each, as I remember, made an attempt to claim it for his or her own province. I wondered, as I have done on other occasions, if our listeners had more precise answers.

They did. It was as lively a dispute as we've had on *Morningside*. But, for my money at least, it's still unresolved. You may disagree. Here are some choices, from all over the country and from throughout our history, beginning with the most modern version I received.

✉ I was recently assured by a friend of mine that the incident happened only last summer, when the Prince and Princess of Wales were in Edmonton.

Patricia Bartlett
Mattawa, Ontario

✉ The story predates the Duke of Edinburgh by many years, although it could have happened to him, too. As children we heard it told and retold at the dinner table whenever we had pie. (I was a child in the 1930s.)

Our family version was brought back from Northern Alberta by my uncle, who had been working as a construction engineer on the Peace River Railway being built before World War One. The event was a visit to the construction camp by the Duke of Connaught, governor-general of Canada, 1911 to 1916. He had been invited to have dinner with the men in the camp and it was one of the workers who advised him: "Hang onto your fork, Dook, we're havin' pie."

Margaret Peyton
Como, Quebec

18

✉ "Save your fork, Duke, pie's coming." The line was a common laugh with my father and his contemporaries, all of whom had lived here – the Northwest Territories, before it became Alberta. It is almost seventy years since I first heard the expression.

Lenore Menard
Lethbridge, Alberta

✉ As a matter of fact, it was told about the former Prince of Wales when he was a very young man and owned a ranch in, I think, Alberta – probably in the twenties or early thirties: The local yokels had a party for HRH and it was on this occasion that the waitress made this remark. What I can promise you is that it happened at least fifty years ago.

I am now eighty-six years old and I remember the story very clearly from my young days.

Mrs. E.W.R. Steacie
Ottawa

✉ A friend of my father's, Don Longchamps, was an aide or assistant to Prime Minister Diefenbaker. It was part of his job to accompany important visitors on Canadian tours, and to make the necessary travel arrangements and make sure that all went smoothly. He accompanied Queen Elizabeth and Prince Philip on a trip to the Northwest Territories (to the best of my father's recollection). It was in a Legion Hall that the famous quote was uttered. When the main course was cleared the waitress reportedly said, "Keep your fork, Duke, there's pie."

My first recollection of the story goes back to when I was about ten or twelve. The Longchamps were guests for dinner and I proudly announced that I had made pie for dessert. You can guess the response! It started a tradition in our house.

Barbara Paterson Robson
Halifax

✉ I grew up on that story, and I'm in my sixties. In my day, it was told about the Prince of Wales (Duke of Windsor), and the admonition made by a mayor of Hamilton, who was purported to be something of a rough diamond. As the story went on, the prince, then quite a young man, broke up and had to be reminded about his dignity by his aides.

Joan E. Brown
Toronto

✉ The Duke of Connaught's itinerary took his train to Grande Prairie first, and then he was taken by motorcade, by way of Spirit River, Dunvegan Crossing, and then to have lunch at a place called Waterhole.

The Duke's equerry was quite a busy man immediately prior to lunch, judging by his inspection and careful wiping off of the cutlery. The lunchtime intermission had been organized by the Board of Trade, which consisted largely of farmers of the Waterhole district.

The set-up for lunch was a long table and, having passed the soup and entrée, a farmer sitting across from the duke noticed his fork being taken away as the dishes were being removed. He made his observation in a firm voice:

"Keep yer fork, Duke, the pie's acoming."

J.H. McRae
Edmonton

✉ I come from Saskatchewan. In 1941 I was teaching in a country school and living with a farm family. Farm families always used their dinner fork for pie. As my landlady was serving pie for dinner one evening she laughed and said "Have you heard the story about the pie and the Duke of Kent?"

The duke had been to western Canada, visiting various air force training schools, and had also gone north for a visit to a hunting lodge. It was there that a waitress was supposed to have said to him: "Keep your fork, Duke, there's pie for dessert."

Ann Dearle
Willowdale, Ontario

✉ I first heard it many years ago when I was a child in Calgary. The incident, as reported then, involved the Duke of Windsor, and took place in or near the E.P. Ranch at High River, where that gentleman used to spend some time. This would have been in the thirties.

Phyllis Fowler
Edmonton

✉ It was in the Northwest Territories, and the dinner was being served by the Métis or Indian people in a large hall. . . . The pie, I'm sure, would have been either Saskatoon or blueberry. I heard it very soon after it happened from a reporter to whom the duke confided.

Isobel Joy
Shellmouth, Manitoba

✉ When Edward, Prince of Wales, toured Canada a few years after World War One, he was in a pioneer part of northern Ontario and it was arranged that he should have lunch with a farm family. When it came time for the good lady of the house to take the prince's plate before serving dessert she uttered the famous words "Keep your fork, Prince, we're having pie."

Humphrey Carnell
Cobourg, Ontario

✉ My husband, a Scot, when there is pie for dessert, sings out: "Hold the fork for pie is coming!" to the tune of an old gospel hymn:

Hold the fort for I am coming
Jesus bids us still
Wave the answer back to heaven
By thy grace I will.

Mrs. E.E. McLintock
Aylmer, Ontario

✉ In 1970, the Prince George branch of the Canadian Federation of University Women put together a history of the street names of Prince George, British Columbia. In it, mention is made of the visit in September 1919 of the Duke of Devonshire, then governor-general:

"The Alexandra Hotel opened September 25, 1915. It was in this establishment that the Duke and Duchess of Devonshire were wined and dined during their visit in 1919. A colorful local legend has it that during the banquet, as the table was being cleared between courses, the waiter leaned over and whispered to the Duke, 'Hold on to your fork, Duke, the pie is coming.'

"The Duke of Devonshire's enjoyment may have been further marred by the presence of an irate citizen, who, resentful that he had not been invited to the banquet, revenged himself by dropping peas on the ducal head."

Rona Larsen
Calgary

✉ In Heather Robertson's book about Mackenzie King, *Willie: A Romance*, this is one of the letters from the girl, Lily, concerning the Duke of Connaught on his way back across Canada after World War One was declared.

"Huge crowd. Singing and cheering. The Methodist ladies gave us a lovely dinner in the station, pickerel fillets and fresh biscuits and pickles. As she was clearing away the Duke's plate one lady carefully removed his fork and set it on the tablecloth. 'Keep your fork, Dook,' she said, 'we're havin' pie.' My heart was in my mouth but the Duke said, 'Thank you madam' very politely and then his moustache started to twitch and his eyes twinkled and his face turned very red and his shoulders shook and he took out his handkerchief and *harrooomphed* very loudly into it and wiped his eyes. There is such a *feeling* in the air, excitement, like electricity, fun and recklessness and good will. All the stuffiness has gone. Everyone laughs and jokes and presses around, and the Connaughts wave and smile and chatter away like they've all been friends for years. It's just like a wedding!

"The pie was blueberry. The Duke had two pieces. Home tomorrow."

Kathy Allan
Iroquois Falls, Ontario

✉ The story is No. 62 in my little collection, now out of print, called *222 Canadian Jokes* issued five years ago by the Highway Book Shop in Cobalt, Ontario. It goes like this:

"In 1951, Princess Elizabeth and Prince Philip toured Canada. They were royally treated wherever they went. They visited a lumber camp in Northern Ontario and that evening were served a hearty dinner in the dining hall. The waitress serving Prince Philip collected the dinner plates prior to serving the dessert. She said to him, 'Save your fork, Duke. You'll need it for the pie.' "

It's vintage Canadian. I can't confirm it, but I am sure you'll find the earliest appearance of the story in Pierre Berton's first book, *The Royal Family* (1954). Where did it happen? Not in New Brunswick, not in Manitoba, but in good old northern Ontario.

John Robert Colombo
Toronto

✉ You may be interested in one more word on the duke. I, too, had heard the legend, but in a version that involved Prince Philip and some isolated northern community. The story has become a family joke.

A few years ago, when I was MP for Okanagan Boundary, I had occasion to sit at the head table with Prince Philip at one of those innumerable banquets that we subject royalty to. When the dessert turned out to be pie, I decided that the opportunity was too good to miss, so I told the story to the prince and waited for the reaction. It was one of astonishment. I wasn't sure whether he was astonished at the idea of someone not having enough forks for proper service or the thought of a serving person speaking to him in such an offhand manner (or speaking at all), but at any rate he denied all knowledge of the incident.

Bruce Howard
North Vancouver

✎ There were other theories, as I've suggested, but Mr. Howard's letter seemed to close the file for a while. Before I put all these explanations in print, though, I called two of the authors who'd been cited as authorities. Heather Robertson laughed with delight. "I just took it from the folklore," she said. "My mother told that story for as long as I can remember." I told Pierre Berton that I hadn't been able to find a reference in *The Royal Family*. "No wonder," Berton said. "It isn't in there."

Did he know where the story came from?

"I thought it was during the tour King George and Queen Elizabeth made in 1939. 'Keep your fork, *King*', I'd always heard," he said.

THE TOUCH OF STUART McLEAN

✎ Stuart McLean, who has appeared on *Morningside* every Monday morning during the years this book represents, is also the head of broadcast journalism at Ryerson Polytechnical Institute in Toronto. He took me over to his class one day and introduced me to his students. In thanking him, I said I hoped they would listen to what he tells them, but that they would never emulate him on the air. By almost every precept of conventional radio – or, I suppose, of conventional print journalism – Stuart gets things wrong. The pieces he does for us, as I told his adoring students, are almost always in the first person; they are flimsy and opinionated, essays in an age of hard news, occasionally sentimental, often self-indulgent. They are about such unimportant matters as the return of a wild duck to a school yard or the art of making hot dogs outside the institution of higher learning where he teaches.

They are also quite wonderful. If the mail and what I hear around the country are any measure, he is our single most popular contributor. The pieces I warned his students about trying to copy are, in his hands, small works of genius, as unique to *Morningside* as, I would like to think, "Talk of the Town" is to the *New Yorker*.

For all my own affection for him – and I like him as much as it must appear on the air – I really don't know him that well. He is a Montrealer, now in his late thirties, who has travelled around, dabbled in writing, and paid some dues. He is endlessly curious, somewhat absent-minded, sometimes ingenuous. He has red hair. When I first met him he was a producer at *Sunday Morning*, the weekly program that is to documentaries what *Morningside* is to conversation. He was so good at putting stories on the radio that they named him executive producer. That didn't work out. It's hard to imagine him as an administrator.

He started doing regular pieces for us about four years ago, and he just grew on us. He goes places that interest him and looks up people he'd like to meet. He tapes some of his experiences – he has spelunked in the sewers of London, Ontario, for us, climbed the terrifying scaffolding of a building under construction, and been pinned by, as he put it, six hundred and seventy pounds of LeCoco brothers in the wrestling ring (while Sweet Daddy Siki played hurtin' music in the background) – and then comes in to *Morningside* and tells me about where he's been, using his tape clips as illustration.

On the air, Stuart sounds spontaneous. He is. But he is also exquisitely prepared. On Sunday evenings, he edits his tapes and actually writes out what he plans to say. He and the producer prepare questions for me, and as he hits his stride on the radio he sometimes holds up a number of fingers, asking for my next interruption. That, at least, is the theory. In practice, both he and I wander all over the place – most notably on the day that has become our most famous duet.

Stuart, on that occasion, had decided to recreate in the 1980s an experiment Danny Finkleman had tried on *This Country in the Morning* in the seventies, which was simply to go out to buy as much stuff as he could for a dollar. Danny had acquired, among other things, a styptic pencil, some penny matches ("one of the great bargains," he had said; "you used to have to rub two sticks together for an hour"), a coat hanger, some city water, and a toothpick. Ten years later, Stuart began by reporting on his own comparison shopping. The styptic pencil, he had discovered, now cost $1.39 by itself. Matches had gone to two cents. A coat hanger? "Who buys coat hangers? They breed in your closet like rattlesnakes." City water, mind you, was still an outstanding buy – one thousand gallons for two dollars – and he put on his list a nickel's worth, twenty-five gallons, enough to fill a phone booth, in case we were wondering – "and no matter what I do to it," he reminded me, "they will take it back." In the 1980s, he said, toothpicks had mostly been replaced by floss, but he'd found some, and with a flourish he presented me with what he called his big-ticket item, a box of "about 725" (he hadn't counted) Megantic sanitary flat-styled picks. "Collectables," Stuart said. Then, he reported, he'd gone to a pet store, to see if he could bring in some livestock on his budget. He'd priced goldfish, he said, but had rejected them.

This is where our duet began. I'm going to reproduce it here, as I've transcribed it from the tape. To tell you the truth, I've long lost a sense of how much of a you-had-to-be-there it is. I know that in trying to get it off the tape a year and a half later, I started to laugh again, and that one of things that made it funny was that on the radio you could hear both of us, throughout, fighting to suppress our giggles. It may help you to try to imagine us now, two grown men, professional broadcasters, already amused by what had happened in the studio, and threatening to break up as Stuart made his proud announcement:

"I got a pet for a dime and I brought it with me this morning. Just let me reach down. . . . "

"This is a live thing?"

"This is a live thing, bought for a dime."

"It's in a peanut-butter jar."

"Yup. Just pop it open there. Oh my God! Oh, no, it's still there. I hadn't checked this morning. No, it's still there, alive and kicking. There you go. Bought a cricket."

"Aw."

"Now, I've only had him since Saturday."

"He's not well, Stuart." (I am starting to laugh here.)

"He is well. He's got the sponge with the water. He's got the Nabisco Shredded Wheat, which you can see he's eaten about half of. Just the one little square."

"He's not well, Stuart."

"Why do you say this? He's fine."

"Have you seen this cricket? This is an insipid critic . . ."

"People, believe me . . ."

". . . cricket."

". . . trust me, the cricket is fine. He doesn't eat a lot, he doesn't drink a lot." (Stuart is almost gone now, struggling for every phrase.)

"This cricket has had the biscuit."

"Listen, crickets don't do much of anything. I got the male. . . . He's supposed to. . . . I got the male, 'cause the male has the wings. It's the wings are how they make the chirping noi – *Don't blow smoke on my cricket.* The wings are supposed to make the chirping noises at night."

"Did he?"

"He hasn't. You know what happened? I got all excited. I had a record on. And the record had a song, and you know the way they make the records now, it had cricket noises in the background. *He* got all excited. I turned the record down and the cricket noises disappeared, and I thought, God, I gotta keep the music up to keep him chirping. Finally, I figured out it was on the music. (A long pause. Stuart is swallowing his laughter.) You know what I like about him?"

"No."

"I don't think he's got the long life span."

"I think he's playing the back nine of cricket existence. This morning."

"I don't think I'm going to have to worry about boarding this little fella in the summertime." (He is regaining control. But by now I don't trust myself to say more than one word at a time.)

"No."

"I think a dead cricket in a peanut-butter jar is a whole lot different from a dead cat on the front lawn. It's going to be a little easier on the family."

28

(I try to change the subject.) "How much was he?"

"He was ten cents. Maybe we'd better put the lid on. I'd hate to. . . ."

"He's not going to get out of there."

"This cricket is healthy. Trust me. I went to a stationery store. I bought a piece of chalk for a penny. (Another long pause. Stuart has broken up.) I'd better get a hold of myself. They had the cardboard box like teachers used to have, about the size of a pound of butter. (Giggles.) You know, if you have a kid under five, a piece of chalk . . . the cricket. . . ."

(Open and uncontrollable laughter. We are gone. For a few seconds, we try to regain control. Stuart struggles to talk about the post office and its thirty-four-cent stamps; I don't help him. Tears are running down my cheeks. We can't look each other in the eye.)

"We'd better play some music," I say, and the control room saves us.

That same season, Stuart and I were nominated together for an ACTRA award for a report Talin Vartanian had produced on hunger in Canada, and there have been other moments we're proud of, too. But the moment with the cricket remains our most memorable on radio; it was added, with J. Frank Willis's report from the Moose River mine disaster of the 1930s and Matthew Halton's brilliant reports from the front lines of World War Two, to the CBC's recording of fifty years of highlights. I still don't know if you had to be there.

What follows is a collection of Stuart's work presented somewhat differently. These are three of Stuart's scripts. Among them is the one that started people writing about chickens, as you'll see later on in "The Morningside Bestiary," and following them are a few responses we received to his fear of basements. Stuart's own pieces have been tailored a bit to appear in print – my parts, for example, have been taken out entirely – but the original flavour is in them, I think, whether you were there or not. So, as I've said so many Monday mornings as a *Morningside* week begins, here's Stuart McLean.

The Dunbarton Duck

This is an unlikely story that began in 1981 in an unlikely way and in an unlikely place. It started, if we can pinpoint one moment and say this is where it began, on a May morning, in a high-school parking lot, in the town of Pickering, Ontario. The high school is Dunbarton High. The protaganists, in the opening scene at least, are the school janitor and the school principal. The principal is Mr. Peleschuck, and as the curtain goes up he is walking across the parking lot on his way from his special reserved parking space to the front door, when out pops, as is the custom, the custodian.

"Good morning, Mr. Peleschuck" is what he is supposed to say, because that is what he says every morning. Except this morning, because it is the beginning of this story, he looks at Mr. Peleschuck sternly, as if he (Mr. Peleschuck) has done something wrong, and then says accusingly, "There is a duck in the courtyard with babies."

Now you have to understand about this courtyard. It is the kind of courtyard that architects like to put into hotel lobbies these days. Dunbarton High is built around it. It is like the centre hole of a large doughnut, big enough to park, say, five or ten cars, if you could figure out a way to get them in there. Two of the walls of the courtyard are glass. They frame the main hallway of the school, so you can look into the courtyard every time you change classes. The other two walls have windows that look into (or out from) the French classes.

So there is Mr. Peleschuck, standing out in the parking lot that May morning. No "Good morning, how was the weekend, you're looking well today," no nothing. Just, "Mr. Peleschuck, there is a duck in the courtyard with babies." Now most principals would probably lick their lips, look around nervously to see if anyone else had heard this, and say, "We have to get rid of them before the kids get here." Mr. Peleschuck is cut from a nobler bolt of cloth:

I said we got to feed them. We have to get them water. In spite of the Migratory Bird Act we can't let the ducks die. I knew that feeding them or anything like that was breaking the law but

I felt that under the circumstances you had to decide what the right thing to do was. We had ducklings in the middle of the school and we couldn't let them die. Not with everybody watching them. So we zipped up to the local feed mill and we purchased some Duck Chow. If you go to a feed mill these days they are quite diversified, you know. You can buy Monkey Chow, you can buy Guinea-Pig Chow, and you can buy Duck Chow.

Now, because he is the kind of guy he is, as well as going to the feed mill for the Duck Chow, Mr. Peleschuck went down to the school cafeteria and got a cafeteria tray, which he filled with water and slopped out to the courtyard so the ducklings could learn to swim. And every day that spring, when he got to school, he changed the water in the tray and poured the ducks some Duck Chow. It wasn't long, of course, before the ducks became a very big thing with the students. The whole school spent a lot of time around the courtyard windows watching the family grow. The ducks became such a big deal that the year-book committee chose a bird theme. Which is why the 1981 Dunbarton High Year Book is littered with quotations from *Jonathan Livingston Seagull*, and more to the point, why, there on the padded brown-leather cover, is a gold mallard in full flight.

One weekend that spring, before the ducklings had fledged – that is, before they got their flying feathers – Mr. Peleschuck and a guy from the Ontario Ministry of Natural Resources netted the family and spirited them away to a nearby marsh. A cafeteria tray can only go so far. The idea was that the duck family could spend the summer in the wild learning to fly before they had to migrate south for the winter. Mr. Peleschuck thought this would be the last he ever saw of the ducks.

I had checked on migration paths and they normally migrate to the southern United States or to South America. So I was perfectly aware, and I told everyone in the school, that it would be very unusual if they ever returned. But the next spring we were looking for them. We started watching for them as soon as

31

the snow left. Well, nothing happened until one day in mid-May someone noticed the duck! And the whole school became excited because the duck had been seen in the courtyard again. And we were into our second year.

The duck was an even bigger hit at Dunbarton High that year. Not only did students crowd around the windows to watch the family, but parents started to come in after school, and then whole buses full of kids on field trips from other schools began showing up. The mother duck had twelve ducklings and Mr. Peleschuck had to replace the cafeteria tray. He went out and bought one of those plastic kids' swimming pools that you have to blow up. Once again, before they fledged, Mr. Peleschuck and the guy from the ministry moved the family to the secret swamp.

The mother duck kept coming back to Dunbarton High like the swallows come back to Capistrano. In 1983 she was there with eleven babies, then eleven again in 1984. The return of the duck and the birth of her family became the true sign of spring at Dunbarton High. One year a senior student presented the school with three representative sculptures to honour the duck. The sculptures are in the courtyard today. One represents the mother duck, one the boy babies, the other all the girls.

The duck became a sort of touchstone for a whole generation of students. Watching the effect on school spirit, Mr. Peleschuck says he came to think of the duck and her babies as a kind of blessing. He says he could never figure out why she had chosen his tiny school courtyard, stuck as it is beside the highway and the railway tracks and the factories.

I used to think about it a lot until we got an aerial photograph. I was getting some photos taken for an explanation of where our school is, and what it looks like, and when you look at the aerial photograph you can see this tiny postage-stamp oasis of green in the middle of all the concrete buildings, tracks, highways, and everything else. There is that little spot of green with some pleasant little trees and I can now understand perhaps why the duck chose this place when she flew over. Now there is no water, but there is a bed of gravel and maybe it was rainy the day she looked at it, and maybe it glistened and looked like water.

On a farm, a duck can live for ten or twelve years. But that's on a farm, where a duck lives the soft life and gets three regular meals with no travelling privileges. But in the wild, four to five years is a good life span for a duck. That's because in the wild they have to fly to South America every year, which is a long way for anyone to fly, especially if you do your own flying, there and back, every year. And especially when you figure that every time you set down for a night's rest, someone is likely to start shooting at you. So for all these reasons, Mr. Peleschuck tried to warn everyone at Dunbarton High not to get their hopes up too high every spring.

I have told the people each year you can't expect the duck back. But we all hoped. In fact it's been quite an object lesson, that if you hope hard enough, things might turn out the way you want. It has become a sign of spring to us. So each spring we kind of hope that something like this will happen once again. So this year the students were looking forward to it once again, especially since some of them have seen the duck nest here every year since they have arrived in Grade 9.

So here it is the spring of 1985 and she has come back again, against all odds, for her fifth spring. She only produced six babies. That is less than any other year, and Mr. Peleschuck thinks that this is a sign she is getting tired, and he worries that this is probably the last spring he'll see her in his courtyard. But he says he will not give up hope, and neither will his students, because everyone at Dunbarton High believes in her. Two students who believe are Mark and Emma. Both of them are in Grade 13; both of them have known the duck for five years. When I met them I asked them what they wanted to say.

MARK: I want to say that we hope she keeps coming back as long as she can, because obviously one year she is not going to show up and people will be . . . not shattered, but they will remember the years that she has come and wonder why she didn't come and hope that she is somewhere. We have been glad to have her these past years. Five years is pretty nice to have a duck come to your school and we hope that she comes back again.

EMMA: I think it is great that she keeps coming back. It seems that all year everybody is always rushing around and rushing to be in class and be in meetings and when the duck is here it is really the first time that everybody stops on the way to class. You may be late for class but you still stop and look. Even if you are in a hurry you stop for a moment to see how many babies there are and just watch them for a few moments. It is really nice.

MARK: And it is kind of neat when you are looking out the window at them from the front foyer and there may be somebody beside you who you have never talked to the whole year and you'll look at them and say something like, "Oh, there's only six this year," or "I sure hope she's back next year," so seeing the duck sort of ties us all together.

By instinct, a mother duck builds her nest at the same spot year after year. Her babies return and build their nests, however, at the place from where they migrate. They don't come back to the place where they were born. Every spring, Mr. Peleschuck and the man from the Ministry of Natural Resources net the Dunbarton duck and her kids, and take them to the secret swamp, where they can grow up before the fall migration. Every year, they are tempted to leave one or two in the courtyard so maybe they would come back there to build nests, but they have never done it because they think the highways and the factories and the railway yards would be too difficult and too dangerous an environment to learn to fly in. So one spring, and it will be soon, the courtyard at Dunbarton High will be empty again. But don't tell Mr. Peleschuck that.

Superchicken

Remember the scene in "Lassie" where the mom comes out of the kitchen holding her apron and scatters stuff around for the chickens and they sort of munch away peacefully at her feet? Anyone who knows anything about chickens will tell you that it doesn't work like that.

Chickens, and I have been told this by many people who should know, are sorry birds. They are, to put it kindly, not smart. That stuff about the pecking order is for real. They will eat each other if they are left alone. According to one man I know, chickens are not far above plant life and deserve to be eaten.

Now that I have stated my bias, I want to tell you about a special line of chickens that have been bred to do one thing: lay eggs. They do it so well that the farm where they live has a trophy room for them, and there are more trophies in that room than Gretzky has in his basement. Big trophies, too, bigger than the chickens themselves.

Before I go much further I should also say that, over the years, I have done many strange things in the cause of journalism. But short of the time that I found myself removing my fingers from Craig Russell's mouth in the steam bath in the basement of the Royal York Hotel, this story, which also caused me to remove my clothes, ranks as one of the stranger experiences I have had.

There are actually two stories to tell. One is the story of the superchicken and where it came from, and we are talking about an entire breed here, not one particular bird. The other is the story of what happened to me outside the chicken house. Which is how we are going to begin.

When I arrived at Shaver's farm I was met by a fellow called Bob. Bob is an employee. I should point out that Shaver's is not a small family farm. Bob and I get into his truck for the two-mile drive from the farm office to one of the barns. It is at this barn that I am going to be introduced to the superchickens. We are driving along what seems to be a perfectly normal country road until I notice that we have obviously been teleported to West Germany and have arrived at Check-point Charlie, a fence across the road with a guardhouse and everything. We go into the guard-house, Bob and I, and as soon as we go in, Bob, my guide, starts to strip.

"You're going to have to take a shower before we go in," he says.

"Of course," I replied.

Now it is one thing to take a shower with a bunch of guys you play hockey with every week. But to suddenly undress with a man you have just met because you are going into his chicken barn is sort of different. While I was in the shower, my tape recorder was fumigated.

I should point out that at the exact moment I am showering, my friend Terrance McKenna, who is preparing a documentary on the artificial heart for the *Journal*, is in an operating room in Ottawa watching open-heart surgery, and no one has even asked him to wash his hands.

In the meantime, I have been told to leave my clothes in a locker at Check-point Charlie and get into the sterilized outfit that has been laid out specially for me.

On the other side of the check-point, in the barns, waiting for me, are millions of chickens. Each chicken is waiting in his or her own private chicken cage. Each cage is about the same size as one of those plastic milk crates that people store records in. The crates are stacked a couple of rows high and the rows go on forever. Picture a grocery store, a big supermarket, where all the groceries have been changed into live chickens. And you know what happens when you walk down one of these rows? The chickens begin stick-ing their heads out of their cages all down the row. You know what it feels like as you walk down the row and the chickens pop out like that? It is like you are the queen or something. As I walked down the row I became quite transfixed with this notion of royalty. The chickens were great. They seemed to understand their role completely: I walked; they poked out and nodded, like they were pleased to see me.

"Thank you, thank you, hello there, thank you." I could spend a whole day like that. The queen has a great job.

Except the queen doesn't do chicken barns, and there is a good reason for that: chicken barns do not smell good, which is basically why, at this point, I suggested we bail out of the barn and go back to the farm office. Now I mentioned before that this was not a family farm. So you shouldn't be surprised that the first room I visited was the computer room, where seven employees spend half of every day studying eggs, and the other half huddle over a terminal entering their observations into the computer. I went up to one of the women in the room and asked her if she could tell me about the particular egg she was logging.

Well, it has a deformation of twenty-nine, which is not so bad. It has a large egg weight. Its color is a fifty-two, which means it is a brown egg but it is not too brown. And it has a good texture score. The only thing wrong with it is it's a little bit out of shape. The albumen height is really well. The ninety-nine there means that there is nothing wrong with it, there is no blood or meat.

We are obviously talking about high-tech eggs here. In the next room is a man in charge of logistics. They don't actually make money here at Shaver's, selling eggs. They don't have to. They have the champion chicken – so they sell it. The guy in charge of logistics is actually in charge of scheduling the hatching of millions of eggs. Shaver's sell the eggs as day-old chicks. They ship the day-old chicks around the world. The man in charge of logistics works backwards. If he knows he has an order of, say, five thousand chicks going out on a five o'clock plane to Morocco, he sets everything up so that at three o'clock, not three-thirty but three o'clock, the five thousand eggs will finish hatching. He sets it up like that because he needs that much time, and no more, to get them out to the airport.

We have to hatch those chicks as close to the flying time as we can. Now this one here is just a small order for 2,200 chicks going to Venezuela. They will begin hatching at one o'clock to be finished at three o'clock, giving us thirty minutes to vaccinate and box them and then get them right out and onto the road. You see, those chickens are out of the shells and then they are gone within two hours. Within two hours of taking them out of the incubator, they are on their way.

Shaver's is the only chicken breeder of any significance in Canada. There used to be hundreds of breeders all across Canada and the United States, but what happened is that the folks at Shaver's developed such an efficient egg machine that they blew everyone else out of the water. They are huge. They have four hundred employees worldwide and subsidiaries in Great Britain, the United States, and France. What I really loved about them is that when Bob Grey joined the company they hardly existed. As Bob says, "I joined a company that had three employees: Don Shaver, a truck driver, a poultry man, and myself."

That was in the 1950s. And there were really only two full-time employees: Don Shaver, the founder, and Bob Grey. The truck driver and the poultry man were part-time.

When Don Shaver was ten years old, in the depression, his aunt gave him two chickens. He saved five dollars, which was a lot of money in those days, and bought himself a rooster. Then he began breeding hens. Because he didn't know anything about genetics, he broke all the rules, and came up, at fourteen years old, with the best egg-producing chicken in Canada. He did it by mating crossed lines or something. He submitted his results to Ottawa. Now every year, chicken breeders have a prize night at the Royal York Hotel, and when they announced the results of fourteen-year-old Don Shaver's chicken, everyone at the hotel nearly fell off the chairs. All these scientists and farmers had to sit there and watch while this kid marched up to collect their prize.

With the reputation he established that night, Don set up a small breeding business that began to grow very nicely, thank you, until World War Two came along. When Don enlisted he was faced with a problem: what to do with his chickens. What he did was set up a deal with an American university. He arranged to ship them all down to the University of Connecticut or Rhode Island or some place like that with the understanding that, when the war was over, they would send him back a load of eggs, so he could get back into business. What the university did instead was to burn its barns to the ground during the war. The fire wiped out not only his complete stock but his genetic pool as well. That left Don Shaver at square one. That's when the current president, Bob Grey, joined the company. The two of them set out to find the perfect chicken again. They bred everything with everything to see if they could come up with a hybrid that would outperform all the other chickens. They went at it for about five years without any success. Then they got lucky.

> It was in 1955 or 1956 that we discovered the combination that is known as the "Shaver Starcross 288." It was through one of our experiments crossing these various lines of stock in different combinations that we hit on this particular one that, from a performance point of view, stood out head and shoulders above anything we had ever produced before. And we were pretty excited about it. We knew if we could have the combination repeat itself then we really had something that was pretty valuable.

Basically, what they had done was build a better mousetrap. The Shaver 288 did the same thing to egg-laying that Roger Bannister did to running the mile. The chicken couldn't do 3:58, but it sure had good numbers. Before the war, if a chicken laid 180 eggs a year, it was doing good work. The Shaver Starcross 288 consistently laid more than 270 and maybe 300 eggs a year. And it didn't only produce good numbers: it did quality numbers. And it did it on – excuse me, but it's the truth – chicken feed. It was a fastidious eater that laid a lot of big eggs. The word spread quickly.

> We really had a tiger by the tail. We had a product that sold well, that people wanted, and we developed a pattern of distribution and modified that from one country to the next, but

*we just kept travelling and adding more countries. Today we are
in over 90.*

Which brings us to the end of our story. What Grey and Shaver
did was what everyone did in the fifties: they franchised the superchicken. Rather than go into the egg-producing business themselves, which is what they had planned to do, they went into the
chicken-producing business. They went to distributors in all sorts
of countries and said: "Okay, chum, you want to sell the Shaver
Starcross here in the Philippines, we'll supply you with the chicken
but you can't sell any other bird. You have to move our bird exclusively." And because they knew they had such a good bird, and
because the distributors knew they had such a good bird, everyone
was delighted to go along with them; they knew the demand would
be there for the chicken. They do more than $15 million in business
a year today, and if you want to go to see the Starcross 288 you
go to Cambridge, Ontario, take a shower, and take a look. There
are great success stories in this country. We have the pumpkins in
Nova Scotia, we have Northern Dancer, and we have the superchickens in Cambridge, Ontario. Those chickens should be there
in the Canadian hall of honour with the zipper, basketball, the plastic garbage bag, and five-pin bowling.

Your Basement is the Scariest Place in the World

I begin with a thesis that no one really likes the basement. I believe
that down there, lurking in our collective unconscious, just waiting
for us, is something scary. When we were kids it was the boogyman. You'd be sent down to get something and you knew *it* was
down there waiting. Going down wasn't so bad. Coming back up
was, because you were always sure that *it* was going to get you
at the last moment. The boogyman is gone but there are still things
down there that are incomprehensible, and equally frightening –
the electrical panel, for instance, or the fuse box. Or the wires-
that-hang-down-that-you-are-pretty-sure-aren't-working-but-you-

are-very-careful-not-to-brush-against-just-in-case. The reset button on the furnace. The lighting. You have to wonder why the rest of the house is lit by Cecil B. de Mille and the basement is done by Alfred Hitchcock. My friend Paul has known many basements in his life, and all of them have been lit, it seems, to engender fear:

In the middle of the ceiling, far away, usually in a tangle of wires, is sort of a socket, and in it is a naked bulb. You have to pull on a little chain if you want to turn it on. But the chain snapped off in 1943 and is about a quarter of an inch long. And you are always entering the room when it is pitch dark, probably when the animals are wandering around in it, and you have to make your way across the darkened room and stick your hand up into this tangle of wires and heating pipes and other things that you don't want to know about and try to find this tiny piece of chain and turn on the light. Of course, half the time the bulb is out, too. In some basements you can only turn off the light by unscrewing the light bulb most of the way. So you tiptoe across the room and you go to turn on the light and you knock the bulb out of the socket and it falls on the floor. So you get another bulb and you are holding it the right way but you are thinking, if I am not careful I am going to stick my finger into the socket. It is a dangerous life.

Now the thing about making your way across basements towards that lonely light is that basements tend to fill up. They fill up with things you don't use very much. Like rowing machines, or old mattresses, or forty years of *Popular Mechanics* that you are going to catalogue one day. You have to go down into the darkness with your hand out in front of you and grope around like a blind person. And worst of all, when you leave these things alone, especially at night, they tend to fall over. Especially if you are alone in the house. Which is why it good to have a cat. Because then you can always say, "It must have been the cat."

Basements are eerie and other-worldly and people do foolish things in places like that. There is something about being down there that puts us all off balance. Michael, for instance, told me this story. It happened in an apartment basement about thirty years ago, down in one of those dusty underground places with all the storage lockers. The story happened in the laundry room.

One of the pieces of equipment was the washing machine, with the wringer that you fed the shirts through after they had been washed. I was down there with a friend and he dared me to put my fingers in the wringer of the washing machine. And I said I wouldn't do it on a dare. So he applied the ultimate sanction: the double dare. And I did – I put my finger in the turning wringer, and it got stuck. Then my hand went through, then the wrist, which is when my friend ran away screaming. Then the elbow – and I started to scream. I don't want to be graphic but it started to peel the skin off at the elbow. The superintendent's wife came down and looked at me and popped the thing. You can still see the scar. My hand was as flat as a board. I ran upstairs; I didn't want to tell my mother that I had put my hand in the wringer of a washing machine, because it sounded kind of dumb. So I told her my hand had been hit by a bus.

I think people do stupid things like that when they're in the basement because they are under a lot of pressure down there. There are a lot of things down there to fear. In my house it's a toss-up between the fuse box and the furnace. I happen to know it's just a matter of time before a fuse blows or the furnace stops. By themselves, these are not catastrophic events. What is frightening, however, is the likelihood that I will be sent down there to do something about it. Now, I don't know how you feel about changing fuses. First, I can never figure out which one has blown. If I ever get past that stage, I am always afraid that one of my fingers is going to slip into the little hole, and I don't want to think about what would happen to me then.

A furnace that has stopped is something altogether different. I will do a fuse – but I don't do furnaces. As far as I'm concerned, you would have to be a complete lunatic to go down there and even think about relighting a pilot light. The notion of crawling around a gas furnace with a lit match, or approaching the restart button, is like thinking about the apocalypse. I understand that I am probably being foolish, that there are people who could show me that these activities are perfectly safe. These same people would have me believe that it is safer to fly to Beirut than to drive to work. They may be right – but I happen to know that if you don't treat furnaces with great respect they are likely to blow up. If the furnace wants to stop, that's fine with me: I won't touch it. When anyone says I'm being foolish, I just smile and point to my friend Paul. Paul is a family man who lives in a good neighbourhood and has a good job. Three times in Paul's life, in three different houses, Paul's furnace has exploded. Explain that.

I know a lot of people who own those new super-high-efficiency modern furnaces will say that guys like Paul and me are living in the dark ages. I disagree. I have seen those things, furnaces that you bolt to the ceiling that are about the size of an electric type-writer. Anything that small that can heat an entire house should not be trusted. Nor should circuit breakers, for that matter. Which brings me to rec rooms and finished basements. Finished basements do not make any difference. Just because you have knotty-pine walls and a bar and a Ping-Pong table, things are no better. The furnace is still down there somewhere, and so is the fuse box. If you have an old basement that isn't fixed up, it's usually one big open space. With a rec room, there are inevitably chairs and sofas and all sorts of other things, and as far as I am concerned, these are just places for things to hide.

Consider all this and add to it mould, floods, animals that can move through the walls, teenagers who sometimes live down there, dry rot, wet rot, rodents, and stairways that have no banisters. If you are going to do anything to your basement, don't add a bar: fix the banister. You never know when you might need it to get out of there fast.

✉ Today I heard about Stuart's uncomfortable relationship with his basement. I fear we wouldn't be much use to each other, because I'm petrified of mine. I wasn't more than mildly uncomfortable about it when I moved into this house seven years ago, but my experiences since have fanned the discomfort into a raging terror. I live in a strange little house, perched on the side of a hill. It has been much added to and tinkered with during its forty-five years; it started as a two-room cabin in the woods. Access to the basement was through a trapdoor in the study, but previous occupants blocked it off, so you now get in by a door at the foot of a rock outcrop in an unlit part of the garden. Apart from hasty hurling in of garden forks and snow tires, I go down there as infrequently as I can manage. The spare bedroom silts up with flower pots and half-empty paint cans; I even keep my bicycle there.

Due to the fall of the land, the basement is about twelve inches high in one corner and more or less adult height at the opposite corner. The "floor" is of earth, a small patch of concrete, and a heap of rocks, some of which seem to be holding up the house. The earth bits are almost permanently damp. After a good rain, the well in the front garden overflows; the water runs down the path, under the step, and into the basement, where it forms a babbling brook.

The ancient water tank, with its leprous blue paint, and the pump, with its hissing flywheel, squat like sinister trolls among the rocks in the nether regions, where you have to crouch to peer at them in the light of your lantern. The kindly man from the local hardware store understands the anatomy of my ancient pump, and stocks spare parts for it. He is stalwart and uncomplaining when he comes to perform his operations while folded up into a human pretzel.

My elderly oil furnace is on the other side of the room. One day it blew up. I wasn't home at the time but the state of the place I returned to was beyond description. It took a platoon of professionals a week to clean and repaint the house and all its contents, and the poor cat had to be surgically cleaned. There's a polite, quiet, efficient propane furnace down there now, but I don't really trust it, either: if its pilot light ever goes out, the cat and I will get in my sleeping bag with a hot-water bottle, then call the propane company.

I have always felt guilty about my fear of basements, thinking it foolish in a practical woman who is able to deal competently with eavestroughs and attics. Knowing that Stuart and who knows how many other men are similarly scared makes my cowardice much easier to bear. Thank goodness *my* fuse panel is in the kitchen above the stove!

Paddy Muir
Halifax

✉ For a guy who overcame abject terror half-way up the ladder of a hammerhead crane; who subdued an anxiety attack while spelunking through London, Ontario's sewer system, that Stuart McLean turns all wimpy when he and his friends can't find the basement light switch. Surely the poor chap isn't afraid of the dark?

Granted, on occasion, a descent into the subterranean area found below most urban homes can be a hazardous undertaking, as when the family pooch decides to come up the steps as you are going down, with your vision somewhat impaired by the vast pile of dirty laundry clutched in both arms and the too-late realization that the handrail is mounted to starboard, and not port.

But what Stuart McLean fails to appreciate is that the Basement – I mean a *real* Basement – is a unique multi-functional area that has been hewn from the bowels of Mother Earth, and is not just tarted-up, wet-barred, dart-boarded rec room adjacent to the laundry chute. In my time, a real basement was for men, not boys. It had a square hole at ground level through which, every fall, would rattle several tons of coal, disgorged from the back of a horse-drawn wagon.

The coal was to ensure regular feeding of a fiery monster through whose cast-iron portal was regularly flung huge shovels full of the stuff, and heaven help any poor mortal who let the fire go out! The ashes were removed for later spreading on ice-covered sidewalks, in temperatures of minus fifty degrees fahrenheit, with six months of snow on the ground. The whole process was a real character-builder; one that Stuart and company missed, or they wouldn't be so distraught over their furnaces' little red reset nobs popping in and out unbidden.

As well, real basements encouraged a strong belief, amongst the young, in the powers of light and darkness, heaven and hell. How could the parent have discovered the pack of Turret cigarettes so carefully hidden behind the second ceiling joist from the left near the stairs? Having been discovered, could Hell be far behind?

Deryck Thomson
Sydney, British Columbia

✉ We refer to our basement in our Quebec country house as "la cave." It's actually a pretty decent basement, with eight-foot ceilings (from which the cobwebs have finally been vacuumed); the light switch is found at the *top* of the stairs, and the recently laid cement floor makes it quite pleasant to walk around down there. This brings me to a feature that Stuart McLean mentioned: stairways and the lack of banisters.

The day I fell into "la cave" stands out as a most eventful basement experience. At the time, the stairs stood in the middle of the basement, with empty space on either side. The entrance was a trapdoor on the first floor – a very heavy trapdoor. As I shuffled around in my flimsy Chinese slippers early one morning (April second, to be exact), I decided to go down to load the wood furnace. Sleepily I opened the trapdoor, set my foot onto the top stair, and lost my footing. I was propelled downward, head first, toward our new cement floor. With arms flailing as I searched for a hand-hold, I grabbed the trapdoor, which promptly slammed it down on me, thus accelerating my descent.

I screamed loudly, hoping to wake my husband, who was sleeping on the second storey. As I landed on the floor in a dive, the impact caused me to pass out. Meanwhile, Brian had rushed down to find no one downstairs – of course the trapdoor was closed. His first thought was that this was an April fool's joke. He wasn't awake enough to realize that this was April second. He opened the trap-door and saw me lying peacefully on the floor, seemingly unharmed.

As I regained conciousness, I saw Brian standing naked at the top of the stairs peering down at me. I felt that I had fallen into a bad dream, which was my basement, and that I was perceiving reality as a shaft of light flowing down from above, with Brian, unattainable, at the top. Helpless, I whimpered and held up my two swollen wrists for him to see. Then the bad dream was over, and Brian was helping me to my feet.

Our stairs now stand in the corner of the basement, still with no banister, but a wall on one side provides a greater sense of security.

Louise Valentine
Frampton, Quebec

WHY I LIVE WHERE I LIVE

I started this myself, as you will see. In the summer of 1985, I had been travelling for television, and, as never fails to happen to me when I wander, was once again reminded not only of the variety of the country *Morningside* serves, but of the special character of so many of its parts. A phrase I remembered from an old series in *Esquire* stuck in my mind, in which, under the title I've stolen for this chapter, a number of American writers limned their home towns. Our thought was much the same. Three of the pieces that follow here – from Sandra Birdsell, Lesley Choyce, and Marlyn Horsdal – were commissioned by our producer, Hal Wake. Sandra is the Winnipeg writer best known (so far) for her brilliant collection of short stories, *Ladies of the House*; Lesley is the Nova Scotia novelist, short-story writer, and broadcaster – his interviews with writers on cable TV are *Morningside*sque in their efficacy – and Marlyn is a writer and publisher on the west coast, whom I had met through her letters to me.

(I wonder if she will mind if I point out she is also a sister of the folk singer Valdy.) The rest of my co-authors here are, so far as I know, just listeners, among those who responded to what I said when I returned to the radio from my summer on the road.

✎ An old friend from my Moose Jaw days who has now settled comfortably into Charlottetown gave me directions this summer to a beach just north of Souris, Prince Edward Island. When I arrived there, by way of a narrow, nearly overgrown road that appears to peter out just before it gets to the dunes and is not, in a province that appears otherwise to mark every tourist attraction as carefully as a kindergarten teacher on the first day of school, advertised by any sign at all, I could see white sand, blue water, rolling beach, and the mouth of a river where, it turned out, there were clams and mussels for the stooping, and, as far as the eye could see, no other humans. The river, whose mouth I explored, bends just behind the beach and its landward bank rises into a copse of trees. If I had the money and could live by my wits, I would build a house there, and live in it.

I would live, too, if I could figure out how to, on another river bend I saw this summer, this one in the Gatineau hills, forty miles from the hustle of Ottawa. Here, where the river snakes, is a gentle waterfall, whose ledge you can ford and whose sounds you can hear from the clearing in the spruce where I would build my cabin.

Or Vancouver. Every time I go to Vancouver I ask myself why I don't live there, and this summer, when the sun shone for seven uninterrupted weeks, and when people bicycled and sailed and strolled and hiked and played tennis and lay on the beach and *used* their city and its God-given resources as no other metropolis I knew uses *its* – this summer I had a harder time than ever coming up with the answers.

I live where I do live – in a trendy condominium at the foot of Church Street in Toronto, across the road from a farmer's market and within walking distance of a galaxy of mediocre restaurants – because I have to. I need to be within minutes of the rickety old building that houses this studio, so I have found a corner of the city that suits my needs. But if all else were equal, I would live on Lake Simcoe in Ontario or North Hatley in Quebec or perhaps Quebec City itself, or overlooking the river valley in Edmonton, or on Cape Breton or in Sechelt on the sunshine coast of British Columbia.

I am not complaining. The lovely job to which I return today takes me around the country more than most people get to go. This was an especially splendid summer, since work took me once again not only to most of the places whose names I've dropped this morning, but to a great many more as well. I swam in two oceans this summer, played golf in four provinces, went horse racing in three others, and was bitten by bugs in nearly all.

But that's my story and I am more interested in yours.

✉ I live in the Red River Valley. I grew up in a small prairie town, moved on, and lived in several others. You know the type: one grain elevator, railroad tracks, train station, general store, and a curling rink with eight sheets of artificial ice. The kind of place people say that, if you blink when you drive by, you'll miss it. Now I live in Winnipeg, and I suppose some may say the same comment applies. But these are just tourists skimming across the valley in their boats or trolling with empty hooks. Valley, they say. Where are the hills?

True, one must travel far to find them – but they're here. Comforting little brown humps on the shoreline. Why do I continue to live here in Winnipeg in the Red River Valley? It's God in a CBC T-shirt, calling to make me think.

I've contemplated moving to Vancouver where they tell me that the difference between Vancouver and Toronto is that in Toronto people dress up in bizarre costumes and pretend they're crazy, while in Vancouver they really are crazy. I don't mind the crazy people in Vancouver. They're like wild flowers on the side of a mountain, pretty to look at from a distance but never meant to be picked and taken home. But I find when I'm in Vancouver that after three days I no longer see the mountains. All I want to do is find a quiet place, huddle down in the sand, and stare at the ocean. And the same thing happens to me when I'm at the east coast. Why do I live here?

I ask a friend. Grasshoppers and crickets sing from either side of the dirt road. It's not quite a full moon but bright enough for long shadows. Perfect night to play Dracula. It's my turn to wear the cape. The question eats at me, interferes with the game. On the horizon Winnipeg shimmers pink and still. You live here, he says, because you're short. You're close to the ground and if a big wind should come along you'd be safe. And yet you feel tall. Naw, that's not it, my daughter says. We've got a curved sky and living here is like living inside a bubble. A small town inside a bubble, she says, jabbing the air with her sharp fingernail.

It's Sunday and the question rankles as I make my weekly trip through the forest where thick, dark trees wrestle the granite boulders for soil. I push the speed limit to get to the lake before all the others and finally I find my spot, huddle down into the sand, and stare out across the water. I think: Why do I live here? Eureka! The answer comes to me. It's not the curved sky or the horizon or because I'm short. It's because when I live in the Red River Valley I'm living at the bottom of a lake. When you live at the bottom of a lake you get cracks in your basement walls, especially in River Heights where they can afford cracks and underpinning and new basements. I like the cracks. The wind whistles through them, loosens the lids on my peach preserves, makes the syrup ferment, and the mice get tipsy. In the potato bin sprouts grow on wrinkled skin, translucent, cool sprouts. They climb up the basement walls, push their way through air vents, and up the windows in my kitchen. I don't have to bother about hanging curtains.

And time is different here. The days piled on top of lake sediment

51

shift after a good storm so that yesterday slips out from beneath today. Or even last Friday with all its voices will bob up from the bottom and it's possible to lose track of tomorrow. You can just say, to hell with tomorrow and go out and play Dracula.

When you live here at the bottom of a lake you can't pin your ancestors down with granite monuments. They slide out of their graves. They work themselves across the underground on their backs using their heels as leverage and they inch their way back into town until they rest beneath the network of dusty roads and they lie there on their backs and read stories to you from old news-papers.

Now, this is something tourists can never discuss as they roar across the valley in their power boats churning up the water with their blink-and-you'll-miss-it view of my place. Sometimes a brave one will leap from the boat, come down and move in next door. I've seen it happen. They become weak and listless, like flies trapped inside a house at the end of summer. And you'll see them walking along the highway in scuba gear muttering to themselves or rowing across the lake in search of a hill. I'll admit, sometimes it's nice to surface, to take off the cape and put on my respectable prairie jacket and boots and do a walking tour of Halifax, sniff a wild mountain flower in Vancouver, get a stiff neck looking up at all those skyscrapers in Toronto, or a three-day party headache in Montreal. But inevitably my eyes grow tired, glazed, and like a sleepwalker I awake to find myself crouched down beside an ocean, a lake, a water fountain, and I now it's time to get back here – to get down in the basement and breathe the wind in the cracks of my walls where, nestled up against the foundation of my house, is the pelvic bone of an ancestor.

Sandra Birdsell
Red River Valley, Manitoba

✉ I remember sitting in a traffic jam one spitefully hot, smoggy day in September 1977. Cars and trucks were backed up for miles outside Yankee Stadium on the Major Deegan Expressway as I tried to fight my way home from a day of teaching at Queen's College. My old Volkswagen engine was overheating badly and I was counting on spiritual forces to get me safely home to New Jersey. If you had to leave your car along this stretch of road for more than twenty minutes the odds were you'd return to find a puddle of oil and a few spare parts. Inside the stadium the fans were cheering; somebody was rounding third and heading for home plate.

Then a week later I was trying to get some end-of-the-summer surfing in at Far Rockaway Beach, the end of the line for the New York subway. The water was brown and warm but the waves were tropical in origin. I was stationed just beneath the landing path for JFK International Airport and in the distance I could see the upthrust of Manhattan skyscrapers. Just as I was about to paddle for a wave I was overcome by a deep, throaty roar that was louder than any sound I had ever heard. In a second I saw a massive Concorde jet dropping down above me as it was about to land at the airport. But as it passed overhead I was still looking off toward the heart of the city, watching for the mushroom cloud and thinking that this wasn't the place I wanted to be when the bombs started dropping.

And it wasn't long after that when I was walking down Forty-Second Street towards the bus terminal. As I stopped for a red light across from Times Square, a taxi backfired. A hundred people around me dropped to the sidewalk. They automatically assumed it was a sniper. I was beginning to get the feeling that there were better places on the planet to while away my time.

So it's now 1985 and I'm sitting in front of a window in my old farmhouse at Lawrence Town Beach on the eastern shore of Nova Scotia. In front of me is a pristine blue lake, a voluptuous green and gold marshland, and beyond that sand dunes and the Atlantic Ocean. It's a clear, vibrant day and I can see down the coast for maybe thirty miles, all the way to the lighthouse at Sandborough. If I linger here like this I'll see a great blue heron land in the shallows, fold up its wings, and stand there on one leg waiting to spear eels. A hawk will zip past my window and patrol the marsh, a deer will casually walk into my garden, or the bald eagle from up the lake will make a foray down this way in search of food.

I live here quite simply because this is a sane, beautiful place. Arriving here as an immigrant it felt like I was, in fact, returning home for the first time in a long while. My childhood home town in rural New Jersey farming country no longer exists. It's been swallowed up by housing developments, industrial parks, and shopping malls. So I had to rearrange my personal geography to relocate the great things that were trampled by civilization. Fortunately, the best of what I was searching for was right here in Nova Scotia.

This year I've been hiking around the headlands along the coast. Each craggy cliff and sea-pounded rock outcropping reminds me that this is still a place shaped by the sea and by the climate, and, despite the awful power and sometimes arrogance of both, I welcome the reminder that man has only barely intruded upon this coast. Maybe I live here because we have some of the thickest, best-quality fauna to be found anywhere. Send me off hiking in the spruce forest behind my house during a warm, woolly, grey fog. Let me get good and lost there, comfortably snug in this environmental cocoon. I'll tell you that I'm just about as happy as a man can be. Or let me go out surfing in January, just a stone's throw from my back door in a cold, clear, semi-Arctic breeze. Let me drop down the face of a dozen crisp, clean North Atlantic waves until the salt water in my hair freezes and I have icicles dangling down to my chin, and I'll say I'm quite comfortable, thanks; no crowds, no pollution, no end of the world Concordes hunkering down above me.

This is a damn fine place to wake up in the morning beside my wife, to take my daughter out searching for frogs and fireflies and starfish and sea urchins. And it's even a good place to give up the comfort of a wood-stove-heated room and walk out onto a frozen lake in winter. Stalk off into the middle of a blinding white nowhere, and let a polar wind clear away the clutter in my mind and the crud accumulated in my lungs.

My personal geography is a map of this jagged coastline. In some inexplicable way I know who I am because I can look out my window every day and see where the land ends and where the ocean begins. There's a vast, beautiful, empty canvas of sky and sea on which to re-invent the world, in imagination and in fact.

Lesley Choyce
Lawrence Town Beach, Nova Scotia

✉ I live in the hamlet of Fulford Harbour on Salt Spring Island, between Vancouver Island and mainland British Columbia. It's a hilly island thirty miles long with one main road, no traffic lights, and a population of around six thousand. I came here ten years ago from Ottawa partly for the climate, because I was fed up with cold and snow; partly because my sister was here, having sensibly trickled out west before me; and partly because I had bought an old wooden sailboat that I was going to live on. I had lived in cities as different as London, England, and Komassi in West Africa; but Salt Spring fits me better. It's nice to shop where the storekeeper will say, "Oh, your husband already bought some of that this morning" and to buy undrugged meat directly from the farmers. Not everybody likes that part. One friend nearly threw up when he realized that the pork we were picking up was half a pig with one ear and one eye, not neat brown packages. Walking over to the post office in Ganges, our biggest village, can mean chatting with a dozen friends and neighbours and probably the world would be safer if we all lived in small communities. Military planners can consider killing a million people in a foreign city because they're abstract numbers. But how could anybody contemplate dropping a bomb on a little village that was just like his own?

There's a wonderful variety of people here. When I worked for the government, everybody I knew was sort of like me – university-educated professionals. And though they were interesting and fun it wasn't exactly a cross-section of Canada's population. Here, I also know loggers and plumbers and fishermen and they're just as interesting, and mostly funnier. Now I know what a backhoe is and a radial-arm saw and a boom chain, and it's fun to learn new things.

People here don't seem to get stuck into ruts and I admire that. We've bought eggs from a dentist and crabs from the rug-cleaning man. There's a clinical psychologist who teaches dance, and the man who owns the pizza parlour used to drive the concrete truck. Louis turned into Luigi and switched from hard cement to soft crusts.

I think living on an island gives you a slight feeling of apartness. There's a cosy, contained element like a little castle inside a moat. Life is simple because the choices are limited in some ways. You can't decide at eight-thirty on a summer evening to visit friends in Victoria because the last ferry has left. It's casual. I can wear jeans to my office all year, which is great because I don't like shopping. The pace is pretty relaxed and the only time you really need to keep an eye on your watch is when you're catching a ferry. I got so used to the rhythm of a weekly newspaper that once when I was in Vancouver I looked at a headline in the evening paper and thought, "How can that be in the paper already? It only happened today." Maybe this is a retreat from a complex world, but we don't turn our backs on it. CBC Radio and the *New Yorker* keep us in touch with reality, if we want, and there are several active nuclear-disarmament and international-development groups, including Voice of Women and Beyond War. So we can all be involved in the issues that are important to us.

I do miss the advantages we associate with city living, like reading good daily papers, eating out, and going to concerts and movies and Expos games. But probably we all make trade-offs wherever we live. I don't miss city noises and crowds and smells, and luckily for me, my husband is kind enough to stay here, designing houses, when he doesn't feel nearly the aversion to cities that I now do.

So I live here because it's quiet and green and the air smells fresh and clean and I like to look up from washing the dishes straight into the eyes of several deer, even though they did munch up my one rose bush.

And you know that boat I came here to live on? I never did

really live aboard her, mostly because I met the man I married. So in the end I sold her to my brother. She stays at the wharf now, but I can look down from our house and see other boats sailing out the harbour.

Marlyn Horsdal
Salt Spring Island, British Columbia

✉ From my kitchen window I see the tundra rolling up and away from Frobisher Bay. The mist is heavy on the hills this morning. Some British friends of ours who live near Winnipeg say pictures of the rolling tundra remind them of the Scottish moors. Perhaps that's why I live here. My maternal heritage is Scottish, and the Scottish part of me is attached to this tundra, its ruggedness, its arctic heather, its elemental beauty. My three-year-old daughter, Kirsten, and her friend Frankie roam about exploring a world of rocks, arctic flora, and wild berries. They can walk for miles, safe from the modern world of traffic, violence, and social despair.

From my front window, I see Frobisher Bay sprawling down to the sea. Its Inuktitut name, "Iqaluit," means "fish." Frobisher Bay inhabitants really live in a transition period: we have all the modern conveniences of southern Canada. We also have the living remnants of the Inuit culture and life-style, which has survived for several hundred years. When these two divergent life-styles clash we have social problems – violence, alcoholism, and family breakdown. But I'm here to experience the northern environment and try to understand it.

People are friendly in Frobisher Bay. Elders are respected; children are loved. We know our neighbours. The isolation and the small population bring people together. My *gallunaau* ("white-person") tongue has a difficult time with Inuktitut phrases, but I've taken two courses already and hope to continue my language training this winter.

Oh, yes, winter! Cold and dark, something to be avoided. Surely, you ask, you don't live in Frobisher for the winter? I guess the answer is yes and no. The winter *is* cold and dark. During November, December, and January the sun just peaks over the horizon and dusk is with us from mid-morning to mid-afternoon. But Frobisher sort of comes alive in the winter. People return from the land and southern holidays, school begins, the swimming pool opens, the Adult Education Centre begins a new school year. This fall's curriculum includes pasta making, introduction to Inuktitut, caribou-skin sewing, snowmobile repair, and basic job-readiness training, to name just a few. And there's still the tundra, now a hard, white expanse, to be explored. The wind-driven snow is the perfect highway for the hardy walker.

My husband will continue to explore this landscape by dog team, as well. We have six Canadian Eskimo dogs and an Alaskan husky to carry him out and away from town. As the days lengthen in January and the sun rises higher and higher each day, travel by dog team becomes more and more enjoyable. This year Kirsten will be able to accompany her dad on many of these outings.

I live where I live because winter turns into spring. Spring explodes on south Baffin. As the snow melts away in April and May, the plants start to grow. By June the tundra is covered with arctic poppy, broad-leaf willow herb, and purple saxifrage. It is truly a beautiful and magnificent landscape.

Nellie C. Dale
Frobisher Bay, Baffin Island

✉ On Christmas Day, 1968, I knew I'd be coming to Canada. I stood for a long time at the mailbox in Bangkok's main post office, holding a letter that contained my draft card and a brief note explaining I would not be going to Vietnam. It was one of those decisions that changes one's life forever.

Almost a year later I found myself in Copenhagen, alone and confronting an uncomfortable choice. Either I could fly directly to Canada, or I could fly home and face the authorities. In those days, Canada had established itself as a place where young Americans could flee. But I knew no one in the entire country. It's hard to go into such an unknown.

What did I know about Canada – apart from the cursory look we'd taken in grade four when I'd done a report on Saskatchewan (I'd picked the topic because I liked the length of the name) – had been gleaned from a volunteer I'd met in Borneo, a CUSO teacher who'd had a poster of Expo '67 on the wall of her bathroom. She told me a bit about her country, about Vancouver Island, where she'd grown up, about the huge Douglas firs and the glacier-wrapped mountains, and the peaceable Canadian people. To underline the attractiveness of Canada, she told me that in Nanaimo, where she lived, the climate was so mild that palm trees flourished.

Palm trees! I'd grown up in Boston, where nor'east snowstorms could – and on occasion did – wreak havoc on Red Sox opening-day baseball games at Fenway Park. So the thought of the palm trees settled into the back of my brain as I travelled across Asia and, I guess, got elaborated on over the passage of time into a Technicoloured, Disneyesque fantasy land. Canada, I told myself, was a country of palm trees and therefore a country of surfing and white sand beaches and year-round tans. I'd go to Canada and listen to the Beatles and eat fresh pineapples and ogle the women in their bikinis.

I stopped in Boston for a while, then drove west in late December and by the time I'd reached the prairies, a blizzard had swept down into friendly Saskatchewan, engulfing me in an icy world that my car's heater could not combat. I wore four pairs of socks. I stopped at innumerable cafés along the Trans-Canada Highway, stomping my feet and gulping cups of coffee. But what fortified me the most, what I clung to, was the vision of the palm trees of British Columbia swaying beneath a hot Pacific sun and the crowds of tanned sunbathers yelling, "Surf's up!"

In Alberta, I thought, surely, I'd begin seeing signs of a more temperate climate. British Columbia lay just a few miles ahead. Maybe, I comforted myself, I'd have to get on the other side of the Rockies to reach the sun. But snow and cold – arctic cold! – surrounded me, buffeted my car, and northern winds threatened to blow me into roadside ditches, there to be buried by some passing highway snowplow and forgotten about until spring thaw. I held onto the steering wheel tightly. I saw palm trees and hula girls beckoning me at the end of the Trans-Canada. They'd sing to me. They'd play ukuleles. And I'd dig my toes into the warm Pacific sand.

Down through the Fraser Canyon, past signs that read "Chains Required," past avalanche sheds, behind semi-trailers that churned up tornadoes of snow, I drove. . . . My fantasy of Canada gradually sprouted icicles. The radio reported that, yes, it was the heaviest snowfall in Vancouver's history, more than a foot on the ground already, and it was still coming down. Drivers were cautioned to stay off the road. So this is where I've come to live, I told myself, with a sense of apprehension. It could have been Siberia.

Later, I learned that there were indeed palm trees in British Columbia – six and a half of them. I saw them the next summer: six stunted, brownish, two-foot-high palm trees, and one entirely dead one, growing beside the highway in Nanaimo not far from the ferry terminal. They'd been planted by the local Chamber of Commerce as a sort of come-on to tourists, to emphasize the mildness of the region.

I don't regret that I succumbed to the lure. I've fit in with all the other immigrants who came here carrying in their heads a vision of a better place. It was – and *is* – a better place. That's why I live here still.

Daniel Wood
Vancouver

✉ All of my life, I've stepped into the back yard and stood amidst what I love; fields of golden corn and wheat, barns alive with robins, whistling swans in March, nights full of stars and crickets and dreaming. I could watch a violent thunderstorm and when it subsided the river would be mine alone. I'd paddle to the sunrise, tasting the puffs of mist on my tongue, touching the breeze of a heron's wings. I lived in an artist's palette. Everything around me was drenched in colour, and life . . . and changes.

But last year, when I was eighteen and just fresh out of high school, I left all that behind and headed north. There is no logical or practical reason I wound up in North Bay. This is simply where the car sputtered to its death. I've not lived in the city before and I'm finding it difficult. I've made a home of a crummy basement apartment with leaky pipes and no sunlight. The view from my window is that of my neighbour's garbage. I got myself a super job but it affords me no time to wander through the forests. To watch a sunrise, now, requires more than a three-minute hike down the embankment to the canoe. Now I cycle five miles, stash my bike in some weeds, climb a barbed-wire fence, thrash my way through a tangle of raspberry bushes, and hike to the spot where the sunrise is most magnificent. The dawn is no longer just a beautiful view. Now it is an achievement. North Bay is teaching me that every-thing that was once mine must be fought for to regain. No longer am I sure that there will be food in the cupboards, a comfortable place to sleep, warm clothes in winter, a good friend to confide in . . . and that incredible view. North Bay has filled me with uncer-tainties, stripping me of everything I've ever leaned on. She has forced independence at me, taking my every weakness to flaunt before me.

This city has shown me alternative life-styles I'd only read of in high-school novels, fiction, I had thought. Now I see the reality of bums sleeping in the streets, poverty, and insanity. She tossed my childhood into Nipissing. She told me to stand up and achieve, and spat on me for enjoying what others had achieved for me.

And just when North Bay forces as much at me as I can handle, making me angry, wanting to pack my bicycle and pedal away, she sends a finger of sunlight into my basement home, beckoning me to a small woods very nearby that I hadn't discovered yet. Just when I couldn't work so hard for another sunrise, the sunrise worked for me.

So to you, North Bay, a tip of my hat. You're exactly what I needed. Soon an artist will scrape me off this canvas and paint me into the wilderness, but this time it will be my achievement . . . and I'll mix my own colours.

Linda J. Berry
North Bay, Ontario

✉ I live on a farm with my wife and two children, the same farm I was born and brought up on, the farm my father farmed before me, the farm I have farmed for the past fifteen years and hope one day to be able to give to my son. I suppose I have always felt that somehow it was my duty or obligation to live here, although that is not the reason I stay.

To say that farming is my life is not necessary. What I do for a living and where I live are one and the same. The two cannot be separated. When I think of living where I do, I think of what I do. Why I farm is a different question. The fresh air, the open spaces, the freedom. All good reasons, but not the ones that keep me here.

Why *do* I live here, so far from the good things in life? Always a two- or three-day or longer wait for repairs if the repair can't be done in town. Shopping and being told, no, we don't have it in stock but we can sure get it. So far from the bright lights and entertainment. So far from a good library or decent bookstore. So far from a good meal and a stage play.

It's the land. When you live and work the land all your life, there is no question. It's like a rock, and will endure long after the oil companies have come and gone with their quick profits. There is nothing like the last day of harvest, or the first time you put your work boots on in the spring. The incredible feeling of looking up and seeing a red-tailed hawk riding the thermals over a summer-fallow field and knowing that that is exactly where she belongs. Hearing but not seeing that first flock of Canada geese flying over late one evening in the fall and praying because all you need is just five more days to finish harvest. The very happy and persistent chatter of the barn swallows as they wheel overhead or sit and criticize the way you repair the swather. Or getting the milk cow down from the pasture just as the sun comes over the horizon on a dew-drenched summer morning. The shimmering bright, hard-on-the-eyes, noonday sun coming off a quarter section of wheat just heading out. That feeling of being able to say that I made it through another Canadian prairie winter.

When it is the only place you have lived, there can be no other place on earth. The thought of moving away from this is terrifying. I live here because it is home. I live here because I want to. Because I always have.

Phillip Hansen
Hayter, Alberta

✉ It all started with my desire to go fishing in British Columbia. I wanted to catch some of those fabled trout I'd heard talked about by some of the well-heeled folks in the small town in Oregon where I was born. My husband muttered that he had yet to fish in all the lakes in Oregon, but if I could save enough money, we could go. We ate a lot of beans that winter and the children (all five of them) wore more patches than usual on knees and elbows.

We finally loaded ourselves, five children and two dogs, into a blue and grey Volkswagen bus. A twelve-foot aluminum boat made a shiny hat on top. Packed into the back of the bus were sleeping bags, food, and an outboard motor that gave off a faint perfume of gasoline.

It was July and we drove for five hot hours to reach the border between Canada and the United States, and another scorching seven hours to the Fraser Canyon. We spent the night in Williams Lake, counting our pennies at the motel.

No one told me about the road from Williams Lake into the "fabled fishing grounds" of Nimpo Lake. The children played submarine. They rolled the windows up tight and closed the air vents with shouts of "Dive, dive," as the bus was engulfed in dust from passing cars and trucks. The reddish-brown soil caked on the windshield. Thank goodness cars were few.

The country was awesome. Deep canyons eroded by the Chilko and Chilanko Rivers; deep holes in the gravel road through which the Volkswagen churned its way west.

During the trip, Roger said little. After a week of evening loon calls and quiet, he stood on the bank of the lake with a far-away look in his eyes. He watched the sun hide behind Mount Kapan. "If I can make a living here, we're moving."

It took three years of badgering Canadian Immigration before our family finally drove over the border at Aldergrove. With the point system, we didn't qualify. Roger was too old; we had too many children; and we didn't have jobs. Finally we squeaked through.

After a lot of stops and starts, we ended up in the Smithers area in northern British Columbia and I have spent the best ten years of my life there, freezing to death in the winter and working fifteen hours a day in the summer between a job in town and separating the rich loam of a farm from the existing brush and trees.

Along the way we picked up two foster children. We hadn't planned it, but there they were, standing on the street corner looking for a home. When there are already five in a family, two more just means two more potatoes in the pot.

Martha Scheel
Halfmoon Bay, British Columbia

✉ As the plane took off from Heathrow we were caught up in emotion. What was ahead? In England lay safety and family. But we were determined: we were going to make it work. We came to Canada from Detroit on the tunnel bus to Windsor. An American lady asked if we were going on vacation. No, we were immigrating, we told her. She said she came to Canada every week for the bingo – better prizes.

And then we were here, really here. We took a Greyhound bus to London, found a hotel, and then a bank. With no previous loyalties, we chose the Royal Bank. It sounded patriotic.

Have you ever tried to open a bank account with some cash (not a lot but more to come), no address except the hotel down the street, no job (but you'll start one on Monday), and no Canadian references? Have you ever tried to get a loan for a car – under the same circumstances – so you can get to work? But, bless her, the loans officer gave us one with a personal reference from Jim's high-school principal who, though we didn't tell her, was also my father.

In two days we had an apartment and walked a mile to the nearest mall to rent a telephone. We walked home with the phone in a plastic bag; we also bought a kettle, two garden chairs, and something to eat. On a bus a man sat next to us reading his paper, but he paused to speak to us. We told him we'd just arrived in Canada. "Oh, you must get off the bus with me and I'll take you home and lend you some stuff!" We protested but he insisted, and I'm sure he emptied his trailer for us. When we returned the things three weeks later, we met his family, who became our first Canadian friends. We have had many a laugh over our chance meeting.

Then work, and getting used to a different country's work methods and expectations. I was lucky to get a job in a furniture store, office work and telephone answering. I was told my English accent sounded good.

We learned the hard way, by making mistakes, and those first few months were hard but they set us on our feet. We worked through summer heat, homesickness, three job changes for Jim, the shock of a different culture.

Jim found a better job in Windsor as a General Motors machine repairman, and we moved there and put a deposit on a house. I was expecting our first baby.

Over the years we had a succession of ups and downs. I stayed home with that baby, and then the next one. Jim worked hard. We enjoyed the good life in Canada, mixing our English family values with the best of Canadian family values. After much thought we decided to have another baby, this one born in July, 1985. We had three Canadian children; we had become Canadian citizens. We had a good life, and many friends. Jim worked hard. I kept asking him to slow down once we were established. The children would be little for such a short time.

Our dreams came to an end on the twenty-fifth of January this year. Jim had a heart attack and died instantly at home. The children were then six, four, and six months old. But I have had a wealth of friendship and in the nearly eight years he was here Jim touched the lives of hundreds of people. He was the sort of man who helped you laugh at life. He was truly a happy man.

Now I must make my own dreams, find my own direction. I must treasure our children and help them know their Canadian identity.

Making a life in Canada was fun. We loved the bigness. Everything was big – the snowfalls, the extremes of temperature, the robins, the cars, the distances we travelled. We liked the freedom to grow. I have much to remember; the memories remain forever.

Margaret Donoghue
Windsor, Ontario

✉ I guess I live where I live because this is where my grandfather picked to homestead in 1906. There have been good years and bad years and the struggle never ends. I, my husband, and two children live near Eyebrow, Saskatchewan, on our 960-acre farm. We are in the severe drought area of southern Saskatchewan and hoping for next year, like so many others. There are years when the crops are so tall and the grass so green and everything seems to be in abundance. Then there are the years like these, when the crops are stunted and empty, the grass that came up in the spring was eaten off by the animals and has not shown its head since. The garden I tried to nurture was cleaned by grasshoppers till you couldn't see where it had been. Then there's the wind, always the wind. It always seems the drier the year the more it blows.

With all this, you may ask, why do you stay there? Some days I wonder, too. I guess the answer is roots. There is no one who will hang on longer for less return than a farmer. If farming was run as a business, like a dry-cleaning shop or a restaurant, for example, there would be very few farms. But to sell your farm is like selling your life, your roots, your friends, your community, your children's friends, and much more. Would you want to be the one who had to quit the land that had been seventy-nine years in the family? Ask any farmer if he left the farm what he would do. Most of them would have no idea. Farmers are jacks of all trades, masters of none.

The greatest problem for young farmers today is land payments. With the return we get on our grain today, it takes all a farm can produce, less in some years, more in others, to pay costs of production. Last year was a bad year and many could not make last year's land payment. With this year's crop even worse, how do we pay last year's and this year's? When my dad retired we had to buy the land from him and my bachelor uncle so they could afford to retire. If we can hold on, how will it be any better for our children? We can't pay today's bills, let alone put away any money for tomorrow. We raise pheasants to sell for meat to make a little extra money. We have our own milk cow, some pigs, and chickens to help with our own food. The banks right now are very tight on their money lending; they'll support you when times are good but when they're bad, too bad, look out for yourself.

Despite all these things, we want to stay here. It is a beautiful country and should offer so much. On a crisp fall morning when you stand out in the yard and hear the geese flying over, you say maybe next year will be better. That is why I live where I live.

Bonnie Mullin
Eyebrow, Saskatchewan

✉ Six years ago I was a legal secretary in Toronto. Now I have a hand-to-mouth standard of living in my bush shack in British Columbia's Chilcotin. I terrify myself felling my own trees for wood; I break my finger in Conibear traps; I get my truck started by putting the Coleman stove under the oil pan (with a cover over the flame, of course); I fight frost to harvest my garden and scythe my meadow for hay. Of course I have a few amenities: propane lights, running water, and a Styrofoam toilet seat in the outhouse! And I wouldn't go back to the city for anything. As a forty-year-old single woman, I seem to have become an exotic figure in my city friends' lives. I suppose I shouldn't be surprised, but this life is utterly ordinary and comfortable to me. I am home.

Penny Simpson
Tatla Lake, British Columbia

✉ Is my antipathy to "the great Canadian landscape" atypical? I often wonder at the vast empty space of the Canadian countryside. Awe-inspiring, definitely, a strange beauty, but to my way of thinking uninhabitable. So I choose to live in a city, Canada's cosmopolitan heart. I live in downtown Toronto, in a warehouse. No trees, no beautiful countryside, no birds or deer for me. I have no forests, no grassy meadows. I have a neo-classical lead factory, the CN train yard, the Gardiner Expressway, Molson's Brewery, and, on a clear day, from my roof, there, in all its vast blue beauty, I can see Lake Ontario. An industrial landscape. And, in the middle of all this, Fort York is comically anachronistic, a touch of our past. Ironic that the neighbourhood is largely Portuguese; on front lawns stand madonnas with neon haloes. In the summer the streets are filled with kids playing street hockey or roaring up and down on their bikes. A far cry from the Battle of Fort York.

Two south-facing windows and two skylights fill my space with light. I never tire of watching the traffic whiz by on the Gardiner. Everyone is in such a rush. I have access to my roof through one of the skylights. This summer I was able to listen to Tina Turner and Bruce Springsteen for free, and every night for two weeks I had the best view in the city of the fireworks at the Ex. Some evenings I just like to go up and watch the CN Tower, its lights blinking in the darkness. And in the place of stars I watch the tiny light specks moving across the sky – planes taking off and landing at the island airport.

Warehouse living has its drawbacks, of course. The communal toilet down the hall often gets appallingly dirty, and there's nothing worse than rushing to the john in the middle of the night to find it already occupied! And of course there is the water pressure, which is low to non-existent at the best of times. Imagine standing in the shower, covered with soap or shampoo, and suddenly the water cuts from full pressure to one scalding-hot trickle! The skylights are prone to leaking, not only when it rains, but every time it snows, too.

Insulation between our living spaces is nil, and the noise level can be excessive. There is the drummer downstairs who likes to practise from 10:00 P.M. to 1:00 A.M.; the family with the baby next door; the artist on the other side of me; and me (I'm certainly guilty of playing my stereo too loud). We all add to one another's headaches. And then, of course, there is the physical danger of living here. Outside one of my windows is a small grey airplane with four white boxes that look like houses. These very attractive little sculptures are in fact functional: they measure the amounts of lead in the air. Lead poisoning is a very real fear, not only for us warehouse dwellers but for the whole community.

The light here is truly wonderful, and the view strangely beautiful. The lead factory is a lovely building; the neighbourhood is colourful and friendly. And this building is always active with creative enterprise. I feel a part of a living, moving, breathing, ever-changing city. I love where I live, for it makes me feel alive.

Sarah MacLachlan
Toronto

✉ Yesterday I turned on the radio long enough to hear you say, "So write me a letter telling me why you live where you do." Must be a contest. Fine.

I live here because it's a small town and all the clichés you've ever heard about small towns are true and I happen to like living those particular clichés.

My only worry is that when all the city slickers find out, they'll move here and it won't be a small town any more. That's why I'm not putting my name or return address on this letter.

Don't try to trace me through the postmark. I drove many miles in the dead of night to mail this letter in a strange town very far away.

Anonymous

✉ When I first learned we were moving to Canada, I didn't think it was good news. I was in hospital at the time, and our family had moved eight hundred miles just two months earlier. And now the Canadian company, which had only a few months before hired my husband and moved us all, was closing down the shipyard where he worked. They offered to transfer him to another yard in Halifax. I still wake up some mornings astonished that outside my window, Canada stretches far, so very far to the west and north.

Unlike many Americans, we did know where Nova Scotia was and had made a vague wish to visit "someday." Now, as we pored over pictures of Peggy's Cove and the Cabot Trail and read descriptions of the expulsion of the Acadians and the Halifax Explosion, we became more and more eager to see our new home and experience its natural beauty, history, and culture for ourselves.

We came for a few days, to look over the city and find a place to live. While we were here, Haligonians were distressed over a murder in their city, the first in three years. When we returned home to organize the move, we learned that five people had been murdered in that city while we had been gone for the weekend.

The April day we officially entered the country, driving up through Maine and over the border at Woodstock, the seven of us – five people and two cats – were storm-stayed, trapped by a blizzard in Moncton, New Brunswick. We spent the night in the Howard Johnson's and woke the next morning unable to see out the floor-to-ceiling window because it was covered with snow. My mother-in-law, who was seventy-four and had seen many a winter, wondered what we had gotten her into. After the tractor cleared a path from the door to the parking lot, we continued on, deciding that if we were going to be Canadians, we couldn't let a little snow stop us.

The first summer we lived here, the Tall Ships came to Halifax. It was a magical time. They city had the atmosphere of a carnival for a week. Something happened, though, to remind me I was still an alien here.

It was the morning the U.S. Coast Guard ship *Eagle* entered the harbour. She is a lovely barque built in the thirties in Germany and confiscated as a war prize by the Americans. The sky that morning was almost as deep blue as the St. Andrew's cross on the Nova Scotia flag. Silhouetted against it were sailors poised one at the tip of each of the ship's yardarms as she was gracefully nudged toward her berth by tugs. On her bow arched a gold eagle, and from her stern billowed an enormous, brilliant, bold American flag. I snapped the shutter on my camera until I ran out of film, with tears running down my face. For the first time, I was homesick. Then I heard a voice in the crowd that had gathered on the pier say, "Those Americans, they're such showboats."

Growing up by the Mississippi River, I had never heard the word "showboat" used quite that way. Now, two years later, I understand a little better. I can feel myself slowly becoming "Canadianized." "Landed" now, I am beginning to find my place.

Nancie Erhard
Halifax

✉ Let me tell you why I, a country-bred, non-skiing foreigner, live in the winter city of Edmonton.

I came as a reluctant bride. That is, as a bride I was willing enough, but I was reluctant to leave the green English hills, the small farms and villages, the seasons, the culture, the history, the

71

safe known ways, and my friends: I was reluctant to exchange all that for this flat, colourless country with only two kinds of weather, and fields as big as whole countries at home, and a city hardly older than my parents, its history enshrined in concrete high-rise and store-front wood. "Here" was too big, too new, too dull, too empty, too hot, too cold; in short, it was not my home.

In twenty years, I have learned to love the subtle shades of the endless level of land, the great arch of sky that smoulders like a massive furnace on winter mornings and fades to the palest eggshell before the night; the gritty, boisterous – promising – winds of March, the sap-smelling mildness of May, and the profusion of daffodils and dandelions, apple blossom and cherry, lilac and lily that all come together in the spring.

I have heard a string quartet playing the "Eine Kleine Nacht Musik" in the middle of a busy shopping mall with the skill and concentration of the Wigmore Hall. I have watched plays in the theatre that equalled the best of London's West End. I have eaten exotically in dozens of ethnic restaurants, and wandered happily through the linking parks along the riverside. I have sung impromptu chorus in a people's "Messiah," marched for peace with mothers and babies down Jasper Avenue, searched for the *Journal*'s hidden gold brick, and watched the high comings and goings of the geese in the spring and fall.

This is a great city. It has a handsome legislative building with bells. It has a fine symphony with nothing – nowadays – to fear from the brass. It has the Strathcona foundation protecting what is by our standards old and interesting, and a wonderful reference library where you can find out anything you want, from the most obscure quotation to the colour of James Bond's eyes. This city has all kinds of fascinating shops, from the rich boutiques of West Mall to stores of thrift and charity and the frankly second-hand. It has impeccable magpies with dinner-jacket plumage and voices like rusty saws, and it has the best free public entertainment of your life at O'Hara's auction rooms.

In Edmonton I have a dear dilapidated house, and the postman shovels the steps for the pensioner across the street. I have a bookshop lady who treats me and my few paperbacks like royalty, a neighbour who makes funny windmills that keep blowing down off his roof; another who gives me more parsnips than I know what to do with, and a third who keeps chickens in the basement of his house – and that's not mentioning my friends.

You see, none of the things I have written about would bring a person to Edmonton in the first place, but together they make reason enough to stay.

Virginia Hobart
Edmonton

⊠ The rabbits ate all the three plantings of beets, a deer ate the asparagus, the dog was decorated by a skunk, and there is a blight on the tomatoes.

Why do I live where I live?

My place, near Crosshill, Ontario, is affectionately dubbed "Mad Hill," thanks to a small boy who, coming for a visit, could not remember the word "cross" (but he knew what it meant).

The time is not distant when I will not be happy about hitching the dog to the sled, strapping on the snowshoes, and beating my way through a blizzard to the car, or spending a half a day hauling in splintery wood for my voracious wood stoves.

In the meantime.

Nothing but a distant, tree-covered ridge impedes the rays of the sun as it rises early in the summer and late in the winter.

Nothing disturbs the silence of the dawn save first one, then several, then a cacophony of bird voices, and, sometimes, in the winter the notes of great horned owls calling from swamp to woods.

The dog, Mindemoya, can spend endless hours searching for groundhogs, and the cats can scramble up and down trees, as cats should.

This morning, from three until almost five, I sat, awestruck, in the middle of my living room and watched a storm of appalling majesty come, and go, and come again.

The rain came like the dumping of a giant bathtub, and once the lightning zinged down the conductor on the corner of the house, and the great dog crept up and put her muzzle under my arm, and the cats came in – you guessed it – dry!

Storms here rate one to five, on the gravel scale. This one rated four and one half hours of shovelling gravel to fill in the wash on the township road, so I could get the car out.

My Shangri-La is not without worries. Snowmobiles are a problem. Hunters are another thing – but sometimes they shoot each other. Probably my greatest problem is the very isolation that seems so necessary. Several times a month, I hie me into Toronto for a feast of friends, galleries, and music – my dose of culture.

I'm always happy to come back.

Frances Gage
Crosshill, Ontario

✉ I enjoy living where I am, indeed I do. And believe it or not, I live in a residence for seniors right in the heart of downtown Toronto. Some people dote on the open spaces and splendid view, or on the quiet forests or the intimacy of plants and animals – but I, despite my rural upbringing, am never happier than in the midst of a lively city. Here the tall, beautiful buildings reflect the sky and they reflect one another. Here the streets are full of human beings, who, like the surroundings, are busy with their own mysterious purposes.

My residence is home – without a capital *H*. It is a nice place to live, like my previous home. The big difference is I have friends to wipe away loneliness, and I have the suffocating chores of home and apartment living removed. I do not ask for perfection. After all, I am eighty years old and familiar with imperfection. I greatly enjoy the casual living, including always available bridge, and I enjoy the excellent programs that I would never take on my own.

The central location permits me easy access to family, and to life-long projects, such as the peace programs, the anti-poverty conference, City Hall doings – even the pro-choice meetings. Downtown keeps me alive today. I do wish our residence were mixed, young and old.

How could I give up my independence? Well, I've never had so much freedom. It's great to live downtown in a seniors' residence.

Avis McCurdy
Toronto

✉ My home used to be a stop over for animals on Fridays, as they waited to go to the Stratford livestock sale. Little pigs would stay in the three small stalls, and many times I would feed and water them. I'd be wearing boots to keep the dirty stuff off my saddle shoes; I'd help to herd the pigs up the ramp into the pickup. But all that is gone now, and *I'm* living in this barn.

The main part of my barn is square and small. It fits me just right, with no empty spaces left over. Since there is just one room, the kitchen and the living-room are just a glance from each other. People who visit me can be right in the centre of things just by sitting at the dining-room table. This openness really encourages communication. There is no isolation when there is but one simple room.

There is no bathroom here. Well, at least, not the civilized kind, the kind that takes you upstairs, away from the crowd, into a hushed, hygienic room. Mine is situated behind the door. It's hidden when I'm letting people into the "foyer," and by the time I close the door, they have already moved into the main room, and it's behind them.

I know of at least three people who have overflowed the pail under the sink. This is a hard system to get used to; you must be able to distinguish the different pitches when the sink water hits the pail water. If there is an echo, you are quite safe. But if there is no sound, the water is probably soaking into all the boxes and rags under the vanity. It's a lot of work when the pail overflows, but usually I say, "Just leave it. I'll clean it up." That's proper protocol for a hostess.

I look on showers and hot-water heaters as other-worldly now. I take my showers in the sink, after I've heated up a kettle full of water. Sure, heating slows me down, but if I had an endless supply of hot water bubbling out of the tap, I would probably take it for granted. This way, every drop of hot water is treasured. Actually, I have a lot more time to do important things, this way. For instance, while the water is heating up, I can write a letter to someone, and while it's cooling down to the right temperature, I can play the piano. If the hot water were ready at any moment, I'd have my routine chores done so quickly, I might be tempted to go into town and stand in line for something.

My barn doesn't have many windows, just three small ones. Often, the sun has to try one, then another, then the last before it can get in. When it does come in, it spills all over the cement floor like jewels. When my cat finds the jewels, she lies down in them and they spread all over her white fur. She loves living here. Maybe she senses the animal history in the old beams behind the panelling.

Last year, a stairway to the hay loft was built. A window was put in at the east end of it. That's where the bedroom is now. If you're not too tall, your head fits right into the keel of the ceiling, and it leads you from the stairs right to the bed. I love the way the slanted walls tuck me in at night.

Every morning, there is activity outside my window. Without any introduction, the sun arrives in its golden chariot. There are no visual interruptions between us and I sometimes dream that the sun and I are companions. We are the only two, for those few brief beautiful moments each morning, I stay awake long enough to fully receive the sun into the day. Then I go back to sleep.

Two of life's important events set the rhythm of my days here: the rising and setting of the sun. I can walk down my lane to the place where the dogs start barking, and there, the most miraculous sunsets happen just behind Reverend Morris's barn. This closing

to each day helps me to remember that human stresses and con‑
cerns are mere triflings against this powerful backdrop of nature.
The wealth and beauty of man's world offers no sustenance to the
soul; they stimulate us only to compete. Here, I feel no such stim‑
ulation. Who would compete with the crashing thunderstorms that
wake me in the night; or the white moon that gets caught in the
apple tree behind Jack and Marg's; or the Pleiades?

Of course, these can be seen anywhere. Iona is not unique for
its natural wonders. But the simplicity of life, here in Iona, Ontario,
makes them stand out. Life is made rich in this way. Here I can
see what is real.

That's why I like where I live.

Susan Fillmore
Iona, Ontario

✉ Why *do* I live where I live? Are there majestic mountains nest‑
ling in the distance? Is the roar of the ocean defeaning to my ear
as it crashes to shore? Are huge monoliths glistening and reflecting
amid the bustle of early‑morning traffic? Is there an idyllic river
meandering past my back door? Does the scent of fresh rain off the
multitudinous evergreen forest waft through my open window?
Can I hear the laughter of sequined patrons leaving various the‑
atres, operas, and opening nights? Is that sky so gargantuan you
could get smothered in its glory? Is the view through my expansive
front bay window so breathtaking that there is no oxygen left in
the room? Is the tumbling snow so brilliant and crisp it is both
blinding and exhilarating? Are the leaves resplendent in gold, crim‑
son, and ochre, and rustling softly in the autumn breeze? Did a
flock of brilliant cobalt‑ultramarine blue jays whisk by my window,
rivalling the luminescent sky? Can I hear the lone, solemn cry of
the wolf, alternating with a reverberating loon's call, as I stroll into
the moon‑swept horizon? Does that sunset saturate the evening
sky in a palette of chromatic splendour? Is that thunderous clamour
a herd of migrating caribou, or an approaching storm about to
awaken sleeping grandeur?

Can I take my brown-paper bag and fill it with an unending assortment of fresh lobster, zucchini, bagels, and tree-tapped maple syrup? Is that dress I'm choosing Alfred Sung, or is that from the new Marilyn Brooks collection? To all these questions and limitless others, the answer is a resounding *NO!*

Toni Nash
Irma, Alberta

✉ I was already a grown man when I moved from tumultuous Tehran to wind-swept Winnipeg. Ten years later, accompanied by my wife and sons, I moved to Victoria. We have lived here long enough to see the trees grow from saplings to sturdy oaks in our yard, and so consider ourselves Canadian, even "Victorian."

Yet it was less of a shock to go from Tehran, in the Middle East, to North American Winnipeg, than from Winnipeg to Victoria.

The Tehran-to-Winnipeg climate change did not shock me, as I was forewarned. One of my brothers, who had recently come back from the Prairies, had told me, "They have two seasons over there: July and winter!" So, armed with this intimidating information, I was even able to survive the great blizzard of 1966, my first and coldest Canadian winter. Yet the weather was much better than I had imagined, the winters much shorter than I was told, and the indoor life and underground connections much warmer than I had thought. No wonder my brother could not perfectly advise me on the type of clothing I needed. For the outdoors, nothing was warm enough; for the indoors, everything was too much. Actually, the mosquitoes, in the short hot summers, bothered me more than the winters.

From wide, flat, modern, underpopulated Winnipeg, Tehran looked like a tumultous sea of people with a mixture of old and new buildings, separated from the Caspian Sea by a chain of naked mountains with everlasting snow streaks amid the peaks. Compared to Winnipeg, Tehran appeared three-dimensional and four-seasoned, full of walls and gates, instead of lines and spaces. I soon

78

learned to respect the Winnipeg lines (whether solid or dotted) much more than I had in the streets of Tehran; rather than putting them between the wheels of my car, I learned to keep my car between the lines. I almost got killed by an oncoming car in the right lane before I learned this simple rule.

As the years went on, I learned that the lines and spaces are not just in the streets or around the houses, but that there are invisible boundaries around the body and the mind of every individual. Touching, which was common in Tehran (even the houses touched each other), was not allowed, and the space around the individual sitting next to you at the table prevented you from moving your arm to reach for the salt shaker. (They prefer you to ask them and they will pass it to you.)

From Victoria, Winnipeg, with its surrounding miles and miles of nothingness, looked more like an island than Victoria, separated by a narrow zone of water from the mainland, but with so many "connections" to big cities and so close to wilderness. From Victoria, Winnipeg felt like a warm and friendly place. I considered myself already a Canadian when I moved from Winnipeg to Victoria, not knowing that I had to answer again the same questions that a newcomer to Canada is usually asked.

In Victoria, nature is beautiful, green, wet, and three-dimensional again. Trees grow everywhere, insulating and separating you from your neighbours, your friends, and the sea.

In Tehran, friendship was necessary (if not compulsory); in Winnipeg it was useful; but in Victoria, Mother Nature seems to try to wean you of this habit. You can go with her fishing, wind surfing, hiking, bird-watching, or just walking . . . with no need for another friend.

I like this city, and I think we are living in the best place in the world. I know it is not perfect – just the best – but the best is good enough for me!

Nasser Shojania
Victoria

EAVER'S HILL AND LONGSHOT

As I said in the introduction (although I'd kept it secret till then), my favourite letter of all in the original *Morningside Papers* came from Krista Munroe. She had written it – it was about suicide, and how she felt about life from the perspective of the debilitating disease that had afflicted her – in September of 1983. A couple of years later, I learned from her brother-in-law that her disease was in remission, and she had had a baby. I called her then, in 1985, to congratulate her, and learned, among other things, that she had called the baby Longshot. She sent me a photo, which hung on my wall for the next two seasons. Then, in March of 1987, I made a speech to some teachers in Medicine Hat, Alberta, and when I had finished, I found a note from her at the podium. I ran to catch her at the door (she had just wanted to say hello, she said) to say how much I had enjoyed her letter, and to see how she and Longshot (actually, he's called Ben now) were doing. She had some news. I asked her to keep in touch. The result is the letter that concludes this chapter. I received it on the very last day of the 1986–1987 season, and read it on the air just after an interview with Pierre Elliott Trudeau that attracted a great deal of attention. I'm very happy to print her letter here, with its happy ending – at least for now.

First, another story, which tells itself, I think, in the letters that precede Krista's. They're from another remarkable woman, Vivienne Anderson. That story has a happy ending, too. I called Vivienne – I had talked to her on the phone earlier when she was in hospital in Toronto – to ask for permission to run these letters in this book. (She's planning to publish a complete journal of her experiences later on.) Before I asked about the letters, I asked how she was. "Fine," she said, "although I haven't eaten for fifteen months. I'm on an intravenous diet." As well, she told me, she had become the music critic of the Fredericton *Daily Gleaner*.

✉ Late last winter I moved to Weaver's Hill, an old farmhouse on five overgrown acres at Charters Settlement, a few miles outside Fredericton, New Brunswick. I have lived in many different places on two continents, and since coming to Canada eleven years ago, I have lived in five towns in three different provinces. Yet I know now that I have finally found the home I will never willingly leave, because I feel a sense of deep belonging here, which I have felt in no other place except the house where I was born.

A cynic might claim that I am living here because I had no other choice, and that is certainly why I came here. When a debilitating illness forced me to abandon my Ph.D., my husband jumped at a permanent job in Fredericton to escape from a cycle of short-term contracts and chronic underemployment. Packing up our books and

81

bags once more, we left the extravagant beauty of Vancouver and headed down east. It seemed just another stage in the perpetual motion for which my family refers to us as the Rolling Stones.

We arrived in January, and found the search for somewhere to live frustrating. No one in their right mind puts a house up for sale in the middle of a New Brunswick winter, and the only properties available were those left over from the previous year because of their ruinous price or equally ruinous condition. Instead of the convenient modern bungalow we had envisioned, we bought our country farmhouse because it was, quite simply, the only house on the market whose generous proportions could accommodate the wheelchair I must sometimes use. But the house and land have captured my imagination and kindled an emotional fire.

What is it about Weaver's Hill that has me so besotted? In winter it is the music of the wind swirling around the hilltop and breathing down the chimney of the wood stove so that it vibrates with an eerie, flute-like note, while I sit snugly beside it. It is the massive twisted pine, sole remnant of the mature forest, which dominates the snow-clad back field. It was once rejected because its curves were unsuitable for ship building: its dignified branches now dwarf the frivolously swaying twiglets of the birches and aspens. It is the tracks of the deer passing scarcely one yard from the living-room window, the scattered marks of the snowshoe hares as they leap prodigious distances, and the daily search for unknown tracks in the snow, in the hope that one day, just one day, like the boy who grew up here between the wars, I might see the rarest of New Brunswick residents, the eastern panther.

In springtime the cause of my enchantment is more obvious. It lies in the exuberant flowering of a Wordsworthian host of daffodils, so lovingly planted here over the years. It is the chorus of bullfrogs who interpret any sound in their own vocal range as the call of a rival, and so break into rapturous love song whenever they hear the metallic clanging of the mailbox. It is the discovery, within a quiet circle of cedars and elms, of the graves of James and Catherine Greer, who built the farmhouse in the late 1840s, their resting place now tended only by the pileated woodpeckers who have carved their appropriately coffin-shaped holes in the surrounding tree trunks. Above all it is the stream of multicoloured warblers performing their ceaseless acrobatics in the weeping willow beside the porch.

In summer, my love for Weaver's Hill has been sparked by the heady sweetness of the clover, alive with butterflies and bees. I have watched the Milky Way splashed across the sky, set amid so many stars invisible in the city that I could not at first recognize the constellations I had learned as a child. I have enjoyed a crop of raspberries so abundant that having filled the freezer, we invited our friends to a U-Pick, and still had enough left over to feed the bear who left his tracks across the garden and trod a fat pathway through the golden rod and fireweed.

My first autumn is just beginning and I am eagerly awaiting the discoveries it will bring. Yet my infatuation is not limited to the natural beauty of the land. I love the clean lines and balance of the farmhouse itself, the combination of the central gable of the early Gothic Revival with the classic restraint of the Loyalist tradition. I love the huge farm kitchen, decorated in primitive red, white, and blue where we serve our friends a Sunday brunch of raspberry pancakes and local maple syrup. I love the panelled oak doors, rescued from another old house, which form the entrance to my studio and serve the useful purpose of keeping out the kittens who would otherwise use my loom as an adventure playground, swinging from the warp like Tarzan of the Apes. When they have reached the age of comparative discretion I shall leave the doors open and then they may play with the balls of yarn, sleep on unspun fleece, and exercise the other privileges they enjoy by virtue of that most favoured of feline professions, the weaver's cat.

We call the farm Weaver's Hill because I am the second weaver in recent years to have set up my studio here. But when Catherine Greer was a young woman on a homestead newly carved from the bush, every farm attic also had its loom. The continuity of the weaving, the enduring elegance of the farmhouse, and the permanent beauty of the land of this understated, underrated province, combine to prove to me that this is a spot that has been especially beloved by others for the last one hundred and forty years, just as I love it now. And that is why, though I came here out of expedience, I want to stay here for the rest of my life. From some-one who has lived here for less than a year and has a track record worthy of a will-o'-the-wisp, this is impertinence. But like so many other things that live at Weaver's Hill, I have put down my roots and I am growing.

✉ When I last wrote, I had planned a quiet and creative fall and winter. I would weave, write, and watch the natural beauty of this enchanted spot come full circle to March first, the date in 1985 when we had moved in. I thought I knew how my life was going to unfold inside the house, and I anticipated few surprises outside. I was even prepared to feel the accustomed tinge of sadness as autumn foreshadowed the coming of winter and the dying of the year.

Nothing went as planned. For several years my health has been precarious, but this autumn my life fell apart, and I have been in and out of the hospital, subject to the whims of a capricious disease with an uncertain prognosis. My exile from Weaver's Hill was to Fredericton. As cities go it's a quaint, overgrown village, but the sense of dislocation was complete.

The contrast between town and country has been a recurrent theme on *Morningside*. The real comparison is not the proximity of neighbours, but between the presence or absence of technology. And there can be no greater contrast than between the natural world of trees and branches pulsating with life-giving sap, and that gleaming temple of high tech, the modern hospital, where the sap is intravenous fluid and the branches are tubing in every imaginable orifice.

Instead of looking out from my bedroom window at a pastoral landscape, in my hospital room I had a grandstand view of the municipal water tower. Instead of the silence of the rural night, my sleep was punctuated by the querulous demands of the patient in the adjoining room, and other more disturbing sounds and smells must necessarily be left unchronicled. It was perhaps for this reason that when I returned to Weaver's Hill between bouts of illness, it was the sounds and smells of fall and winter, not the visual images, that imprinted themselves most indelibly on my mind.

This sharpening of the senses was less marked in early fall, but even then I was moved, not by the brilliant display of scarlet and crimson that I had anticipated, but by the golden days of Indian summer: when sulphur butterflies spiralled upward into the sky, while buttery aspen leaves spiralled down to join the soft drifts beneath the trees. As I stood under the birches, I could actually hear the leaves falling. With every breath of wind there was a sputtering crackle as the stems separated cleanly from the tree and the leaves descended, brushing against the seared foliage as they fell. On the ground the ripening leaf-mould gave off a smell as appetizing as any loaf of newly baked bread.

It was when I came home again after the leaves had fallen and the trees stood stark and grim that all my expectations of fall and winter were violated. I discovered that winter was not a time of death, but the season of teeming promise. On my favourite tree, the massive twisted pine, the needles nearest the trunk had earlier turned a rusty, stricken brown, so that in my ignorance I had feared they were diseased. Now the autumnal gales had stripped this biennial harvest and the pine was confident in its coat of fresh dark green, as newly minted as a spring-clad broadleaf.

I had never really looked at twigs before, and when I did I realized how false are all those springtime clichés of the budding of the year. It's true that buds swell and burst in spring. But they are formed in summer, and throughout the winter they sit sleekly on the twigs, already holding the promise of their future. As for the alders, those otherwise undistinguished weed trees, they even flaunt catkins in December, miniature pairs of dessicated prongs on the end of each branch, like tiny pairs of trousers hung out to dry.

When I went back to the hospital, I carried this renewed hope with me. And then I found that even there, surrounded by suffering and death, Weaver's Hill looked after its own. For the querulous voice in the next room turned out to belong to the great-great-grandson of the pioneers who had built the farmhouse one hundred and forty years ago. And I talked to the man's wife, and learned some of the early history of the house and of the family who had lived there.

I have been at home now since a few days before Christmas, and as the festive lights go out and we come to the bleakest time of the year I do not know what lies ahead. But just before the first deep snowfall came, I discovered the final unexpected lesson of winter. One evening at dusk Richard was frantically digging manure into a new flower-bed before the promised storm could arrive, when he called me to come and see the source of a curious green light he had unearthed. At first it did not seem to come from a living creature, for it shone with the greenish glare of neon hotel signs or phosphor computer screens. It was a glow-worm, the larva of the fireflies that flash so frivolously through our summer skies. But unlike the gleams of those ephemeral beetles, this light was steady and unwavering. And as I face into the darkness of the new year, I take comfort in the knowledge that here at Weaver's Hill, as at countless other wild places in Canada, deep under the snow and ice of winter, there are a myriad living lanterns burning unseen, the colour of hope, potent symbols of life, not death.

✉ I last saw Weaver's Hill, my beloved home, in early March. I saw it for just half a day, a moment of cruel, biting beauty in the aftermath of an ice storm. Then I went back to the hospital again, this time to Toronto, where my exile was complete.

As my health gradually improved I began to read again, and started with the work of another exile, Isak Dinesen's memoir *Out of Africa*. This is not the high-class soap opera of the movie, but the spare and utterly beautiful recreation of her life in Kenya, the magical world that had meant so much to her before she lost it forever.

When I turned to her biography I learned that she had written it not on her return to Denmark, as I had thought, but several years later. As she herself said, "One must have things at a distance." And as I read those words, the image of Weaver's Hill seemed clearer, and I realized that when I am at home the notes I scribble each day in my nature journal are merely the Beaujolais Nouveau of memory, and that deep in the dusty cellars of my mind a hidden vintage may be ageing in the dark.

But every cellar needs a key, and it was not until several days later that my husband provided it when he arrived at the hospital with an armful of budding maple branches. The maples at Weaver's Hill are some of the oldest trees on the property; they stand in two crooked lines and arch across the driveway. They date from the years when the farmer's horses would pull a cart down the rutted hill on a hot summer's afternoon, or drag a sleigh behind them, its runners carving a pair of hissing blue snakes in the snows of winter. The trees are past their prime now and have not aged gracefully. In summer and autumn the dying, broken branches are all too obvious. It is when the leaves have fallen that they come into their own again, their twisted limbs framing the house from the road, a classic title-page from a childhood fairy story. And that was how I had seen them last. I thought I could remember nothing else.

But the crimson maple buds clustered in succulent bunches at the end of each twig reminded me of the gentle, teasing quality of spring in New Brunswick. The most obvious prankster is the grass, which performs a tantalizing Dance of the Seven Veils with the final snowfalls before turning, chameleon-like, from brown to green, with a progression so subtle that while you are making up your mind which colour it is, it has vanished beneath a carpet of dandelions that sprouts overnight.

The maple trees have a special version of this magician's sleight of hand. When I lived in the city I used to think that they were red only once a year. Since moving to Weaver's Hill I have discovered otherwise. The winter buds are softly shaded with rose, though you need to be up close to see them. But there comes a moment in early spring when, just before the swelling bud scales split apart, they take on, in gaudy profusion, the very same scarlet hues the leaves will flaunt in fall. It's an explicit promise to tide us over the tattered drabness of their summer green.

As spring began to unfold this year, the flowers sent by friends provided other keys to memories I did not know were there. A bunch of daffodils recalled the day the ice of a particularly late snowfall slid off the steeply sloping roof onto the crowded flower-beds that line the farmhouse. The damage to the flowering bulbs seemed beyond repair, and I was near tears at the loss of so much beauty, only to see the daffodils appear almost to burn their way back through the snow, cheerful and radiant, quite untouched by their close brush with death.

One day last week an elegant arrangement of blue iris arrived beside my bed, and looking at its velvet serenity I recalled the day when a much-loved friend was due to visit Weaver's Hill for the first time. Although it was pouring with rain, I had gone searching for flowers to welcome her discriminating eye. Hidden amid the unlikely fronds of the asparagus bed, I found the perfect flower: an iris whose convoluted petals contrasted with the piercing purity of its spear-like leaves, a timeless Chinese water-colour. As I lay in bed, I remembered that flower, and the taste of the rain on my face, the squeak of slippery grass under my boots, and the sheer exultation of springtime after the rigorous New Brunswick winter.

I've always found Keats's poem "Ode on a Grecian Urn" to be faintly ridiculous, romanticism carried just one step too far. But now I realize that I was the one who never understood. There's a haunting phrase in the poem: "heard melodies are sweet, but those unheard are sweeter," and now I know exactly what he meant. In a few weeks' time I shall be going back to Weaver's Hill with a new lease on life, and until I do, although I shall be deprived of this year's spring, I have my cellar well-stocked with memories; I have opened up the door, dusted off a few of the cobwebbed bottles, and found that the vintage is good.

✉ It is May, and I have returned to Weaver's Hill.

When I left Toronto, Ontario was already beginning to shift towards summer, but New Brunswick is rarely a pioneer, and was still firmly in the throes of spring as I came home. The daffodils and tulips had splashed their bold colours around the farmhouse, while the trees, in counterpoint, were at their most delicate as each new leaf slowly unfolded to reveal the same perfection as the tiny hand of a newborn child.

The kittens, now sedate young matrons indoors, have reverted to their kittenhood outside, and gambol on the grass with unrestrained enthusiasm, chasing bees and moths and pouncing on the dandelions that pepper the rampant lawn. The bleeding-heart bush beside the porch has stretched out its swaying fronds and is once more the favourite resting place of the ruby-throated humming-birds, which play at hide-and-seek all day around the feeder hanging above it. For the first few days after their return, which coincided with my own, the hummingbirds recuperated from their long journey, but now the males have begun their semicircular display fights, zooming up and down and twittering with ridiculously high-pitched machismo. I saw both kittens sitting on the lawn beneath one such strutting male, and as he swayed back and forth above them they sat entranced, their heads turning endlessly from right to left, and left to right, like avid spectators at the Centre Court of Wimbledon.

Walking through the rough grass beyond the raspberry canes, I found a silvery fragment hanging from a hawthorn. It was the newly shed skin of a garter snake. Like the snake, I have had to shed the protective covering of my old way of life, slowly and painfully, and take on a new life, which will restrict me henceforth. But like the snake, I am renewed and can feel all that surrounds me with the heightened sensitivity of a skin long insulated from the outside world.

Mine was no dramatic brush with death, or mystical return of a silenced heartbeat; just the painstaking resolution of a seemingly intractable illness. And now I am free to take up the threads of my life again, and I mean to do that quite literally, by sitting down once more to the hypnotic rhythms of the weaver's loom that gives the farm its name.

The greatest joy of my return has been to learn that, though fresh discoveries lie in wait for me every day, the house that captured my imagination when I first saw it less than eighteen months ago has grown to fit me like a comforting shell. When I first came to Weaver's Hill, I was frequently startled by the unexplained noises of the old homestead. As time passed, I came to recognize these one by one: the insect-like ticking of the studio roof as it expanded in the sunlight; the moaning vibration of the hollow bedroom door in a summer gale; and even those thumps and creaks that to this day remain a mystery are now, on my return, as familiar as my husband's step on the stair or his breathing at night. As darkness falls at Weaver's Hill, this gentle lullaby of sound is as soothing as the movements of a cat that washes its paws, turns itself around, and settles down to sleep beside the fire.

Vivienne Anderson
Weaver's Hill, New Brunswick

✉ I've wanted to write to you for a long time but for many reasons I talked myself out of it. For one thing, I subscribe to Walt Kelly's principle that nothing is so urgent now that won't be urgenter tomorrow.

The last little while has been interesting for me. For one thing, my Hodgkin's disease recurred. After a few delays and a confirming biopsy, I finally started chemotherapy at the end of August. I wonder if I can even describe how nervous I was before I started the chemical warfare again. I talked to a kid who had this treatment for a whole year, and he told me a bit about what to expect. I thought I could survive anything, but I really dreaded the thought of losing all my hair, especially since I thought the wigs were *so* awful. And I resented having to do this again. I asked myself on more than one occasion whether I was really going to do it. I was convinced that I'd just get over this batch and have to do it all again and again and I'd end up dying from the disease (or the treatment) anyway. And this time I wasn't just going to miss getting old: I was also going to miss watching my son grow up – last time

I didn't have him. (It's funny, but the longer I live, the more I feel I'm going to miss when I die. I always thought really old people felt like they'd done everything and were ready to die. Just shows that if you've never been old, you really don't know what it's like!)

After the required self-pity, I got tough. One can only wallow so long and then it gets tedious. Besides, with six months of chemotherapy ahead of me, I didn't have the luxury of time. And there's nothing special about this whole thing – everyone alive gets their share. Mine happens to be cancer. Someone else's is paralysis; another's is a jerk for a spouse, and so on. If you're alive, you've got things to deal with, and it's only a result of being alive, nothing else. It's also not fair or unfair. It just *is*.

I always felt like I had a choice: take the treatment, with all its problems, or don't take the treatment. By making an active and positive choice, I believe that some of the discomforts were easier to handle.

Well, thank heavens *those* six months are over! I really didn't think I was going to survive sometimes. I have never been so tired (there are six stairs from my kitchen to my son's room and I used to have to rest after climbing them), or so down. (Cesamet – synthetic dope – did help with the nausea and vomiting, but it made me so depressed and paranoid that I can barely stand to think of it even now.) I spent most of that six months feeling really good, though. The reality of chemotherapy is that your life doesn't stop while you get it – you just have to schedule things a little more carefully than other people do. The days you get the chemicals and the next few days are probably not good ones to plan to do anything, but after that you may have to go a little slower but you can still go. I had the good fortune (because of my wonderful husband) to get to play with my kid nearly every day of the week. Not only that, but because of the chemotherapy I am still alive to hear him count to ten for the first time, to hear him sing "Bawett's Pwivateews" (he loves Stan Wogers), and to watch him go down the slide *all by himself*. So you see, I was telling the truth when I said that the recurrence wasn't really a tragedy. It's a hell of a setback, but at the least I've got a little while longer, and at the most

I could even be cured. (I hate all this stuff. I hate the times I'm sick, I hate being unable to do some of the things I want to do, I hated losing my "immortality." I hate the thought that I probably won't be spending the next fifty years with my husband. But who ever gets any insurance in that department? We're all subject to the bus factor, aren't we?)

I have managed to stay busy these past few months. I am now vice-president of the local unit of the Cancer Society and I'm involved in a public-education study that is using some of the Steve Fonyo money to supply information to people about preventable types of cancer. It has always seemed more practical to me to try to prevent those diseases we *can* prevent than to concentrate on treating the sad results the general neglect of preventive medicine has engendered.

I also work for the SPCA as its secretary, and consequently I occasionally get involved in the controversies surrounding rodeos, cat control, and fur coats. I've discovered just how emotional people get when it comes to "their" animals versus "someone else's" animals. I find it quite amazing that some people are so preoccupied with the effect that cats and dogs have on *grass*! Oh, to have such an uneventful life that grass could be my major concern!

I've taken a couple of courses at the college here, and I've managed to keep up on some other things as well. But the most important thing of all is that I get to spend some great time with my kid. I had no idea that a little kid could be so much fun. (This is just the ignorance of inexperience, of course, but it has been quite a discovery for me.)

Speaking of Ben, he just woke up from his afternoon nap and is asking me to read "And to Think That I Saw It On Mulberry Street." In fact, he's saying, "Mum read 'Marco keep your eyelids up.' " It is fascinating just how much little kids can remember. So I'd better go rescue him.

Krista Munroe
Medicine Hat, Alberta

92

ALL FROM THE LOVE OF MS. PAC-MAN...

This is a collection of what we called Private Passions, or part of it. I think it's self-explanatory: I started with some confessions of my own; listeners responded. It's "part of it" only because as I mulled over the entire collection – even after I and my editorial collaborators had boiled down the collection that had been read on the air to what we thought worked best in print – I realized we still had far too many to include in one chapter. So some more, some of those we received about passions for food, appear later on, in Chapter Twenty.

Actually, I still haven't explained it all. At least one of the passions in this first selection, Margaret Taylor's intricate composition about her love for crossword puzzles, wasn't read on the air at all, for obvious reasons, and some of the others. . . .

Never mind. Here are some things some Canadians were privately passionate about in the late 1980s, beginning with the video game that has its hold on me – although, as it was to turn out, I was not alone.

I

✎ To the tell-tale imprints of a misspent life that have set themselves on my right hand – the splayed nail of a childhood football injury, the yellow smear of my unbroken nicotine habit, the all-but-permanent inkstains – I have added, in middle age, a horny callous on the inside of the first knuckle of my second finger.

It would please me (not to mention my hungry publishers) to announce that this latest scar marked the energy expended as I hunched over a manuscript, squeezing a pencil as I honed my prose, or even that I had gained it on the golf course, working so hard on a proper overlapping grip that I had stamped my gloveless right hand forever, and was now, as the result of my dedication, shooting regularly in the low eighties.

But the cause is, alas, a more prosaic one. The newest callous on my gallery of passions marks the entry into my life of Pac-Man, or, to be more proper, *Ms.* Pac-Man, a video game designed to suck quarters from the pockets of aimless adolescents in shopping malls, which has, in the hermetically sealed eyrie of my downtown Toronto apartment, captured me.

I love this game. I bought my own edition last Christmas, as a gift (ostensibly) for the person who shares my eyrie and my life, but also (or so I pretended) as a lure to my children, all young adults, whose lives are now so full, or so I feared, that a visit to their ageing parent, who goes to bed at sunset, needs an extra incentive. Those purposes worked. My lady broke into giggles of pleasure when I whipped Ms. Pac-Man's dust-cover off and she now plays the game in the high eighty thousands. My kids pretend to ignore the arcade corner of my apartment, but they visit me steadily, to my delight, and sometimes I have to pluck them away from the Pac-Man board as, on Saturday mornings long ago, I had to stand beween them and Roger Ramjet – except now when they stand up I move into their place or, at the least, insist on a game of doubles.

Ms. Pac-Man – or the version I have, which is a self-contained table, with flashing lights and a twinkling tune – is not cheap. Since

Christmas, though, if I had continued to sneak down to the ice-cream parlour in the main concourse of my building, pumping quarters into the slot of the game that had hooked me there, I might well have paid the price of ownership ten times over. Besides which, as I cackle to myself each evening, punching up another free game (dare I admit that sometimes if the early play is not going well I have found a way to abort that effort and start again – the Pac-Man version of a mulligan?), it's an awful lot cheaper (not to mention more realistic in today's crowded housing) than having your own golf course.

Even now, eight months after I unveiled it in my home, I cannot explain Ms. Pac-Man's appeal. Other electronic games, from Space Invaders to Centipede, appeal to me slightly less than an evening of watching the parliamentary channel in translation. And every-one I know young enough to have experienced the video revolution in person warned me that, however entranced I'd been by my early excursions to the ice-cream parlour, I would tire of it soon – even though my personal game has its own counter-ennui device, a secret button that increases the speed.

But here I am, an eight-month veteran, still rushing through the door when I return from the road or from a hard day here at the world's most pleasant job, dropping my briefcase, pulling up a chair and, before I can pour the evening's first libation, scrunching over the blinking lights and darting images, and smiling quietly as I add a new layer on the callous.

Part of it, I think, is that practice makes you, if not perfect, then at least better, and Ms. Pac-Man rewards you with measurable returns. I envy athletes, as I've said before, in that when they get home at the end of a day and their loved ones ask them how they did, they can say simply that they won or lost, while the rest of us grope with qualifiers and moods: the first interview went well (I think) but then there was that dreary meeting with . . . . And so on. Ms. Pac-Man is an athlete: thirty thousand one day, forty thousand the next. And the better you play, the more interesting grow the challenges, until one magic day when you've dodged your way through the first two screens, gobbling up the opposition after a clever manoeuvre has given you the power, running cleverly for cover when the power runs out, then scampered your way through the next and more difficult three, then, keeping your cool as the pace grows ever more frantic and the demands ever quicker, you survive the tension of the four red screens and, as the machine tootles out the strains of the theme song announcing its most challenging set of screens and the picture of a stork floats across the screen, and you . . . .

But I am fantasizing now. I have never reached this plateau – although some of the people for whom I pretended to buy it have, and reached numbers in the eighties and nineties of thousands that I can only dream of. But in the hours during which I try, while the tensions of the real world drain from my weary mind, and the news blares unheard from the TV and the newspapers lie unread on the floor, I wiggle happily at the controls of my machine, the smiling figure who represents *me* on the screen darting blithely among its enemies, holding to its tenuous freedom.

"Pac-Man is a silly idea," wrote Martin Amis (Kingsley's son) in a book I treated myself to when my addiction was first flowering, "but a good game." And maybe the world needs more of both those things.

For now, though, it is among my private passions, and I feel better this morning, on this first day of a new season of *Morningside*, for having bared my chest about it – callous and all.

II

✎ The second in the series of private passions I want to admit to bears all the earmarks of classic addiction. It began innocently, when I was young and carefree, and at first I was sure that whatever pleasures it gave me I could take or leave alone. It grew quietly over the years, and even my best friends – or so I was sure, although in recent years I have found some of them looking quizzically about my apartment – were not aware of how deeply the hook had been planted. And only now, in the terminal stages of fixation, do I realize how much it has taken over my life. It has, I now understand, brought me close to financial ruin, and I pursue it not only at home (sometimes even alone) but when I travel, seeking out the back-street haunts of its pushers, and feverishly writing cheques in darkened rooms.

I bought my first Canadian painting, painlessly enough, in the early 1960s. I had sold a magazine article I had not expected to sell and I had some of what we have later learned to call "disposable income." I disposed of it on an oil painting, by the rising young west-coast artist Claude Breeze. If you are an astute listener to *Morningside* you will have heard the later fate of this work, for it is now in the collection of the noted Vancouver connoisseur Ron Longstaffe, and he mentioned it while he was here a couple of years ago talking about the show of his collection at the Vancouver Art Gallery. If you *did* hear that interview, in fact, you may have inferred that I brought an exquisite eye to my early investments – but the truth was that after a few months of displaying our one-painting collection, my wife and I admitted to each other that, however fashionable it was, we didn't *like* the painting very much. I mentioned our feelings to the gallery owner who'd sold it to me. "Oh, really?" he said. "Give it back to me for a while." And, not long after that, he called to say he'd sold it again – not yet to Longstaffe but at a price much higher than I'd paid and, to my delighted surprise, half the profits were mine.

Looking back, now, I can see here the beginnings of my addiction. Where else, I wondered, could you spend money on something that – at least at first – brought you both pride and pleasure and then, when you tired of it, sell it for a profit?

I put my winnings into a William Kurelek prairie landscape ("Poisoning Gophers," it was called, and if I close my eyes I can still see its vivid greens and cruel, contorted figures), hung that for a while, grew not only weary of, but actually uncomfortable in its presence and, wonder of wonders, sold it again, through a different dealer but once more at a profit.

It would please me to report now that, having realized the emptiness of buying for a profit and not love, I turned instantly away from the seductions of commerce. The truth is I learned that lesson gradually, and before it had sunk in I had blown the windfalls of my early adventures on a piece of sculpture I bought for my office at *Maclean's* that still sits, so far as I know, in a dealer's basement, and on a series of original prints that lie in mine – or would, if I had a basement. But along the way I *did* learn that art galleries are not intimidating, that there is a sense of excitement in spotting a new talent, that there is as much pleasure in browsing as in buying, that a painting can grow on you and become part of your life – I have a prairie landscape by the mature artist Winona Mulcaster that is probably worth three times what I paid for it ten years ago but which I would no more sell than I would hock my great-great-grandfather's ring – and that for those of us who are willing to forgo the occasional vacation or, perhaps, drive an older car, it is possible to enjoy the thrills of the rich and famous – or some of them – without the income.

Most of what I've bought is, like my beloved Mulcaster, landscape. I have an Anne Meredith Barry of Cape Breton Island, four small oils of Ontario by Denise Ireland, a little mountain gem by Cathy McAvity (I cannot tell you the pleasure it gave me to see a larger work of hers this summer in the Edmonton Art Gallery, among works by such more celebrated artists as Dorothy Knowles, whom I love and admire but cannot afford – though I do have a water-colour by one of her daughters), and a few others that transport me on wings of colour and energy and memories on long winter evenings. One or two might be for sale if the mood strikes me, but my walls would look emptier without them than I could stand. I see the country now through clearer eyes – I saw waves by Ron Bolt roll into Sable Island this summer, and stopped beside the Old Skagway Highway in the Yukon to soak up the exuberant colours of Ted Harrison at Emerald Lake.

I grow steadily more adventurous – the addict seeking his ever-stronger fix. I spent more than I could afford this summer on a Hudson's Bay blanket painted in rich patterns by the Métis Robert

Boyle; I covet a K.M. Graham from the Arctic, a Harold Town, a Shadbolt, a Lemieux, a Pratt, a Bobak of either sex.

I will settle, of course, for those I can more nearly afford, and continue to press my nose against the windowpanes of the rest, revelling in their prints, thumbing the books of their collected masterworks. But someday, who knows? I was pulling away from a helicopter shack near Canmore, Alberta, this summer, after an excursion up one of the Three Sisters, when I saw a weathered board, with a brilliant totemic image drawn in what appears to be charcoal and poster paint. I stopped my car and offered the helicopter man thirty dollars. The painted board is mine now. I can't read the signature on the bottom. But, I can't help thinking, I couldn't read Claude Breeze's signature when I started, either.

III

✎ Once I saw a couple win a million dollars. U.S. dollars, too, which is worth pointing out at those levels. They did it by naming six different kinds of cookies: chocolate chip, oatmeal, brownie – I was too excited myself to remember them all. They didn't have to name the cookies from scratch, mind you. There was a screen in front of them, with a series of blanks, and as a clock ticked in the background – they had about thirty seconds to get all six – letters would fill in alphabetically: the *a* in "chocolate," then the three *c*s . . . they got chocolate chip, then, I think, and the blanks appeared for "oatmeal." When they filled in their last blank, horns blared, storms of confetti fell from the ceiling, strobes stuttered, and their children ran out of the audience to start hugging them. The million dollars in cash was on a table. Actually, we'd met one of the children before, a boy about six. When the parents were going into the isolation booth – so no one could shout "macaroon" to them, I suppose – the master of ceremonies had asked them what they'd do first if they did win the million, and the camera had shown us the little boy while the mother said if they won they were going to get an operation on his ears. I think they forgot this after they won, by the way. When the strobes were still flashing and the confetti was still fluttering, the MC asked them again what they were going to do first and the mother said, "Go to New York."

This was on a TV game show called "The $1,000,000 Chance of a Lifetime." I suppose I ought to pretend I saw it by accident, that I was flicking around the dial one afternoon looking for a Jacques Cousteau special on snails and just happened upon this couple who'd chosen to name cookies instead of, I think, white things or countries in Asia. But the truth is I watched it on purpose. I'd seen them win the day before – you have to win three days in a row to get a crack at the million – and I tuned in to see how they'd do.

I don't watch the Million-Dollar Et Cetera all the time, mind you. I much prefer the "$100,000 Pyramid," even though, obviously, the money's not as big. As a matter of fact, "$100,000 Pyramid" isn't even for $100,000 all the time. Most days you can measure the big winnings in hundreds, give or take the odd vacation in New Zealand. What happens on the Pyramid is that if you win one of the preliminary rounds you get to go to the winner's circle, and your first time there you get to try for $10,000 (all these figures are U.S.) and your second time for $25,000. The $100,000 only comes into play every couple of months or so, when Dick Clark, who is not only the MC of the Pyramid but owns the whole caboodle, gathers the three winners with the most impressive scores and has a play-off, a kind of masters' invitational.

I shouldn't really be talking about money at all with the Pyramid. Unlike, say, "Press Your Luck," a horrible game where you can be blown out of the water if you press the computer button one too many times, or "Card Sharks," where a jack when you expected a six can cost you thousands of dollars, the Pyramid is a game of skill. Not intellectual skill, perhaps (I know Ph.D.s in biochemistry who couldn't get past the warm-ups), but a certain adeptness with words, and a quick wit. Anyway, that's why I watch it – that, and to marvel at Dick Clark, who has found, if not the fountain of youth then the mother-stream of black hair dye, and looks younger now than when he hosted "American Bandstand."

I realize I'm saying some controversial things here, but I'm prepared to live with them. I know people of otherwise impeccable taste, for instance, who think "Wheel of Fortune," on which, as on "Chance of a Lifetime," you try to fill in words from alphabetic clues, is a more stimulating program than the Pyramid, and once in a while, when those of us who admit to watching television before dark get together to compare notes – this sometimes happens by accident, the way people in adjoining cabins on a cruise ship will discover they went to the same dance teacher – you'll get a traditionalist who'll stick up for "Jeopardy." These people are well intentioned. But they're wrong. "Wheel of Fortune" hasn't been the same since they started trying to make Vanna White a personality instead of a fashion mannequin, and as for "Jeopardy" . . . well, it's a serious game, all right, and perhaps the only contest left on television you can actually win by *knowing* something, but the contestants are all too solemn, if you ask me – the last of its invitationals was even won by a *Canadian* – and no one ever hugs anyone. Some game show.

✉ Welcome to the club! I am delighted to know that someone else older than fifty is also addicted to Ms. Pac-Man. I am sixty-two and have a sixteen-year-old daughter. That's how I was introduced to the game. We went to Michigan to visit friends during the March break in 1982, and they took us to an arcade. We came home to Ottawa and started visiting various arcades around Ottawa. Those were the days when the game was new to everyone. We would meet the same people wherever we went – hooked on the same game. We would stand in line to take our turn at the machine. It was at least a year before we learned there was a fourth board.

My daughter, of course, learned a lot faster than I. Her reflexes were better. I'll never forget the evening she ate her first banana! Our euphoria accompanied us out of the arcade. Jan kept saying, "I ate a banana! I ate a banana!" Later, we found a restaurant that had a table game, and we would order canneloni, and take turns eating and playing. Invariably we would put the top score on the board. Then she broke a hundred thousand. That was her goal, and her enthusiasm waned from then on. Other games claimed her interest . . . .

Not me! Ms. Pac-Man has remained my favourite game. I am the one who begs my daughter to play just a couple of games at the arcade.

Sometimes I play alone. Can you see a sixty-two-year old "little old lady" wandering into an arcade and playing a couple of games? Sometimes I have callouses on the second finger of my right hand. I can only play two, three, or four games before my arm gives out. I still haven't reached a hundred thousand.

Oh, but I remember those olden days when we were first learning. Now we have worked out our own patterns; but then we did not know the tricks. I admire my daughter's savvy. She can still play a better game than I because she takes more time than I do. She never wastes a point. We have always played the game for points rather than trying for the next board.

Have you tried Baby Pac-Man or Junior Pac-Man? I can't find anyone my age who will come with me to play.

Gweneth A. Yates
Ottawa

✉ As you were revealing your Ms. Pac-Man addiction to all, I was engrossed in a long-forgotten addiction of my own. That particular day was the occasion of my oldest daughter's eighth birthday, and after the excitement of her new, very own hamster and its accessories had worn off, our family proceeded to work on her new five-hundred-piece puzzle, which depicted about twenty-five cute teddy bears.

The puzzle brought back memories of Christmases past, when I was growing up, and my parents would set up five hundred, eight hundred, even thousand-piece puzzles during the holiday season. I would spend hours, long into the night, adding just one more piece, and another and another, until I could hardly keep my eyes open. Over the years, I forgot about my puzzle addiction. I became busy with other things, like raising three little girls.

Then suddenly, uncannily, on the morn of your own confession, I realized that old addictions never die. By noon of that day, hours after my husband and children had gone off to other activities, I was sneaking trips to the dining-room table to search out just one more piece. My youngest child was still in her nightgown, waiting for Mum to get her dressed. My husband, a partial addict himself, joined me for brief interludes through the afternoon, until the border and the more colourful of the teddy-bear outfits were completed. Thankfully, he barbecued supper for us, allowing me time to find some of the trickier pieces. Fortunately, I had baked my daughter's birthday cake the evening before, and I even resorted to paper plates to speed up the meal. My husband finally put his foot down when, after bathing the children and getting them into their pyjamas and reading them stories, he insisted I should go upstairs and kiss them good-night. Later in the evening, he questioned the mess on the kitchen table (just a few supper items not put away), but his words fell on deaf ears. Much later, I finally pushed myself away from the now ninety-per-cent-completed puzzle. My pile of mending, children's clothes to be hemmed up or let down for the impending school season, lay nearby in a heap – a reminder that I had spent almost a whole day on a jigsaw puzzle!

And the eight-year-old for whom the puzzle was intended? The next morning, she gave it only a glance and went on with feeding the hamster.

Janet Mather
Toronto

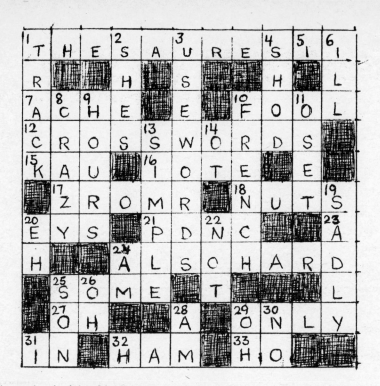

My passion is doing 12 ACROSS.
11 DOWN a puzzle before me and I am 31 ACROSS a state of euphoria-ee.
5 DOWN guess you'd say that I 28 DOWN hooked
And spend my waking 9 DOWN consulting every kind of puzzle book,
1 ACROSS and dictionaries, encyclopedia-ii, and glossararies,
And 10 DOWN and Latin vocabularies.
Maybe you think I'm 8 DOWN, 20 DOWN,?
25 ACROSS people think I'm really 18 ACROSS.
They shake their heads and 19 DOWN say, "She's 23 ACROSS 10 ACROSS to waste
her time that way."
I track down words like 4 DOWN and 15 ACROSS. Kau?
Oh that must be the bird from Chihuahua.
27 ACROSS why must it be 24 ACROSS??
If 29 ACROSS they'd use 13 DOWN clues and not 3 DOWN that just confuse.
Like, 33 ACROSS is not Santa's 'Ho, Ho, Ho,' but the first name of Chi Minh!
And is 32 ACROSS something to put on a bun?
Certainly not. It's Noah's 25 DOWN.
And 17 ACROSS is......? Zromr??
Oh God I am undone.
I'm feeling 6 DOWN. My head does 7 ACROSS. My 20 ACROSS go dim.
I really 28 DOWN 31 ACROSS pain.
It's all too much for this small brain.
Now what the heck's this......North Carolina Police Department??
Police Department in North Carolina.....?
29 DOWN Boy! I think I've got it! 21 ACROSS !
What could be finah!

Margaret Taylor
Calgary

104

✉ My nemesis happens to be crossword puzzles. It started several years ago when my husband and I would buy the *New York Times* on Sundays. We'd stop at the library, where I would Xerox the big puzzle, then we would each settle down with our own copy (we tossed for the original) and have at it for speed and accuracy. I am alone now, but because I am alone I enjoy them more and more.

The *New York Times* zoomed to $3.50 a copy, so out of desperation I answered an ad in the *New Yorker* and subscribed to Will Wong's crossword puzzle club – talk about a junkie! I now get four great ones a month, plus the odd bonus. I enjoy the club puzzles the most because they are clever and literate and do not use fillers such as "a South American pepper tree" and "a three-toed sloth from Borneo."

Is there a name for someone addicted to graphs? When I am not crosswording, I am knitting to a pattern, or, more happily, plotting bargello designs on a needle-point canvas, which I lovingly and patiently stitch as I watch television in the evenings. Am I hooked on squares, or am I a square? I hate to think I am such a passive, sedentary person, but at seventy-plus, I guess my crossword passion at least keeps my personal computer on its toes.

Jane E. O'Flynn
Hamilton, Ontario

✉ At the age of twenty-three I'm ashamed to admit it. While others my age are traipsing through the Australian outback, my passion sounds mundane and dull: bridge, the game of one's dotage, played by those who announce their bids in frail, thin voices, then peer intensely at their partners through bifocals, gauging their reactions, searching for a clue.

I think my parents have always fantasized about having competent bridge players living at home, but two attempts to teach my brother and I the game when I was sixteen were abortive. The bidding was incomprehensible. "Why on earth should I bid two clubs when it's my weakest suit?"

But the disease grew insidiously, erupting at the end of my university years. One by one my friends took up positions on the game. Sitting on the fence was not permitted. Those opposed stood up and said nay, those in favour sat down and said, "Deal the cards." Gradually, fatally, I was hooked. It's not that I wasn't warned. One Ph.D. student, who speaks from years of experience, advised me, "Bridge has destroyed many a university career." And a work acquaintance who had played nationally confided, "I found I was living, breathing, sleeping, and eating bridge." He gave it up cold turkey. Did I heed these warnings? Of course not. I compulsively read books, gleaned clues, and struck up conversations on the game. My parents couldn't believe their good fortune. Games enthusiasts, they had watched in dejection as one by one I had lost interest in cribbage, backgammon, hearts, euchre, and even Scrabble. Now I was ready to play. The only one left to convince was my brother. It took only a week.

We started playing every night. The scenario is simple: during dinner, I innocently ask, "What's everyone doing tonight?" My brother looks up suspiciously, "I'm not playing bridge tonight, I'm painting." Protests and pleading are not necessary; the strategy is to coolly assume he's said yes. My mother ponders a moment, then observes that she really doesn't have to attend her appointment. The dishes are cleared, my brother mumbles that he will not play past nine o'clock, and the cards are dealt.

The chair in the other room that needs fixing remains on three legs; the filling made this afternoon for tonight's pies remains out of the shells; upstairs in my brother's studio, the canvases cry out from neglect; and my own thesis is as yet unwritten. Like four fiddling Neros, we sort our cards.

The bidding begins; the emotions run high. I'm furious with my mother for putting us in a no-win slam. My brother grumbles in frustration because I did not return his lead (I happened to be void). Our inexperience weighs heavily on our resentment, yet my parents are patient. I've learned a lot about them this month that I didn't know before. My father plays a mean defence; my mother, the wizard, makes tricks appear on the table like a rabbit out of a hat; and both of them know, as the game winds down, whether that third card in your hand is a six of clubs or an eight of hearts as they rake in that last trick.

As my father tallies the grand score, I also discover that they're a well-matched pair. Over all the nights we've walled ourselves in to indulge our private passion, shunning friends and associates, and neglecting our duties, they've amassed scores of more than thirty thousand, separated by only a hundred points. What marital bliss, to have a compatible bridge partner for life. My brother and I, trailing ten thousand points behind, are left to compete with each other, honing our skills.

I don't know how long this passion will last. I only know that its momentum increased when I bid and made my first grand slam. Gaining rudimentary knowledge in the art of bidding, that subtle and intricate word play that is a language unto itself, has opened a whole new world. After having learned a smattering of French and German, I am proud to say that with bridge, at last, I am functionally bilingual.

Lisa Lajeunesse
Carleton Place, Ontario

✉ I hum.

Well, *mostly* I hum, but when there are no critics, I sing out loud.

I've been doing this for years, and rarely get caught.

Once, however, when we lived in an apartment in Toronto, I was singing at the top of my voice in Ukrainian. My next-door neighbour, not a devotee of Slavic music, slammed her door in disgust. After that I sang in Swedish.

When I find situations stressful, I hum. So I hum at work. Humming is like bacteria: you can infect a whole department. With practice, you can start good-sized groups of people on "Annie," change them to "Amazing Grace" over the lunch hour, and send them cheerfully to their cars at night with "Don't Cry for Me, Argentina."

Humming to car music is singularly unsatisfactory. Car music *requires* loud vocalization. People in traffic beside you understand that you are making a statement, and you can dispense with the apologetic smiles and self-conscious waves that normally accompany traffic *faux pas*.

You may hum when you shop, and, in fact, I get some of my best humming done in the produce section.

I've found it quite appropriate to hum while examining labels in the designer shops, but here it is most important to hum some Julio Iglesias or Vivaldi. You will lose credibility with the elegant saleslady if she so much as *suspects* the tune is "Born in the U.S.A."

When my son was a baby, my husband and I were sitting in the family room one evening.

From behind his newspaper, my husband casually said, "Your son hums."

"Hm?" I said incredulously.

"Your son hums," he said, quite loudly. I guess it's in the DNA.

Gail Mackay
North Vancouver

✉ My wife is having a love affair.

I suppose it should not come as a total shock. After all, we have been married fourteen years, time enough for that initial spark to fade a little, perhaps. The hard part to live with is that my competition is much taller and quite a bit older. It must be the matured, weathered look that she finds so attractive. Most of these doors are well over sixty years old.

Yes, doors – the passion of my wife's life.

I should be so lucky to have a rival of the two-legged variety. How do you compete with a French door quietly beckoning to her

108

with all fifteen panes, or an oak door with stained glass delicately reflecting prisms of coloured light in the sunshine, or a solid pine door standing majestically with gleaming brass hardware?

It would be simpler to tolerate her hanging out the car window, Peter Pointer and Toby Tall strategically positioned in her mouth, whistling madly at some sweaty jogger on the street. It's another matter to handle a situation where she dreamily sighs, "Did you see the bevelled glass on that front door?" A favourite pastime is driving through town scouring the houses for unique entrances.

This past summer the passion became more intense when she discovered screen doors. I don't mean the standard suburban home aluminum screen door with your last-name initial sitting prominently in a circle. No, the screen doors that caught her fancy are the ones you see on many old farmhouses in the country. They are made of wood, usually with some type of interesting carving or scroll work.

I thought I had lost her completely the other day. We were walking around downtown Toronto and accidentally stumbled into a three-storey shop that specialized in – you guessed it – *doors*. I say accidentally because if I had known that such an emporium existed, believe me, I would have steered the door detective in the opposite direction, even if it had meant ending up at Waddington's and bidding on a Ming pot.

Three floors of doors. Old doors. Some with different types of glass. Some just solid wood. Some refinished. Some still in need of work. The thought of my wife's hands lovingly caressing and sanding one of these musty artefacts made me want to throw out every last can of Polystrippa in our basement.

I had to rescue her. Never before had she been surrounded by the loves of her life. She walked aimlessly around the store, her eyes glazed, softly bumping into plain back doors and ornate front doors, whispering softly into their keyholes.

To me, doors are just a functional part of a house. You shut 'em in winter to keep in the heat, you open 'em to welcome guests, and you slam 'em on siding salespeople. You paint 'em every five years, and wipe 'em off twice a year.

My wife disagrees. She says a door symbolizes the *character* of the household.

I hope her passion for doors is temporarily satisfied. The question is, if I have to handle our doors with care, how can I deal with those pesky siding salesmen?

Peter Young
Oshawa, Ontario

✉ When a dinner conversation turned to private passions the other night I found I was able to immediately name my husband's, it seemed so obvious to me. How many normal people can spend hours looking at, polishing, and organizing doorknobs, hinges, plates, and all the other little insignificant pieces that hold a door together?

Then, this morning, I turned on *Morningside* and heard you discussing someone else's private passion. Doors and doorknobs. My husband's soul mate exists! All the kinds of doors that are sitting in her garage are in our house somewhere. Our kitchen and living-room have the pocket doors (without the little things to open them; the perfect ones haven't been found yet). Our front door is the front door that was my husband's as he grew up. When he heard the house was being torn down, a three-hundred kilometre trip was necessary to save the door. I'm not complaining; it's a lovely door.

I used to ask where he found all these doors and hardware. I don't ask any more. Nor do I ask where does this end. Do we move when there are no more doorways to complete and no more room to store the doors that are beautiful only to him?

Lynda Roach
Meaford, Ontario

✉ The instant you began to describe your private passions, I knew what mine was: listening to Talking Books. Don't confuse this with merely liking to read. Most blind people listen to Talking Books sensibly: they spend a reasonable amount of time sitting by their tape recorders. I listen every conscious minute I can steal away. I listen while I make the bed. I listen while I walk my seeing-eye dog, Zephyr. When he sees me put on the earphones, he sighs. I used to talk to him more as we went along. Now I get caught up in the book and only remember him when he stops us for a curb. I listen to them when I'm falling asleep. If I have to share a room with someone, I listen through my pillow speaker. I take them with me to the doctor's office. I have one on while I wash dishes. I have a tape deck in the car. I own seven tape recorders.

When I meet another addict, we can talk for hours. We don't merely discuss how much we loved Timothy Findlay's *Not Wanted On the Voyage*, as sighted people do. We discuss the way it was read. Some of us like people who read straight ahead and don't use different voices for the various characters. Some of us like foreign accents. I love it when the reader puts in extra touches like a sigh, a chuckle, a snort, or a grunt. I like certain readers so much that I'll listen to books I wouldn't have bothered reading in print, merely because those people read them so well that they make the medi-ocre sound good.

These readers feel like close friends. I know many of their voices as well as I do those of my family and closest friends. I even think I know which are kindred spirits.

Although my vision has always been poor, I used to be able to read. When I studied English Literature at university, I skimmed through mounds of Great Literature. I didn't guess how much I missed till I could no longer see well enough to read. Jane Austen, for instance. I skimmed through a couple of her books and found them tedious and slow. But listening to Jane is sheer delight. When I whipped through *David Copperfield*, once in high school and again in college, I missed whole chunks. I didn't find out about Uriah Heep's behaviour in prison until I listened to the book.

What proves that this is a Private Passion, a decided addiction, is the fact that, were I to wake up tomorrow with perfect vision, I would not tell the CNIB. I'd love to be able to read printed books again. But, even in my sighted days, I never could read to myself the way certain readers can read to me now. It's like going to the theatre, for free, whenever you choose.

Jean Little
Guelph, Ontario

✉ The enjoyment I get from the colour yellow goes beyond just a liking. It pushes the pleasure button in my brain and feelings of warmth and happiness, or whatever sensation this colour and the object it's on evoke, are released.

This passion is most delightful in private moments with as simple an object as my yellow plastic pencil sharpener. Or even the mundane soy beans I cooked this morning, that popped yellow out of their translucent waxy skins as I ground them for making milk. To spice and colour other foods, I have soft-yellow ginger and brown-yellow curry sitting on the shelf above my stove. As I cook I wear a banana-yellow apron my mom made.

I love the growing floral yellows in daily walks through the valley fields nearby. Bright yellow petals of the false dandelion, growing tall this year because of so much rain, reach out to me. Ever-present on these excursions is the orange-yellow of my golden retriever Samoyed dog, Juneau. Dying grass and turning leaves give an ode to yellow in their final farewell before winter.

At home, when I curl up in a yellow and white sling chair, absorbing the sun through the window, I wish I could paint my room with yellow-white light to keep me warm through cold mountain winters. Light and yellow I also associate with the intellect and energy. Sometimes I smear a sheet of paper with yellow pastel simply to feel it.

When I was a child, my favourite dress was yellow. My son is a tow-head, his hair bleached over the summer, a living creation of my passion.

June Waters
Canmore, Alberta

✉ My private passion is cruising. On sunny and rainy days, spring, summer, and fall, I slip into my blue Nissan and start the engine. My right hand fingers the radio, turning the knob to the classical-music station. My left hand quickly turns down the window, as the corners of my mouth turn up – I am commencing my cruise. As I leave the outskirts of my small seaside community, turning right on the highway, my fingertips turn the volume to loud – I mean *really* loud. My ears luxuriate in the whirl of stereophonic sounds. Whether the music is Beethoven or Bach, harpsichord or flute, a Broadway chorus or Gregorian chant, all ten toes wriggle in my vamps, and two palms thump out the beat on the steering wheel and car roof. Wisps of hair waft across my forehead. I brush them away, delighting in the speed, the sound, the scenery of the Maritime coastline. There's a certain exuberance in listening to a symphony by the sea.

Joan Bond
Hubbards, Nova Scotia

✉ I am seventeen years old, technically not yet an adult. One would probably expect to see me with my nose in some wildfire-first-kiss-bleeding-heart-teen-romance rather than *Alice's Adventures in Wonderland* or *Charlie and the Chocolate Factory*. Yet, to me, there is nothing more cosy and comforting than curling up with a cup of tea and a stack of books that might include *Winnie-the-Pooh*, *The Wizard of Oz*, *Jacob Two-Two Meets the Hooded Fang*, or a favourite book of fairy tales.

I do read "grown-up" books as well. I have slogged my way through Hemingway, Steinbeck, Shaw, and Shakespeare. My friends are constantly recommending Jane Austen, Virginia Woolf, James Boswell, and Somerset Maugham, and so I dutifully borrow such books and, with the best of intentions, begin to read them. I usually don't finish. It's not that they are bad books. Far from it. The ones I finish I almost always find excellent. It's just that . . . well, they're not as *nice* as kids' books. When you read a kids'

113

book you just know that things are going to turn out all right. Dorothy always finds her way back to Kansas and the handsome prince always falls in love with the beautiful princess. There aren't any horrible, irreparable tragedies. Winnie-the-Pooh never plunges to his death while being carried off by a balloon, and Roo never contracts botulism from a slightly off batch of watercress sandwiches, or a bottle of strengthening medicine past its prime. Everyone always lives happily ever after.

It is sometimes embarrassing to be the only one over four feet tall in the children's book section in stores, and I often get strange looks from librarians as they see me sign out a pile of "juvenile fiction." I endure the giggles and quizzical looks, though. I'm a sucker for a happy ending.

Pam Nichol
Saskatoon

✉ For three years now I have succumbed to the temptations of pop culture by adoring a rock singer. This is no different from millions of teenage fans who worship the heroes of the music business. But I, alas, am thirty-four years old, happily married, a small-business owner and mother of two growing sons. I have collected, studied, taped, videoed, and researched my idol (who is a few years older than I) beyond the call of someone half my age. Astonished friends accept my madness but never let me forget its outlandishness.

Being a staunch Canadian nationalist, it is entirely inappropriate for me to be so taken with someone "Born in the U.S.A." There was the time I had to stay home from my women's problem-solving group (none of us *ever* misses this) to watch the "Much Music Spotlight." Knowing I could not lie to these people, I admitted the truth. They decided something serious must be going on in my life that I could not discuss. And then there was the time I hired a baby-sitter in order to stand in line for five hours, the oldest there; I came away without a ticket, but was desperate enough to pay scalpers' prices to get into the concert. What about the hours I spent sitting with headphones writing down the words to his songs while the kids watched TV? Or my friend, who flew with five bootleg albums from her visit to the west coast? Or the *Rolling Stone* magazine I stole from the public library? All of this in between the daily routine of making suppers, reading bedtime stories, shopping, and working.

My friend summed it up when she saw my newest poster of Bruce in our main-hall foyer. "Have you no shame?"

My answer: "No, no shame at all."

Susann Hoffman
London, Ontario

✉ I absolutely love letters from my family. In this day and age, a student at university is supposed to look at his or her family as though they are a slight inconvenience. They're the ones who occasionally buy you dinner, and maybe if you're really good, a bag of President's Choice chocolate-chip cookies, which you die for, but can't afford on your own. You go home at Thanksgiving and Christmas, and come back laden with goodies from the freezer, and that's about it.

Somehow, I missed out on the necessary requirements for coolness. A letter from my parents is something I treasure.

When I first started school, I thought everyone felt this way. I would fly up from the mailbox, proudly waving the trademark long envelope with Daddy's unmistakable scrawl, or Mom's hand (they alternate, each week), and skip, beaming, into the lounge. No one understood. When I laughed aloud at a particularly good episode in one of Mom's chronicles, everyone looked at me as though I was missing something up top. Parents aren't supposed to write to you, and if they do, it's only on your birthday, or to send you a cheque. When you throw in the fact that my grandparents' return address graces my mailbox at least once a week as well, you know that I am definitely considered an oddity. It's got to the point where

I creep upstairs with my precious cargo held tightly to my body, unlock my door, tearing envelopes open eagerly to discover what my family has been up to lately. Sometimes little bits and pieces of family life flow out, maybe around the breakfast table in my new house, but then I realize that no one is really listening, and I quietly return to my bowl of Raisin Bran.

Maybe sometime, all those people who have a secret passion for their family (and I know there are some other people out there reading letters in their rooms, and laughing out loud) won't have to keep it a secret any more, and it can be cool to like your parents.

Lisa Kowaltschuk
Ottawa

✉ You won't find my lake on most maps. It's at the edge of our property. Because it is muddy-bottomed, no one ever swims there. It has no beach. It is weedy. It has a shallow sand bar of an outlet to the creek, so no power boats ever get in it. And because the creek is shaded by overhanging branches no sail boats are ever in there either. So it is *my lake*. Well, more or less. A man puts up his eel or gaspereau nets there in the early spring. A couple of women sometimes venture across a corner of it on cross-country skis, and the odd skimobile tracks cross it once in a while, but that's about it. The whole community drives past it two or three hundred yards away every day of the year. They admire its sunsets and curse the northwest wind that tears across it in winter, and they never go nearer than that.

But it is so beautiful, bound on one side by a wooded hill, on another by some small hillside farms, and for the rest by marsh grass and maples. Even when the wind whips the surface into whitecaps or Cindy-dog and I battle across it in blinding winter storms, it is balm for the soul.

I set my canoe on the bank of the creek and always feel I am sneaking up on the lake as I paddle up to it through the long grass. I usually drift into one of the reedy banks just before I get to it to

116

see if the loon family is close by, or to count the ospreys fishing it. I try to converse with the loons by blowing between my thumb knuckles into my cupped hands. Sometimes I flatter myself by believing they reply.

There are seldom ducks there. Usually it is just the loons, ospreys, the occasional heron or bittern and, of course, the eagle family.

And then there is that magical week in early December before the snow flies when you can look through the clear ice almost to the bottom of the lake. That is when it becomes my own private rink and the crack of my skates can be heard a mile away at the store. I am sure heaven must look a lot like my little lake.

Max Wolfe
Jemseg, New Brunswick

✉ Blue jays are my secret passion. I try to keep it secret because blue jays are not held in high esteem by the bird-watching community. They are bullies at the feeder. Worse still, despite their remarkable colour, they are *common*. They don't migrate or pass through or even hide themselves away in the deep woods. There they are, loud and flashy, right in our back yards, season after season.

Why do I love them the way I do? I run out into the yard or peer out the windows when I hear that imperious "jay!" from nearby trees. They are gorgeous! That colour – blue, blue, electric, stolen-from-the-sky blue. And we're treated to that flash of colour all year round.

I have a four-year-old daughter. Her nickname, shortened from Jennifer, has always been "Jae." She loves the blue jays, too, because they tease her and call her name. Best of all, though, her eyes are bright blue-jay blue.

And this is the heart of my secret passion.

Peggy Hopper
Caledonia, Nova Scotia

✉ Living on the Saskatchewan prairies, one experiences a love-hate relationship with rain. We yearn for it to nourish our slender green grasses in the spring, then curse the leaden skies when it outstays its welcome and ripe golden swathes lay sodden in the fields. And so my passion for long strolls and contemplative lounges in misty rains of all seasons remains private. These last three weeks of soaking drizzle, while disastrous to the harvest, have wreathed the inside of my face with smiles of sweet contentment.

This passion was born in the Mendip Hills of England. Rain there was not a thunderous cloudburst that shattered the breathless heat of a summer afternoon. It was fine warm rain that caressed my skin and fluffed my hair into a downy halo. I was hooked. Colours and smells close to me intensified, while horizons were softly shrouded in a fine gauze of rain.

I was able to indulge my gentle addiction while mapping rocks amid mosquitoes, trees, and sapphire lakes in northern Saskatchewan. We worked from a central camp and relied upon small bush planes to ferry us to and from our traverse areas. Rain became more than just beauty to me then. When fat rain clouds settled their bellies on the hills, our planes remained bobbing serenely at their moorings, earth-bound for the day. Freed from the rigours of traverse, I'd snuggle deep into my warm sleeping bag, lulled back to sleep by the rain pattering on my tent. The wonderful smells of wet spruce and pine mingled with the pungent odour of revitalized lichens accompanied a leisurely day of reading, card playing, and office chores. I always took a few hours to sit on the shore scrubbing my soul with the breathtaking beauty of that quietly powerful landscape.

If I sit still amid the happy chaos of my home and look deeply into myself those moments of magic exist again.

Rainy days mean black-rubber boots with red soles, a cotton coat stuffed with me and a favourite sweater, and my son bundled against the damp. Curtains twitch in disapproval, his stroller wheels hiss through soupy mud and rattle over the gravel as we amble along, day-dreaming contentedly. I'm still amazed at the way vibrant watered colours emerge from my prairie's drab dusty coat.

I'll always love the rain, regardless of the time of year and its result-ing hardships or benefits. Rain delights me in the bush, on the prairies, and in the city. Trees and grasses shaking droplets of water from nodding leaves, or black wet pavement reflecting the kalei-doscope of city lights, all satisfy my private passion.

Mary-Lynne Gillespie
Yarbo, Saskatchewan

✉ Give me a flower catalogue and I'm gone. In winter I spend hours at my private passion, planning the colours and contours of the garden; matching seeds to soil conditions, moisture levels, morning sun, and afternoon shade; charting heights so that the feathery Astilbe doesn't overpower the delicate campanula; choos-ing colours to blend and complement each other and put on a splen-did display all summer long. This, I have discovered, is easier said than done.

My private passion also presents a paradox. All the best advice, including the homely little tips squeezed in at the bottom of columns in the catalogues, says that planting masses of one variety makes a more pleasing and effective show than planting dozens of vari-eties. But the people who write the catalogue descriptions obviously don't want me to follow this sage advice. If they did, they would never have told me that the Blue Giant Poppy is "a brilliant Cambridge blue with golden anthers for contrast," or cas-ually mentioned that the colour of the Carved Ivory Zinnia has the "purity and richness of soft butter-cream."

The fact is I find it impossible to order just one of anything from a catalogue, whether it's a snapdragon (Carioca Blend, Little Darling, or Madame Butterfly) or an aster (Pinocchio, Heart of France, or Early Charm).

Finally, after hours of agonizing, I make out my order – a draft first, of course, in case I mistake anemone for Adonis and so I have a record of what I've ordered. Then I fill out the order in my best printing, always imagining the order filler at the other end, in

119

Georgetown or St. Catharines or Toronto or Brandon. She opens the envelope (for some reason I think they're all motherly types, sitting at long counters wearing sturdy canvas aprons) and sees that I've taken pains to copy neatly and correctly the name of each species, each variety, each catalogue number and price. Will she read the order and comment to her neighbour, "What ever is she going to do with all these sweet peas?" or "This garden has too much pink in it; what it needs is a shot of scarlet lychnis and that sapphire-blue lobelia we had last year."

In late winter and early spring, the seeds start arriving, ready to be tucked into their tiny peat pellets, watered, and covered with plastic and set in my south-facing bathroom window. When all danger of frost is past, the tiny roots of lily of the valley and baby's breath arrive, along with the plantlets that will become day lilies and phlox and lupin, and with them, the summer bulbs and the dry sticks that miraculously become forsythia bushes and honeysuckle vines.

At the height of summer, when the lilies reach their peak, the fall bulb catalogues arrive.

Kathryn Randle
Ottawa

THE ADOPTION TRIANGLE

The first trigger for the series of personal stories that came in to *Morningside* about having a child and giving it up for adoption, about adopting a child born by someone you haven't met, about *being* that child, and about other aspects of this whole complex and disturbing subject, was actually a drama that ran in our usual spot at the end of the program. The drama was called "Birthright." It ran in December 1985. It was written by J.J. McCall, of Vancouver, about a mature, unmarried woman – J.J., whom you may know as an actress, is mature and unmarried herself, but "Birthright" was not her story – trying to decide whether to keep a child she was carrying after an affair with a married man. It drew more, and more personal, mail than our dramas usually do. Among those responses were the two letters that begin this collection, which represent, as you may notice, precisely opposite views: the child who longs to meet her birth mother; the natural mother who fears discovery. Each of those letters arrived pseudonymously. But in each case, there was a traceable address. Wanting to know more, producer Susan Rogers and I sent telegrams asking the writers to call us. Both did, and after some talk and assurances that we'd respect their privacy, they agreed to talk to me on the air. Their stories brought still more stories until, for a few weeks, my morning mail became a kind of national bulletin board of individual variations on a theme. As we did on the radio, I have respected the anonymity of an unusual number of these authors, and kept even the place from which they've written confidential, although in every case I know the stories to be real. I think the reasons are obvious.

I've called this collection "The Adoption Triangle," after the three main figures: the child and the two sets of parents. But, as you'll see, it's really more than that: a polygon. This is how it looks from some of the sides.

✉ Each day I eagerly await another episode of *Birthright*, and each day I find myself getting curious, jealous, and angry. At twenty-seven, I am just embarking on a search for my mother, who is now sixty-one. Don't blood mothers know what a nightmare it is on our end of the line? To pass people on the street and wonder if we are related to them?

Fortunately, giving a child up for adoption these days is not the living nightmare it used to be, although it still takes as much courage and love on the part of the mother. Several of my girlfriends, now between the ages of thirty and forty, gave up children for adoption some ten or more years ago, and all of them have registered with the Canadian Adoption Registry.

The Canadian government has a stone-age attitude to adoption. I think I have the right to documentation, and in particular a genetic history of my birth, diseases, and so on. Both parent and child are mature enough to exchange information and shall respect one another's private lives.

Lindsay Lewis
Ganges, British Columbia

✉ I have taken some time to calm down after hearing part of your drama about an adopted child. As I tuned in, I heard one of the actors state that eighty-eight per cent of mothers of illegitimate children want to see their child again.

I am a mother who gave a child up for adoption, and I know many other women in the same position. I do *not* want to see the child. I made a painful decision years ago, and it was the only wise decision for each of the women that I know. We are not criminals. Most of us were children who got pregnant because we thought we were in love, or because we didn't know enough not to, or because we were raped or abused. We pay for our "mistake" forever: we fear being found out, or coming face to face with the child. I know of women who keep moving or have changed their names for this reason. Why do you not often hear our side of the story? Because we are trying to keep our mistakes a secret, and cannot afford to expose ourselves. There is still a great stigma attached to an illegitimate mother who gave up a child.

We cannot come forward. If the door was not pushed open so often, children would be more contented in their adoptive homes with their "real" families. There are two sides to this story – or three – and one side is very much being ignored.

Anonymous

✉ My twin babies will be born in May. I'm thirty-four and I'm living on welfare in a housekeeping room. I was living with my parents until last August, but I left my wonderful twelve-year-old daughter with them and went to see if I could find a better life.

I've never earned more than $1,500 in a year. I can no longer live with my parents, and I can't afford my daughter.

I really would like to know my kids but they'll be adopted when they're ten days old. I can leave them a letter and a gift but I cannot leave them anything that would identify me. I can't even tell them any place names, except where their ancestors come from.

I wanted to leave them their genealogy. I wrote a twenty-two page letter but I was told it wasn't allowed. I wrote a shorter letter describing my physical appearance and naming four places in Europe that our ancestors come from.

I'd really like to meet the kids one day and let them know their beautiful sister. I hope the babies will be like her.

Bev McCuish
Vancouver

✉ When I was separated, I gave my illegitimate child up for adoption. I was treated like dirt at the clinics and hospitals because I was giving up the child. I had no proper counselling about the adoption, and there was no follow-up. When I went to the registrar to register the birth, I had to give a name. No one told me I would have to do that – and do this day I cannot remember what I said.

All this happened twenty years ago in Scotland. Thankfully, treatment and counselling have greatly improved since then.

As I recovered both my health and my mental equilibrium, I vowed I would never see or acknowledge the child. I had to make my way with my four-year-old daughter, and I put the bad experience behind me. In all those years, only once has the child come to my mind with any force, and that was when my daughter was being married. It struck me that she had a sister who should be standing with her as a bridesmaid. Now I'm in Canada. I've changed my name, I've changed my address. I hope I'll never be traced. I could not agree to any pressure to see her. Too much time has passed for any relationship to develop.

Anonymous

124

✉ This past year, an accidental pregnancy resulted in the birth of a beautiful, happy baby girl whom I placed for adoption with the family of my choice. Her new family have extended their love to include me, and a friendship is developing. There was a great deal of pain, but knowing the family helped me to overcome the hurt. I couldn't give my daughter what she needed as she grew up; but childhood is short. When she is ready to become my most valued friend, there won't be any shame or fear. I consider myself her "godmother" and guard my relationship with her family with the utmost care.

Sharon Laszlo
Inuvik, Northwest Territories

✉ I gave birth to a child sixteen years ago and gave her up for adoption. It was the most difficult thing I have ever done. I've never been convinced it was the best thing to do; thoughts of that child have been with me constantly for the past fifteen years. I wonder what she's like, what she looks like, whether she's happy or not. I love her. Even though I don't know her, she is very much a part of my life, always has been, and I hope always will be.

I am married, to her father, and we have three children. We have never spoken to our children of their "sister." But I have always wanted to meet her. In my fantasy, she becomes part of our family, and everything is wonderful, and I am happy because I can give her the love I didn't give her when she was little. I missed out on so much by not being part of her growing-up years. I think of her as a tiny baby and she is now fifteen years old.

I am also afraid of meeting her. I recognize that it will be a very difficult meeting, and I know I will be very nervous. Yet I feel confident that it will be good.

Anonymous

✉ Many years ago, I managed to get my girlfriend pregnant. She decided to have the child. Her parents tried to persuade me to

125

marry her, but I refused. Her girl was put up for adoption. The mother has since married a decent husband.

Now I am a successful businessman, and my one fear in life is that my daughter will find me.

I feel responsible and downright guilty over the pregnancy. The birth was my responsibility as much as the mother's.

I believe there are many fathers out there who got a girlfriend pregnant and did not marry her who have the same feelings I do.

Anonymous

✉ My husband fathered a child before he married me. The child was given up for adoption. I knew all this before our marriage. I thought he was irresponsible not to have taken precautions. I guess I still think that, but I forgave, or at least tried to forgive. Now we're in our forties and trying, not always successfully, to make our marriage work.

I dread the day that child makes contact with my husband. If the child does, and if he or she has problems that require care and attention, our already shaky marriage will be unable to take the strain.

This letter may sound like the writing of a very selfish person. However, I wanted to emphasize that other people besides the mother and child are affected by these searches. I can imagine other families who would be affected more dramatically than our family.

Anonymous

✉ My husband and I adopted a twelve-day-old baby four years ago and it doesn't matter which side of the issue one is on – one is deeply involved with all aspects of adoption.

As an adoptive parent, I shall never try to conceal from my daughter the fact that she is adopted. When she is old enough to understand, we will tell her. I don't want to make a big issue about it.

We also have an eleven-year-old son, and it's nice to balance our family and tell our son that he is especially precious to us because he is ours, that I actually gave birth to him; and to tell our adopted daughter that she is especially precious because she is adopted and we wanted her so much. She is ours as absolutely as our son is ours.

Adopted children have "birth mothers," but we, the adoptive parents, are the child's real parents. We are the people who love and nurture our child. We stay up nights with her, feed her, comfort her, support her.

If she wishes to search for her birth mother, we'll help and support her, but perhaps not encourage her. If we support her in this it will cement our love and our family rather than cause an alienation.

Sometimes I wish we never had to tell her she is adopted – but that is a coward's thought!

Anonymous

✉ We adopted three unrelated babies. Our children always knew that they were adopted; when they were old enough to understand, I told them how difficult it is for a woman to give up her baby, that it requires love and unselfishness. The woman who gives up her baby for adoption wants the child to have a secure, happy family life.

When the question of finding a birth mother came up, I had to do some soul-searching, because when we adopted our children we were told that this would never happen. In spite of trying to feel objective, there was an element of possessiveness, and perhaps fear of the unknown. What if the child should love the birth mother more than me? What if the birth mother might interfere with our family? At first, I didn't talk about it at all to the children. But eventually we did talk about it. Our two girls said they have a somewhat ambiguous curiosity about their birth mother. They would like to see her from the distance, or perhaps see a picture, but they weren't sure they wanted to meet her. Our son recently said he never had any desire to find his "mother" because he already had one.

I have often thought I would like to tell the mothers of my children how thankful I am to them for letting me have their children. We have had ups and downs, bringing them up; there were worries, tears, pain, and frustration. But the joy of seeing them develop into responsible, loving adults has outweighed all the rough times so far.

Our children are free to love who they want. No one owns them. We always shared with them all we had to give and there are no strings attached.

Ursula Soper
Orillia, Ontario

✉ Some years ago, my husband and I adopted a group of children, all siblings, who had been removed from their home because of neglect, abuse, and suspicions of incest.

I've read and heard about children placed for adoption "out of love" and "in the hope of a better life." All our children were over the age of two and one was a teenager when our lives came together. They know they weren't put up for adoption out of love. We know that if their birth parents were to seek information about our kids, it would be devastating. It has taken four years of love for us to come together as a family. When, if, our kids want to know about their birth parents, we will be at their side, but if we are approached by either of the parents, they will receive a firm message that they are not welcome.

Our children have struggled with the truth that they were not wanted by their birth parents. Our gift to them has been love, security, and self respect. They have grown from sad-looking waifs

128

who had little reason to trust anyone into bright-eyed capable children.

When I think someone might some day find these kids and claim them as their own, I feel a powerful defence welling up inside me. No one will take peace away from these kids. When *they* are ready to take a risk, okay. But until then, laws or no laws, this adoption will remain closed.

Anonymous

✉ Most people seem to think the father of an adopted child just walked away, happy to be out of a sticky situation when young love turned sour. This is what I thought also, until I found out about my father.

My father did seem to feel pain, a lot of it. It was my father who wanted to stay with my mother. It was my father who put me into a private foster home, even though he was trying to get through university. It was my father who visited me there.

I feel him inside me. I feel him running through my blood. My mother, it seems, wanted little to do with me. You yearn for those you feel are with you in some way, and I yearn to see, meet, and know my father.

Sherrie King
Birth name Sherrie Charron
Salt Spring Island, British Columbia

✉ I am one of the more fortunate people who was able to trace my birth mother and meet her.

After contacting the social-service agency, placing telephone calls to prospective relatives, and telling outright lies, I was finally able to find my birth mother. I phoned her at her home in another province, told her who I was, where I was born, and that I felt she was my birth mother. There was a long silence (though likely not more than about five seconds) and then she simply said yes, she was.

At that point, after having so many doors closed, all I could think to ask her was, "How are you?" I really did want to know how she was. I told her I had begun the search thinking I did not want to disrupt her life, but only wished to meet her and then go on living as we had before. I asked if we could meet in her city in a few weeks, and she agreed.

Between our telephone call and our meeting, I spent hours poring over photograph albums with my Mom and Dad, and together we assembled an album containing baby pictures, school pictures, newspaper clippings, and things that were pertinent to my growing years. My parents were almost as excited as I was about the meeting, but they kept reminding me that things might not be as rosy as I thought. They wanted to shield me from any hurt that I might encounter.

When it was time for the meeting, I went to a hotel coffee shop and was approached by an attractive, dark-haired woman. One theory went flying right out the window – that you will know your birth mother immediately. I would have passed the lady on the street a thousand times and not known who she was.

We spent the next couple of hours in the coffee shop talking and looking through the album. I found out the circumstances of my birth and the trouble she had making the decision to give me up for adoption. I thanked her for making a very difficult choice, because I have had a very happy life. (I was adopted by a most loving and caring couple.) She said she had a niece only a couple of months older than I and she would often look at that little girl, wondering if I was developing in the same way, and if I was being loved and taken care of.

I wish more people could be successful in their searches for their birth mothers, to enable them to have the satisfying experience that I have.

Gerry Postnikoff
Saskatoon

✉ I am a child who was given up by her mother and I am a woman who in later years gave up her child for adoption so I can see both sides of the situation.

My mother gave me up for adoption when I was about six months old. She never realized that I could not be adopted because she had said she was epileptic and because my father was not a full white. My childhood consisted of being bounced from foster home to foster home with stops in between at the orphanage. My teen years consisted of being filled with a blind rage, which sent me to various provincial jails or to mental hospitals to recover from despair. I had no sense of self-worth.

The years rolled by, and time, like onion skins, gradually covered the scars and fears of my youth. I had a child and determined that I would be the best mother Canada had ever seen. But I had never been raised in a home with a family, and I had absolutely no conception of what a child required. For the child's sake, I finally gave him up.

I married and had children of my own. They grew and went on their own, and finally I decided to see if I could locate the rest of my family. This was not an easy decision; I did not know if I was strong enough to withstand another rejection. But I persisted.

My mother was found, and there was a reunion. I touched her cheek ever so carefully, absolutely amazed that this woman, there, *right there*, had carried me in her womb. That niggling thought that perhaps my mother gave me up because I was so repulsive was gone, forever.

Now my child is twenty-six and I wonder about him. I knew that what I did was the best thing: I was a young teenager who knew nothing about the reality of life. I wanted him to have a home with one family. After I found my mother, I went looking for information about my son. I learned that he had been raised in a wonderful, loving home.

I live in fearful expectation that this young man may look for me, yet I am hungry to find him and tell him that I love him, even though the circumstances surrounding his conception and birth were not the best.

This young man – I know I would be proud of him – deserves to know that his mother gave him up with love and hope for his future. I think the most unselfish act a mother can do for her child is to provide a good future. This I did. It was a most difficult decision. I gave up a part of me, forever.

Anonymous

✉ I'm thirty-two years old and I was raised by the Children's Aid in Toronto. I grew up in numerous foster homes and institutions. I never knew my real mother and I doubt that I ever will. Your show opened up a lot of emotions and feelings for a lot of people, myself included.

I haven't the slightest idea of who I am. I know my mother's first name and I have her last name, but that's all I know. There's no family history behind me. This fact has always been extremely difficult for me to handle. I still go through times of great loneliness and depression. I long for the day I could sit down and talk to my mother and perhaps, just perhaps, start a friendship. For me, there are two sides to the question. Should I try to find my mother? Or should I just try to forget? I've tried the latter, but it hasn't worked.

I would love to meet my mother – but I can't just barge into her life. She has the right to be left alone. There are no easy answers here. I want to meet her, but I do not want to hurt her. My question now is this: how would I respond if I did find her and she were to say that she didn't want to see me? I'd be hurt to be sure. Do I want to take that chance? I'm not really sure.

It just may be that the best thing to do is to leave it alone. However, I'm not completely sure that's the answer either.

Peter Allan Brown
Saskatoon

✉ I have never wanted to find my biological mother; nor have I desired to meet the man who contributed to my conception. I have a mother, and a father, and while (as for most children) there have been times when I would have liked to trade them in, *they* are my real parents.

If I were to meet my biological mother, I doubt that it would suddenly solve my problems or allow everything in my life to make sense. She would be a stranger, though a stranger to whom I could owe a word of thanks.

Let me tell you about my real mother. We look nothing alike: she is under five feet tall and has black curly hair and dark eyes, I am five feet eight with fair hair and green eyes. Funny, but people often tell us that we look alike. We do *sound* identical, we move similarly, we use the same gestures and expressions. People assume that the bond between us must be blood, but really the ties between my mother and me go beyond blood – after all, she *chose* me. How many children can boast about that with assurance?

Maura McIntyre
Toronto

WHAT STARTS WITH A AND ENDS WITH A DOUBLE DACTYL?

Answer: The Great Canadian Alphabet Contest of the 1980s.

✎ This is a first, I think: a light-verse collection with a plot. The plot started at the end of January 1987. I had been looking at the alphabet that had been assembled in the early 1970s for *This Country in the Morning*, a collection of couplets with a prescribed scheme of rhythm and rhyme that I'd read on the radio and later put together in my own first anthology – "D's for the Dief, a right jolly old elf, and I laugh when I see him in spite of myself," will do for an example – and I began wondering what would happen if we tried it now, a decade and a half later. I started talking it over in the early mornings with Gary Katz, our studio director, and a fan of light verse. What, or who, we wondered, would the subjects be now? Would people be more cynical? More bitter? What would we learn about the nation's mood? Then again, who cared? It would be fun to try. I read part of the old alphabet on the air, and invited listeners to try their hand at updating. Glen Allen would help me judge.

That, as I say, is how it all began. But almost before we could start putting together the new alphabet, the contest took on a life of its own. Among the samples I'd read from the old collection was this one, from someone I knew then only by his name in the 1974 collection: Arthur Hister, as he'd signed himself, of Vancouver. He had written, and I quoted:

B is for Barrett. Dave's giving them hell.
First auto insurance. Sweet dreams, B.C. Tel.

In citing it again, I not only remarked on how much water had passed under that particular bridge – Barrett's controversial premiership seemed historic now, as did, in fact, even his regular appearances on *Morningside*'s Tuesday panel – but wondered what had become of the author, if, indeed, he was still among us. Then, in the mail that arrived with the first batch of new entries, I received this:

H is for Hister
Yes, I'm still alive
But rarely catch Gzowski
I work nine to five

So imagine my wonder
When out of the blue
A friend phones me up
Says "Pete's asking for you."

"Oh, happy day," I
Cry. "Whoop-dee-do.
This is great news. But
First tell me Pete Who."

"You know that guy Gzowski.
He's on CBC."
I remembered some effort on
Late night TV.

"He mentioned your name on the air
Several times.
He wanted to know if you're still
Into rhymes."

So, Peter, listen
Here's where I've been
I'm still in Vancouver
My cat's seventeen

I now have two children
My wife runs a store
My hairline's receding
My kneecaps are sore

I bought IBM
When I ought to have sold
My Mazda still stalls
When the weather's too cold

But guess what, dear Peter
There is something new
I host my own program
It's on channel two

It's finally happened
That us, you and me,
Are brothers-in-arms
At the old CBC

But tell me, my comrade,
I've been in arrears
What is it you've done
These past fifteen years

You still smoke those ciggies
And dream "Just suppose?"
And your glasses still cannot
Stay perched on your nose?

Have you interviewed all of
Cape Breton as yet?
Is there any Canadian
You still haven't met?

Why don't you move to
The coast for the air?
And join with refuseniks
Like Laurier La Pierre?

So write me, dear Peter,
And try to compose
Some couplets, a sonnet,
And not just some prose

But in case you are shy
And won't really try it,
I'll wait till you publish
This poem, then buy it.

Dr. Art Hister
Vancouver

✎ Before I could respond, we began relishing some of the new entries on the air. A lot of them were political, and did, as we'd expected, reflect the changing times. Here are some couplets that caught the eyes of our distinguished panel of literary judges, which is to say Glen and myself:

✉ B stands for Brian, majority shrinking,
Can't seem to learn, before talking comes thinking.

D's for the deficit and the horrors it brings.
I'm sure Mike will solve it when he dies and has wings.

Roy Shephard
Scarborough, Ontario

✉ M's for Mulroney, and for Mila his mate
She shows us style, he Tunagate.

Lynne Collard
Nepean, Ontario

✉ S is for Stevens, Noreen and Sinclair;
"How was your day dear?" is answered with care.

Gail Norcross,
North Vancouver

✉ T is for Tories, sitting at third.
They're "pour les oiseaux" – i.e., for the birds.

Peter Scholes
North York, Ontario

✉ V is for Vander, in Hoof and in Zalm.
What a difficult choice, the town or the man?

Gail Norcoss
North Vancouver

✎ But some were more general – just comments on Canadian people, places, and . . . well, things:

✉ A is for acid on forests and lakes.
The rain that was gentle now drips our mistakes.

Samm MacKay
Waterloo, Ontario

✉ E is for Edmonton, the Ghermezian grail.
The only attraction they lack is a whale.

Darlene Roth-Rehn
Yellowknife, Northwest Territories

✉ E is for Elbow, a fine lakeside point
Once was a quiet place, now quite a joint.

Lois Finnestad
Saskatoon

✉ F is for French. Our nation's bilingual.
Put the kids in immersion and then let them mingle.

Pamela Kent
Surrey, British Columbia

✉ H is for Halifax. Here there's no failures,
With its fog and its mist, it keeps us in sailors.

Rosalie Rivers
Ottawa

✉ K's for the Klondike. We find it divertin'
To bone up on History, chronicled by Berton.

Kerin Spaargaren
Calgary

✉ K is for Knowlton, now there's a smart fellow
He reads all the news like he's playing a cello.

Marshall Skinner
Windsor, Ontario

✉ L's for Liona, our lady guitarist
Whose image has changed to strummer bizarrest.

Samm MacKay
Waterloo, Ontario

✉ M is for mainland, the little hors d'oeuvre
Sandwiched between St. John's and Vancouver.

Eric Mendelsohn
Toronto

✉ M stands for Man., preceding "itoba,"
Halfway between coasts, a good place to stop ova.

Sheena McKinnon
St. George, Ontario

✉ O is Orillia – you'll know it best
As the home of Steve Leacock, the Anacin test.

Joan Harnock
Sault Ste. Marie, Ontario

✉ T's for the trauma of transferring to Trawna,
Some may be happy, but most just don't wanna.

Catharine Hay
Ganges, British Columbia

✉ W's for Winnipeg (my brother lives there)
It's so cold in the winter his tires go square.

Jacky Bramma
Whitby, Ontario

✎ Meantime, I'd decided to answer Art Hister – sorry, *Doctor* Hister:

Dear Arthur: Congrats
On what's happened to you,
The stories, the stats
And the kids numb'ring two.

141

But your verses, I fear,
Omit one bit of news
(Or so 'twould appear
From the parts I peruse).

I knew you as Mr.
But now, as I see,
You're *Doctor* Art Hister –
How come the degree?

Is it new? Is it earned?
Did you get it for free?
For something you've learned?
Or are you like me?

Did somebody call you,
And say, "Better sit.
We'd like to install you
As Gzowski, D.Litt."?

Forgive me for boasting –
And probing the mystery.
I'd love to be toasting
This bit of Art Hister-y.

Can you fill in the blanks,
In (if possible) rhyme,
I'll reply with deep thanks,
And a new story: mine.

✎ I read that on the radio, and a few days later, fearful that he hadn't heard me, called his office in Vancouver to check. That caused some confusion, I learned. Art Hister wrote:

✉ Let me tell you what happened
When you phoned me last

My secret'ry woke me
From sleep with a blast

Her voice was quite frantic
"Ontario called.
I'll spell out his name
Gz," then she stalled

"I think that he's Polish
It ends with a ski
He said 'Call collect.'
Must be CBC

"His voice was quite friendly
He just asked for Art
I looked everywhere
But I can't find his chart."

She'd honestly never
Listened to you
Just Willie and Waylon
All else is taboo

You wanted to know
How I got my degree
Did I actually earn it
Or did it come free

My mother was shocked
She thought in her heart
The whole country knew
I was Doctor Art

This diploma I got
It's called an M.D.
I got it quite young
I was just twenty-three

I saw whilst a babe
That this name of Hister

Required a title
Not simply mister

Though it's yellowed by now
It still hangs on the wall
Of my mother's abode
In cold Montreal

The reason she has it
It's hers by decree
She claims that M.D.
Stands for mother's degree

She worked hard to earn it
With the sweat of her brow
So her son the doctor
Is Doctor Art now

✎ And that, for the time at least, seemed to be that – the score,
if I can paraphrase Janet Bruce, whose letter about winter appears
in a later chapter: Hister 2, Gzowski 1.

We began to choose the winning alphabets, those that seemed
to us either to have a theme that held together, or to contain so
many clever couplets that the entire work was worth celebrating.
Here are four:

✉ A is for Acid, free-traded in rain
    and for AIDS sown in love with a harvest of pain.
  B is for Big Foot, and if poor old Brian
    swore that he had seen one, we'd say he was lyin'
  C's for our Culture, dependent on Flora
    to say what it is that we ought'a have more'a.
  D is for Dief, whose statue, I hear
    under each gimlet eye grows a tiny bronze tear.

E's for Election a long time to wait
   but we still won't forget about Tunacodgate.
F is for Fission . . . the nuclear kind
   thanks to which just one finger can cancel Mankind.
G's for good neighbour, Canadians rue,
   whereas they don't have any, their neighbour has two!
H is for Hull. Who says it's not pretty
   enough to be part of our capital city?
I is for Inuit, inexplicably sore
   as low-flying Yanks suck the roof through the door.
J is for Juniors. It could stand for Jerks
   or Jesuitical coaches of young Russian turks.
K is for kilometres. God only knows when
   I'll give up computing "times six over ten."
L's for the liquor I drank to relax
   'til I found out how much of the price was the tax.
M's for Ma Bell, extortionate tart!
   If they'd give me her number I'd phone her a fart.
N's for the News on my CBC station
   compelling incentive to defenestration.
O is for Ozone. Why can't we cajole
   what is here on the ground to get up in that hole?
P's for the Post, which costs us too dearly.
   If I thought they could read, I'd stop writing clearly.
Q's for the Question not easy to answer:
   "By what right do you smoke and give other folks
   cancer?"
R's for the Railroad "uniting the nation"
   in disgust as they cut one more train, one more station.
S is for Soft, as in wood and in heads
   whereas one makes for forests the others make Feds.
T is for Tuna and Tainted and Tin
   what it was, how it tasted, and what it was in.
U's for the Universe duly unfolding
   But where is Pierre, and who is he holding?
V's for Victor. Deliver his plunder
   to the radioactive debris that he's under.

145

W's for the Women, with Justice in sight
    when, in fear, come the "real" ones to put out the light.
X is for Christmas, or so it would seem.
    Even X-ians write it. By X, I could scream.
Y is for Yippie and Yoiks and Yaroo!
    Peter likes to read glad ones. I hope this will do.
Z is for Zoske, the spelling's phonetic
    So he'll end what he started, bad rhymes alphabetic!

We know you like couplets that uplift and cheer
But Goddamn it, Peter, you *did* pick this year!

Patricia Smith
Duncan, British Columbia

✉ A is for AIDS, one of two epidemics.
    The other one, drugs, fairly reeks of polemics.
B is for blab, and it gives me the shivers,
    to think of the toxic sludge in our rivers.
C is for content, Canadian-made
    without which our records would never get played.
D is for Darlington, and nuclear power,
    a pork barrel the contents of which have gone sour.
E is for Edward, who wouldn't have the – –
    to enlist in the Navy of West Edmonton Mall.
F is for "free trade," which Simon's all for
    but each day it costs us a thousand bucks more.
G is for Gainers, where gain is the rule,
    and the working man's nothing but a greedy man's tool.
H is for hunger strike, on Parliament Hill,
    of which all but Senator Jacques had their fill.
I is for inmates, who may soon be deciding,
    who gets elected in Brian's home riding.
J is for Jesus, on coins stamped in gold;
    one of the few things of which Noreen told.

K is for knowledge, as in "Who knew what, when?"
  Is Brian embroiled in a scandal again?
L is for lumber, a taxing dispute –
  the precepts of free trade it appears to refute.
M's for Minaki, lodged in our mind,
  as the whitest of elephants to be seen in our time.
N is for nude, how they dress in the bar,
  where Coatesy-poo got caught with his hand in the jar.
O's for Olympics, one of Calgary's treats;
  if you know the right people you might even get seats.
P's for our parrot, who uses his mouth,
  to echo the hype of his master down south.
Q's for Quebec, where all Brian's cannon
  are loose on the gun deck, and firing at random.
R is for rain, a problem politic,
  that wipes out our lakes by its nature acidic.
S is for Sondra, our Miss Etiquette,
  Our ham-fisted hostess, our graceful Rambette.
T is for Turner, a bumbling phoney,
  whose only sound asset is Brian Mulroney.
U is for "P-U," a distasteful smell,
  wafting up from the tuna that Fraser would sell.
V is for Vander Zalm, vapid and void,
  of any sound program to get people employed.
W's for Women, who may not be REAL;
  the best way to tell is to give them a feel.
X is for exit sign, aglow in the gloom;
  Brian's only bright light in the cabinet room.
Y is for yawn! a view apathetic,
  of Mulroney's performance; so far, so pathetic.
Z is for Nazis, which I understand,
  still languish, perhaps, on Canadian land.

Chris Jinot
Guelph, Ontario

✉ A is for Arctic, the top of the map.
   Our icy ice sea 'neath the peaked Polar Cap.
B is between the two Cs on the band.
   the network that broadcasts to showcase this land.
C for the charter that rights all the wrongs
   for one who believes or belies or belongs.
D is defrost: pastime of the nation.
   if given a choice, though, I'd choose hibernation.
E is for English or sometimes Anglaise:
   a word on a sign or a turn of a phrase.
F is for flat, from horizon to eye,
   as big as the prairie and wide as the sky.
G is for guard, what we stand on for thee,
   to keep our skies clear and nuclear free.
H is for hockey. I'm sorry to say
   It's "go fight, win, break, bruise" instead of just "Play."
I is for Frob – I mean Iqaluit.
   No longer a sailor's name, it's Inuit.
J is for jellyfish, a blob all afloat.
   Next time on a ferry look down by the boat.
K is for kist (no longer a star).
   A nose out of sync gives the catch mal de mar.
L is the landslide that brought in the Tories:
   four years of hearings, mix-ups, and I'm-sorries.
M is for muskrat, not a real fast liver.
   Lots flat on the road along the Detroit River.
N is for new, as in Brunswick and foundland,
   Scotland (or Scotia) help compose this renowned land.
O is for Ostler (some call him the Speaker).
   Fired if he's stronger, chastised if he's weaker.
P is the pause inside procrastination.
   You'll get a free vote during this generation.
Q is for quiet, as noisy as stars,
   A Canadian night far from bustle and cars.
R is for red-caps; that is, it once was.
   Now it's for rent-a-cart, whatever *that* does.

S is for Sunday and shopping and sin.
    They tithe, tax, or fine you for being where you've been.
T is for tariff and T is for trade.
    Nothing's for free when there's coin to be made.
U is usufruct: the neighbourhood comer
    who'll sell you the tools that he borrowed last summer.
V is for Velcro, attached to some lips;
    those wearing this will not likely sink ships.
W's water, and sometimes it's ice,
    and sometimes it's both when one would suffice.
X is in front of country and skiing:
    blazing and trailing and falling and treeing.
Y is for yard, given way to the meter.
    It just made no sense marking each centifeeter.
Z is for zed, not for "zee" like the States.
    (We may be good neighbours, but not linguimates.)

Patrick McWade
Madsen, Ontario

✉ A's for Americans, boisterous race
    Who seem to enjoy kicking sand in our face.
B's for our Bashfulness, well-documented,
    Which looks on flag-waving as slightly demented.
C's for our Consciousness, prefixed by "self-".
    (The books on this subject would fill a whole shelf.)
D is for Danger, which gives us dismay.
    When the game gets too risky, we'd rather not play.
E is for Effort, which none of us spare;
    We'll always try harder, though winning is rare.
F is for Fortitude, stalwart and steady;
    Though loath to attack, to "stand guard" we are ready.
G is for Gusto (embarrassing trait!),
    Which is never a part of Canadian fate.

H, for Humility, lowly, debasing,
Ensures that our country remains self-effacing.
I's for Identity, and ours is split
'Twixt Brit and American. (Thus spake Can Lit.)
J is for Just, which describes our society.
But to be "just" Canadian quells notoriety.
K is for Killing, an act we abhor.
So our country's a good place to hide from a war.
L is for Loyalty, our grand solution,
Much neater and quieter than revolution.
M's for the Margarets who pour words in torrents:
The brilliance of Atwood, the greatness of Laurence.
N is for Nash – not the Ogden of verse,
But Knowlton, who tells us that things could be worse.
O is for Optimists. We don't have many.
(The last one, I think, was a premier named René.)
P, for Polite, is the way we are seen.
And Americans notice our subways are clean.
Q's for our Quirks, like the infamous "eh?"
And the well-known "aboot," and Victoria Day.
R's for Resistance to cultural swamping,
Which keeps Gordon light-footed and Stompin' Tom
stomping.
S is for Sex, which we never discuss.
(Dr. Ruth, it is clear, could not be "one of us.")
T is for Tea, the kind only sold here.
(Red Rose is our next-favourite beverage to beer.)
U is for Unity, and I'd avow
That we've managed it somehow, but don't ask me how.
V's for our Valour when put to the test.
But unless we must fight, we would much rather rest.
W's Weather: a major frustrater.
If it's nice out today, then we'll pay for it later.
X is for Exercise: meaningless action,
In Canada, subtitled "Participaction."

Y is for Yearning to know who we are.
  (Pierre Berton has taken this subject quite far.)
Z is for Zed – for we never say "zee."
  It's one of the reasons that we remain "we."

Margaret Gunning
Hinton, Alberta

✎ And finally, the grand winner of all – or so Glen and I thought.
Our reasons? We liked it.

✉ A is for André, the minister who's making
    Us pay through the nose for the drugs that we're taking.
B is for Brian, for bull, and for blarney,
    And Bonzo (that other true son of Killarney).
C is for Carney – all three hundred pounds of her.
    (But Calgary's Pete Club sure liked the sounds of her.)
D is for Dustbowl – divine retribution
    For failure to fund Bible Bill's institution.
E is for Everyman, paying the freight
    For a whole herd of feds who can't hit their own weight.
F is for Follies, parliamentary and ice,
    Skate around all the issues and always dress nice.
G is for Gzowski, that silver-tongued critter
    Smoothing out all the airwaves that were riled up by
    Ritter.
H is for History being repeated.
    It'll repeat again when Mulroney's defeated.
I is for me, an incontinent man
    Who is hooked on the buy-now and pay-later plan.
J is for Jobs, so Jump on the bandwagon
    For Jobs building Jails down in Manicouagan.

K is for King; Frank's number-one mover
  In OCO's fiasco-recovery manoeuvre.
L is for Leveraged buy-outs of assets
  By the Reichmans, the Pocklingtons, Bronfmans, and
  Bassetts.
M is for Missiles all cruising so errantly
  With computers that can't read a compass, apparently.
N is for New Democrats, earnest as preachers,
  Wistfully watching the game from the bleachers.
O is for Optimism burning so bright.
  (It snowed? Ah, but it'll chinook overnight.)
P is for Pessimism. (Look at that snow.
  There'll be accidents all over town, don't you know?)
Q is for Quinn, an ex-Flyer, ex-King,
  An ex-Leaf, and ex-Flame, and now ex-everything.
R is for Reagan, bombs bursting in air
  Inspiring the colour that he dyes his hair.
S is for Sinc. Just like me (so he said)
  Because my wife and his never talk much in bed.
T is for Turner – neither Tina nor Ted
  But the man from Glad's hair on J.K. Galbraith's head.
U is for U-boat prowling our Arctic waters.
  Manifesting your destiny again, Yankee rotters?
V is for Vander Zalm, upbeat and chipper,
  So porcelain of tooth and so wooden of slipper.
W is for Winter, our Parliamentary season.
  It's windy and long and makes no rhyme or reason.
X is for Xenophobes – both French and English,
  Who can't live together and can't make it singlish.
Y is for Yahoo, a Calgarian rowdy
  Unabashed that his mascots are Hidy and Howdy.
Z is for Zephyr wafting over the mountain
  Only eight days left till spring, and I'm countin'!

George Berg
Calgary

✎ We *still* hadn't heard the end of it. After hearing me announce his victory on the air, George Berg wrote:

✉ The Calgarian's high times are both few and flat
    But there's one who's forgotten about all of that.
He's forgotten Mount Allen, all snowless and rocky.
    Doesn't mind that the Russians have stolen *his* hockey.
He's forgotten both ends of his budget won't meet,
    And the times that he's opened his mouth to change feet.
He's forgot all the pot-holes, the long winter's chills,
    All the posties who bring only junk mail and bills.
He's forgotten the search for the Final Solution
    For those who claim cigarette smoke is pollution.
He's forgotten the times he's been arrowed and slung
    By the fortunes that hang around life's bottom rung.
He's forgotten the welts on his old aching frame,
    All the scars that one picks up by playing life's game.
Now he thinks of the times when his dreams have come true
    (As his days dwindle down, he has had precious few).
Now he's all giggles and smirks like a sinner
    For under the calloused old hide, there's a winner!
Now the old gent's in clover (that location so rare)
    'Cause he's just heard his alphabet read on the air.

                              George Berg
                              Calgary

✎ But even with that final celebration, the plot that had begun with Art Hister had not ended. In March – this had begun in January, don't forget – I received this:

✉ C is for contest with answers in rhyme –
    My mind remains blank till it's long past the time!

The above couplet seems the story of my life. Almost twenty years ago *Maclean's* magazine ran a contest for which the entries were to be what they called "Double Dactyls." A Double Dactyl is a diabolically contrived verse with a tightly structured form. The best way to describe it is to give an example – the following was given in *Maclean's* at the time:

Higgledy, piggledy,
Benjamin Harrison,
Twenty-third president
Was, and as such
Served between Clevelands, but
Save for this trivial
Idiosyncracy
Didn't do much.

Two quatrains, of which lines 1 to 3, and 5 to 7, are to consist of two dactylic measures each. Lines 4 and 8 are to contain one trochaic and one iambic measure as shown, and are to rhyme. Line 1 is to be a nonsense line; line 2 is to identify a notable; one of the double dactyl lines other than the first two is to be a single word; and the entire poem is to be amusing, preferably epigrammatic. As I said, diabolical.

I played around with this form for a while at the time, but got nowhere. Now, almost twenty years later this form has come back to me, and almost without effort, I jotted down the four that I enclose. Indeed, even better than the couplet with which I began this letter would be the following:

Scribbley, scrabbley,
Poor Eric Channen – he
Sometimes writes poems – his
Verses are great!
Must find a contest with
Retroactivity –
One that takes entries full
Twenty years late!

My wife, who regularly listens to *Morningside*, assured me that I should send them in, even though they do not conform to your current competition. Here are four of them:

Jiggery, pokery,
Brian Mulroney is
Premier of Canada –
Two years to run.

Due, I suppose, to his
Mandible-arity
Leads with his chin in more
Senses than one!

Fiddledy, diddledy,
Handsome John Turner is
Leader of Liberals –
Longs for a break.
Overimpatiently
Waiting for Brian to
Trip on his bootstraps – a
Pratfall to make!

Higgledy, piggledy
NDP's Broadbent seeks
Balance of power – seems
Wise among fools.
Someone should tell him that
Ultracentrality
Leads to the place where you
Fall between stools!

Hickery, dickery
President Reagan is
Ultraconservative –
Patriot proud.
See him there standing so
Tall in the saddle – his

Head is so high that he's
Lost in a cloud!

Eric Channen
Windsor, Ontario

✎ Bemused again, I read Eric Channen's letter and double dactyls
on the air. And lo and behold . . .

✉ Higgledy-piggledy
Peter of *Morningside*
In bringing the subject up
Little did wist
Verse makers would reckon that
Double-dactyllery
Offered a challenge
Too hard to resist.

Dickery-Dockery
Marconi (Guglielmo)
Receiving from Cornwall
On Signal Hill.
If only he'd foreseen
Teevee-nauseaitis
My guess is he'd likely
Be up there still

Jiggery-pokery
John A. Macdonald (Sir)
Socking the Grits with a
Speech to the chin.
Responding to plaudits
Bibuloustically
With " 'T'wasn't me, fellows,
Must be the gin."

Ken Cheetham
Willowdale, Ontario

156

✎ And after which, in turn, I received, among other correspondence, these:

✉ Higgledy-piggledy,
Jimmy G. Pattison,
Builder of empires, of
EXPO the Groom,
Such a fine Christian man,
Orthodoxarian,
Ready on Monday to
Lower the boom.

Hickory-Dickory,
William A. Vander Zalm,
Built him a Fantasy
Garden – with glades,
Now he's in Wonderland,
So-Cred-Utopian,
No one is needy and
No one has AIDS.

Alan J. Tolliday
Vancouver

✉ Rondelay, sondelay
Peter G-zowski has
Let an idea most
Insidious drop.
Following this rhythm is
Ultrahypnotical.
Once you get started
Just how do you stop?

Mary Chapman
Elrose, Saskatchewan

✎ Which in turn – and this may be how you stop – brought it all back to the *Morningside* office. Waiting on my desk one morning were these double dactyls, from the man with whom I'd talked about it all in the first place.

✉ Higgledy Piggledy
Juliet Capulet
Cried to her Romeo
"Too bad you're You.
Open hostility
Interfamilially
Makes you less welcome than
Shylock the Jew."

Higgledy Piggledy
Baron von Frankenstein
Genius creator of
Life from the dead.
Now he's eponymous
(Uncomplimentrily)
Only for bruisers with
Bolts in their head.

Gary Katz
Toronto

✎ And so, for the time being, at least, it ended, although it occurred to me when I met Arthur Hister's wife at the Canadian Booksellers' Association convention in June (the store she runs is a literary one, apparently) not only that he had been right in his predictions about the future of his verse, but that he and I were still not finished. In any case, *Morningside*'s creative writers were ready to turn to another form of expression.

SHORT SHORT STORIES: PART ONE

The first story in this first of three fictional inter-ludes in this collection is what started all of them. Pat Wolfe, who was doing some work with the native community in Saskatoon, sent it in. He had no evident purpose, except, perhaps, that I might like to read it on the air. I had no particular purpose when I did so, either, although, after all these years, perhaps I ought to have known. "Why, this letter is a self-contained short story," I said naïvely and aloud when I read it. "I wonder if anyone else is interested in trying the same thing, writing a story as concise as this."

They were. In the next several weeks – actually, Pat had written early in the spring of 1987, not long after our poetry exchange was running down, and since each batch we read on the radio brought in more, they were still coming in the summer – I received more than a hundred. Among the first that arrived (and I've put it second here) was one that picked up, in a way, where Pat Wolfe's had left off. But very shortly a lot of other themes emerged. Eventually all that our contributors were doing was writing stories that could be told on one page.

✉ The water is running in Saskatoon today. I got a phone call from the post office that some mail had arrived. I walked across the iron bridge over the South Saskatchewan River and saw, lying on the ice, a rainbow kite. It was beautiful and sad, close to the water's edge yet impossible to reach by foot because of the melting snow. It sort of reminded me of a painting of a burning giraffe. Giraffes have no vocal cords, they say.

I got my mail and in it was a letter from my mother. Her mom, a beautiful lady with long braids and smiling eyes who was born in Algonquin Park, had died, at the age of eighty-eight. They were together and all was peaceful.

I walked home, past the kite, and dug out some fluorescent purple fishing line and a little lead weight. Back on the bridge, all it took was a No. 2 Len Thompson spoon tied to the line, and a toss of a hundred feet or so, and the kite came flying up to me like a frightened butterfly that had landed on the wrong flower.

As I wound up the string, a woman and a brown-eyed boy walked up to me and asked if I had *found* the kite. The day before, a beautiful kite had been lost to a tree. The boy had bought it with his own money. It was a wonderful creation in nylon patches – a rainbow phoenix with a bright-red tail. I handed the string over to him and he left. Then I went down to the gardening store and brought back some shamrock seeds for Grandma's grave. As I came home, the footprint the kite had left was smiling.

Pat Wolfe
Saskatoon

✉ I can tell you something about the kite your friend rescued from the ice. I can tell you that it was bought from the Cumulus Shop by Cumberland Park, right here in Saskatoon.

The first morning the snow melted I was driving past the park with my grandson, Gabe, when we saw a guy flying not one but *two* kites, one in each hand, and both as big as boxcars. All colours of the rainbow, they hung in the air like sun dogs on a forty-below morning. Gabe was on loan to me and Grandma for two days while his parents packed their things to return to Africa, where they work for CUSO. He said they didn't have kites in Africa. I didn't believe him but we stopped anyway to go into the Cumulus Store and look.

There were all kinds of kites there – box kites, Malay kites, kites like dragons, and a kite with a mile-long tail. It was difficult to choose. But when another boy bought a multicoloured lozenge-shaped Flyer, Gabe opted for one just the same. "This kite could fly all the way to Africa," he said. I tried to explain that if he let go of the string, the Flyer would drop to earth. But I'm not very good on the principles of flight.

After lunch we set off to fly the kite in Rotary Park, which is on the river bank behind our house and just below the iron bridge. (Grandma said to be sure not to go on the ice because it was rotten.) After a few false starts the Flyer shot up into the air, dived and rolled, and then soared again. The wind freshened and Gabe let out string until he came to the end. Just then I had to answer the call of nature. When I got back the Flyer was missing. Gabe said he had let it go. I looked all around. We went up on the iron bridge and there, on the ice below, was the multicoloured lozenge. "That's not my kite," Gabe insisted. "That's the other boy's. My kite is flying to Africa."

George Piper
Saskatoon

✉ I live in a small rural community in the Gulf Islands of British Columbia. The roads are dirt and the cars kick up dust and stones when they pass. The houses are mostly home-built and friendly, and not having cement foundations they often settle into the ground a little, but like the crooked smiles on the old-timers around here, the lopsided houses with their tilted floors just seem to belong. There's a magic on this island. You feel it when the last ferry boat leaves at six every evening, and there's just the islanders left behind. No police, no hospital, no stores, no street lights. Just stars and hoot owls and the big black silhouettes of the Douglas firs.

It's spring on the island now, and as I walked home from a friend's house this afternoon, I was delighted by the clear blue sky and the fresh sound of water running in the ditch beside the road. I was enjoying all nature's treats so much that I practically walked straight into the old green Plymouth that was parked on the side of the road.

I started to walk around the car when I noticed a little person sitting on the hood. It was Jenny, a beautiful brown-haired, blue-eyed six-year-old. I was no more than ten feet from her but she didn't notice me, being as absorbed in her world as I had been in mine. She was talking to herself. I stayed perfectly still and tried to listen. Then I moved a little closer and saw what she was doing. She was blowing soap bubbles with one of those rings that you dip into the soap and blow through. There were dozens and dozens of bubbles all around her, all glistening with pinks and blues and all moving and floating upwards with the breeze. She seemed dazzled by the sheer numbers of bubbles that mysteriously flowed from her wand and she kept dipping and blowing faster and faster and then there were hundreds of them spreading out everywhere as if multiplying on their own. She was talking to them and I moved a little closer to hear what she was saying.

"Be the one, be the one, be the one that lasts forever." Her eyes were fixed on one bubble, the one that still had not burst after the others all around it had disappeared. When it finally burst, she dipped and blew more bubbles and again waited till there was one that stood out from the rest and again she said, "Be the one, be the one, be the one that lasts forever!"

We watched the bubbles drift away, up into that blue sky, and watched them burst one after another. They were so suddenly gone. Once in a while you would follow one up, up, and so far up that you lost sight of it. You couldn't tell if it burst, but you couldn't see it either. They were so perfect, so beautiful. All gone, all except maybe for that one.

Stephen Arthurs
Hornby Island, British Columbia

✉ The sirens were not a new sound. We had heard them before in practices. The wail seemed to rise from the pit of the stomach, reach a peak, and then fall, churning the insides again and again. In later life I was to associate the nausea of air-raid sirens with the inevitable rise and fall of seasickness.

But this was no practice. It came less than half an hour after Mr. Chamberlain had been on the wireless to tell us that we must now consider ourselves at war with Germany. "This is his *answer*. This is Hitler's *answer!*" screamed the lady next door as she ran for the shelter of her house, her hands clasping her head as if to protect it from whatever might fall from the sky.

The wailing ceased and all was still. The whole neighbourhood stopped and listened for any sound of the approaching terror. My mother and father began removing everything from the cupboard under the stairs. This was a special place. Apart from the larder in the kitchen and the airing cupboard built around the hot-water tank in the back bedroom, it was the only storage space in the house. It was wedge-shaped, with two doors: one opening into the end that was almost high enough to stand in, the other opening into the pointed end of the wedge. I was allowed to keep my toys in this lower space but the other end was for more important things like the ironing board, brooms, polishes, and the new Hoover. All of these things were hurriedly piled in the hall because the government had told us that in an air raid the safest place for us was in the space under the stairs.

I knew that war was a serious business and that there were things to be afraid of – but it was exciting as well. Now it had come. Things were happening. Everything was out of the cupboard under the stairs and we were inside, taking shelter.

Then my whole world came apart. For the unexpected, the impossible, happened.

My father's voice broke.

My father was afraid.

David Sage
Burnaby, British Columbia

✉ I never did find out who brought it. It arrived among the steady stream of food and flowers and neighbours and sat reeking of sugar on the kitchen counter. It was the kind of cake you'd expect to find laced with nickels and pennies at a birthday party: the pink icing practically fluorescent, the top dotted with silver candy. For two weeks no one cut into it. Nor did anyone put it away, and I found my eyes drifting towards it again and again. Perhaps it stood in contrast to the bitterness of everything else that crowded the waking hours of those days.

She was soon to be nineteen and life sprawled ahead of her, or so it had seemed. Now there was only an empty car on a hillside, a lack of clues, and our heads swarming with scenarios. The unspoken lurked in everything: the smug poplars turning their backs to us, the miles of ditch scoured for keys, for a scrap of her clothing, the bitter dregs of coffee gone cold and gulped down anyway just to keep going.

As each day passed, our hopes flared and fell with a rhythm of their own and we took turns breaking down or comforting each other as the cycles happened to mesh. Only the children remained immune to the frightful greyness of the sky, to the stretching out of night when we lay awake waiting for the muffled weeping to

164

begin again. And who of us could help but envy the way my two-year-old nephew still crawled under his uncle's chair and twisted his face into an imp's idea of *horrible* – before overflowing with giggles? Yet rooted in that envy was also a worry of how we would tell him, later, when he was old enough to understand.

I suppose I should have stopped him when I spied him alone in the kitchen, sliding the chair across to the counter. But something in me went out to him and I watched in silence with a strange sort of joy rising in my chest. He struggled to get the chair into position and, with his tongue set between his lips in determination, crawled onto the seat. The chair teetered a moment as he pulled himself into a standing position and I almost called out to him then, though I doubt it would have stopped him. He didn't hesitate. He didn't look around guiltily to see if he had been found out. He just opened his two-year-old mouth as wide as it could possibly open and sank himself into the sweetness of that pink cake.

That was more than two years ago, now. Soon I will show him photographs and tell him how he had an aunt who loved him just as I love him, who would have continued to love him just as I love him. In the meantime, he likes to visit his uncle because of the crazy games we play and the sweetness of the cakes I feed him.

Derek Hanebury
Buffalo Head, Alberta

✉ A Chevrolet, an old Chevrolet, is parked right next door. It's rusted and incapable of motion. However, it has new functions. It is now home to mouse families. It protects and helps to nourish weeds. And, most important of all, it lends shade and shelter to Thomas. There – beside the right-front tire and behind a barrier of long grass – Thomas spends many hours in passive reflection. He never moves, not for a field mouse strolling by, not for group of juncos. His claws are bared only during his stretch, though his ears are always flicking. They look like leaves on a tree swept by wind.

Just as one can ponder the chicken-and-egg dilemma, I spent

many hours, in many frames of mind, wondering if it was Thomas who taught the seasons their stubbornness, or the seasons that taught Thomas his. This was the only place I ever saw him, and he was always there. Perhaps he never left it. Perhaps he had always been there. But when the snows come, his path is revealed. I have followed it on numerous occasions, through neighbours' yards and across the back alley. Every year it remains the same, and every year I fail to find its source. I think maybe I've been looking for the wrong end. And I know the neighbours find it strange – unnerving – that an old woman who rarely gets out during the year should venture out in the middle of winter and so doggedly walk this odd route through the snow. Maybe one year I'll discover where Thomas's tracks lead. Or maybe I won't. I kind of like a mystery.

Phil Henderson
Vancouver

✉ I was eight years old and I skipped and dawdled and ran my way over to see Aunt Katie. She wasn't really my aunt; everyone in the country community just called her Aunt Katie.

As I approached the door, the aroma of oatmeal cookies worked its usual pull on my senses. Even to my young eyes, Aunt Katie's kitchen was plain. A widow longer than my memory, she managed on thrift and generosity. Her giving always came back to her.

This morning the cookies were forgotten when I skipped into the kitchen. There were new curtains – and such beautiful curtains; all the lovely colours of my crayons beaming at us from the material. Aunt Katie glowed, too. She was so proud, having made them from an end given to her by the woman she nursed through the flu.

It was June. School ended and I spent most of the summer being busy. Aunt Katie was forgotten for the summer. September, school, and a need for cookies and comfort took me back. I was crushed. The beautiful curtains had faded to a dirty grey.

"Oh, Aunt Katie, what happened?"

166

Smiling, she passed me a cookie for each hand. "It's all right. Don't cry. You see, God needed all that colour for rainbows, and can you imagine – He chose my curtains."

I'm Aunt Katie's age now. She's gone, but whenever I see that marvellous coloured arc after the rain, thoughts of her curtains warm and comfort me.

Ruth Leonard
Sydney, Nova Scotia

THE JOYS (MOSTLY) OF CHRISTMAS

Christmas stories have become a *Morningside* tradition. We collect them in advance now, and often record a few in the weeks leading up to the holiday, so that we too can have the day with our families. One of my own Christmas rituals, in fact, is to turn on the CBC in the house where my children gather, so they can hear their father wish them the best of the season and then see him opening the gifts from the stocking they've prepared for him. (I know it's supposed to be the other way around, and the kids have stockings, too, but now that they're in their twenties, they make their mother and me hang ours up as well. Maybe it's Santa Claus.)

It pleases me this year that the Christmas season in which this collection sees print – actually the best of the past three *Morningside* Christmas yields – will also be the first in the world for Stephanie Ann Gzowski Zufelt, my first and perfect granddaughter. If Stephanie could read, the first story she would find

168

here is one its author first heard from *her* father, the Reverend Murray A. MacDonald, and the author's grandfather is involved, too. Mardie MacDonald, who sent this story to me on the letterhead of Coleville-Smiley Pastoral Charge (United Church) in Saskatchewan, still reads it herself each year as Advent begins, and remembers it from her childhood, but, as she writes, "I was an adult myself before I realized that the storekeeper in the story was Dad's own father, Willie R. MacDonald of Glace Bay."

So Mardie MacDonald first, and then other Christmas memories and images from Canada and elsewhere – all told by Canadians over the years.

✉ One year during the thirties, Christmas was especially bad in Cape Breton. The miners had gone on strike in mid-summer and the strike had dragged on and on, well into the fall. A miner with a family could go to the Union Hall every Saturday, give the union official his empty potato bag, tell them how many children he had, and be given the standard ration of staples for his family. When all the miners' resources were exhausted, the strike fund gone, and the miners' families deep in debt, they would have to end the strike and go back into the pits.

It wasn't too bad for the men who worked on contract, cutting the coal and blowing it down with dynamite and loading it into the pit boxes. They could work doubly hard and make up to twenty dollars on the one shift they worked.

It was different for Johnnie and miners like him. They were on one day's pay. They worked one day a week for three dollars and twenty-five cents. For a man like Johnnie, with eight children, it meant he still had nothing and was still deeply in debt as Christmas drew near. Three dollars and twenty-five cents might buy almost enough groceries and some kerosene for the lamps. But there was nothing left over for shoes or clothing – or Christmas.

His wife was desperate. She told Johnnie the children had been talking excitedly about what Santa Claus would bring them. She told him he'd have to go to the store and ask for something extra for Christmas. Johnnie said he couldn't do it. He just couldn't face the storekeeper and ask for more, owing so much already.

In desperation, she sent two of her little boys. They entered the store with their father's pay envelope, with its three one-dollar bills and its twenty-five-cent piece. They said, "This is Daddy's pay and this is Mama's list of what she wants, and she wonders if you will put in something extra for Christmas." The storekeeper looked at the money and the list. He had heard all the hard-luck stories ever invented. He'd promised his wife he wouldn't extend any more credit. She knew he wasn't sleeping at night, worrying about the way the wholesalers were hounding him. He knew he couldn't afford to be taken in again.

He started to tell the two kids what they could say to their mother, when he happened to glance down at their feet. There were holes in their stockings, but it was their shoes that got to him. Not shoes, really – just two pieces hacked out of an automobile tire, tied on the boys' feet with string.

The storekeeper phoned his wife and asked her to phone the neighbours and round up some old shoes – real shoes. When she started to ask him why, he cut her off with, "Never mind, just do it. And try to get some underwear and stockings, too, and pants and sweaters and anything else you can get your hands on."

He lifted up Johnnie's little boys and sat them on the counter and gave each of them a piece of hard candy. He placed the things on "Mama's list" into a box, added some extras, looked at the box for a moment or two, and then added a big chunk of bologna. He looked at the boys again and at the box again. Then he went into the back of the shop and got the two chickens he'd been saving to take home. He took out the bologna and put in the chickens.

Soon the storekeeper's daughter arrived with an assortment of shoes, rubber boots, underwear, stockings, some pants and sweaters, and some toys that were only one or two years old. The storekeeper locked the store, hitched up his horse, and loaded the three kids and the box of groceries on the back of his wagon.

When they arrived at Johnnie's house, the storekeeper wouldn't get off the wagon. He didn't want to hurt Johnnie's pride. He told his daughter to help the two little kids take the stuff to the kitchen door.

"Don't go in," he said. "Mind you just leave it on the step and come right back here." She was barely back on the wagon before the horse was moving. He didn't want Johnnie's wife embarrassing him with her thanks.

The storekeeper's own kids weren't very happy about eating bologna for Christmas dinner the next day. The storekeeper said he wasn't very happy, either. His wife just smiled.

She knew he didn't mean it.

Mardie H.C. MacDonald
Coleville, Saskatchewan

✉ My husband came home last night, December ninth, with the Christmas tree. It's bushy and dark green and beautiful and has the wonderful perfume of balsam fir. He bought it at a tree plantation down the road and watched the grower cut it down, so it couldn't be fresher. When he got home, he sawed off a slice of stem, so it would be sure to absorb the water; we put it in a bucket in the pump house, where it would stay cool and out of harm's way until Christmas.

The fragrance immediately filled the small building, and every pore of me, bringing back the smell of all the Christmas trees I have ever smelled – and that's fifty-seven trees!

They didn't quite all smell this good. One year we had what my mother called a "cat spruce." Not only was the sweet perfume missing, the needles all dropped off and we were left with a twelve-foot-high skeleton and a drift of brown needles underneath. That year was the beginning of fibreglass angel's hair, and this apparition was draped with it. It looked like the cobwebs on Miss Haver-sham's wedding cake when Pip came to tea. The fibreglass prickles got into our woollen stockings and we itched the rest of the winter.

In Halifax, where I grew up, the same man brought our tree every year. He would arrive about a week before the twenty-fifth and if he was late we children were beside ourselves, thinking he had forgotten. His wife often came, too, with evergreen and moss wreaths she had made and decorated with rose hips. The tree was then put in a safe place, guarded against cats and dogs, until it was time to bring it in and put up in the bay window.

After I was married, it became our custom to go to a friend's wood lot and cut our own tree. We drove the twenty-five miles or so down to the shore of St. Margaret's Bay and tramped through the woods, looking for the perfect tree. Some years there was deep snow; our search was not easy, with two parents, two children, their friends, and a dog to bark at squirrels and get in the way of the axe. But we always found the perfect tree.

Since we have lived in British Columbia, we have had to give up our tree cutting. Ironic in this province of so many trees, but Douglas firs are just too big.

This morning when I went into the pump house, the powerful smell that yesterday nearly knocked me over had subsided a bit. The tree was snuggled in amongst the wintering geraniums. I took the slice that had been cut off the bottom of the stem, brought it in the kitchen, and put it in a warm oven to release that perfume again. The slice of stem is here beside me, and that sweet, fragrant, pungent smell sweeps me away again to the dazzling excitement of Christmas.

Patsy Hayward
Victoria

✉ The best part of Christmas in Vancouver is the night the Carol Ships pass.

We eat an early dinner, scramble through closets to find our waterproof boots and wet-weather gear, and drive to Ambleside Beach, where huge crowds of families are assembling.

The beach is covered with a narrow wedge of snow, which at the ocean's edge looks like stencilled eyelet lace. Low waves shingle one upon the other, making a continuous wash up to the Capilano River. The ocean is cold, and as transparent as Saran Wrap.

A solitary Cates tug, a Christmas tree lashed to the mast, ruffles its white foam petticoat and moves into the narrows. The superstructure of the Lions Gate Bridge is a moving marquee of rhinestone lights.

Giant log bonfires are built on the beach, and children rustle up pieces of driftwood and add them to the fires.

Beyond the black headland of Prospect Point, a tall triangle advances, draped in red lights, and the convoy of Carol Ships slips out of the darkness, reflected accurately in the black sea mirror. They move, generators lub-dubbing, into a huge circle.

From Point Atkinson, along the West Vancouver shore, the ships are strung like an unclasped bracelet. We can hear the children singing far away, and the sound escalates gently as the ships move towards us. We have to move back up the beach as the ships' white wakes erase our footprints.

Beyond, into the inner harbour, the sounds trace back to us. Even after we can no longer hear the children, we feel the cherished Christmas music in the cold sea air.

Gail Mackay
North Vancouver

✉ Recalling the Christmases of my childhood, I'm struck by the part played by Eaton's, not Eaton's of the Eaton Centre and of the various suburban shopping malls, but the T. Eaton Co. Ltd., of Yonge and Queen, before there was even a College Street store. There was, first of all, the Santa Claus parade. Fortunately for us, we lived within walking distance of Eaton's west-end warehouse, where the parade formed, because we certainly could not have afforded carfare to go to a downtown viewing spot. My mother was glad when my older brother and I were old enough to go by ourselves and she didn't have to interrupt her Saturday baking to take us. The parade was held on Saturday mornings then, early, to minimize traffic disruptions, and I recall that it was barely light when my older brother and I left the house, bundled up against the cold with warnings ringing in our ears to behave ourselves and not to throw snowballs at Santa. When we got home, it was still early enough to do whatever Saturday chores my mother had lined up for us.

It is only proper, I suppose, that Eaton's figures in a story my mother told and retold about me. She had gone downtown Christmas shopping, and taken me with her. I would never have been taken downtown purposely to visit Toyland, but as long as we were in the store anyway, there was no harm in going up to the fifth floor, and, as long as we were in the toy department, no harm in lining up to speak to Santa. He took me on his lap and asked me what I would like him to bring me. It would have been a short list; we weren't conditioned by television commercials then. Later in the day we crossed the street to Simpson's and went to their toy department as well. I lined up to see a second Santa Claus. He, too, took me on his knee and asked me what I would like him to bring me. "I've already given my order at Eaton's," I said.

Fred C. Farr
Thornhill, Ontario

✉ My mother was the organist in the United Church. The organ was the kind with a hand-cranked pump in a little well at the side of it. The boy who pumped the organ had grown too tall to fit into the well so, as I was smaller than he, I fell heir to the job.

On Christmas Eve, the little church was packed. The choir had practised Christmas anthems and the senior Sunday school kids had learned their scripture readings. Green boughs and red berries decorated the church window sills, and everything was beautiful. To

174

set the tone of the service, one of the older men in the choir was to sing "The Holy City."

Mother played the introduction and the gentleman stood up and began to sing. I pumped mightily. The verse went just grand; the singers' rich bass voice fairly rattled the windows. Then came the chorus. The great voice boomed, "Jeru-thalem, Jeru-thalem," with a sound something like steam-relief valve in the centre of the word – he'd forgotten to wear his teeth.

The sound repeated in the chorus with such volume was my undoing. I started to laugh, and lost my rhythm with the crank. Before I knew it the crank had pulled out of its slot in the bellows.

I tried to catch the slots, as it went up and down, with the end of the crank. The organ was losing volume, and my mother stage-whispered: "Pump, Bevie, pump," while she played on near-silent keys.

Finally, one of the men sitting behind me reached over my shoulder and slipped the crank into the slot. I pumped like one possessed, and the final chorus of that glorious song echoed in the church.

I turned to my rescuer, who was all doubled over, with tears streaming down his face.

"Thank you," I stammered.

"You've made my Christmas, damn if you didn't!" he said, thrusting a quarter into my hand.

Beverly Walker
Picton, Ontario

✉ Not all Christmases are happy. Even though I can now see the humour in the event I want to tell you about, and laugh, I can also still cry about it.

It was my first Christmas in Canada, when I was in grade one. Santa Claus was a new phenomenon to me. I knew all about St. Nicholas and his servant Peter, from Holland. We had celebrated that event with our Dutch friends on December fifth. But here in Canada they had someone else, Santa Claus, who came on

December twenty-fourth and left gifts for everyone. This person knew if you were bad or good; he came down chimneys and drove a sleigh with reindeers. I was awestruck.

I asked friends all about the great event, and I relayed the valuable tidbits to my parents. I wanted them to be ready for Santa Claus. But they laughed and told me he wasn't real, just a person who dressed up: my mother explained why we celebrated St. Nicholas on December fifth, so we wouldn't overshadow the true meaning of Christmas. I wouldn't listen. What did they know? This was Canada.

On Christmas Eve, I went through my usual bedtime routine, with one exception. I took a long brown stocking out of my drawer and hid it under my pillow. I said good-night to my dad and mom, turned out the light, and crawled between the chilly sheets.

When my sisters were asleep, I quietly pushed back the covers, slid my feet to the cold floor, and hung my stocking on a nail in the wall, then crawled back into bed. Through the window I could see my neighbour's house, especially their roof. Wouldn't it be neat if I actually did see Santa go down their chimney!

I couldn't sleep. The excitement of waking up to a stocking full of gifts was too much for me. Yet I knew that I had to sleep, because Santa wouldn't come if I was awake.

A few times during the night I awoke, but the sky was always dark. I didn't check the stocking; I would leave that thrill for the morning. I closed my eyes very tightly.

When I finally woke again it was light. I excitedly turned over in my bed and eagerly looked at the wall. There beside the window hung my stocking . . . limp and empty.

What had I done wrong? Why had Santa forgotten me? For weeks I had honestly tried to be good and kind. I did not dare to ask my mom, or even admit what I had done. I couldn't ask her to hold me. I had been so sure that Santa was real.

I put my stocking back in the drawer, crawled back into bed, buried my face in my pillow, and wept.

Gertrude Adema
Weston, Ontario

✉ It was the usual Christmas Eve at our house. We were woken up about nine or ten o'clock. We got dressed and went downstairs for the big treat, which made our eyes shine and brought a smile to our faces, the milky sweet cup of tea and a raisin bun. We didn't get many treats, which made it all the more worth waiting for.

We, all hundred or so of us, were the orphans at Nazareth House, all girls, and we would be singing at Midnight Mass.

The choir was at the back of the church. We climbed the stairs and found our places on either side of the organ, altos on the right, trebles on the left. We warmed up the congregation with Christmas carols sung in Latin, such as "Adeste Fidelis," until it was time for the priest to start High Mass. Being awake at midnight was a heady thing to a nine- or ten-year-old, and it was sheer joy to be a part of that choir and give glory to God.

Maureen Edge Newby
Dollard des Ormeaux, Quebec

✉ On Christmas Eve, 1914, I was a sapper, aged twenty, in the Royal Engineers, Seventh Division, British Expeditionary Force. I was on night duty with a junior NCO, making a patrol of the wire defences of the front line.

At about midnight when we were ending our wire patrol and returning to our own lines, someone from the German-Saxon division hoisted, above the parapet of their trench, a small Christmas tree illuminated with candles. They started to sing "Holy Night." The night was so still that the candles did not even flicker. The carol singing was soon taken up on our side, and continued through the night.

Then, just after dawn on Christmas Day, shouting was heard from the Germans: "Don't shoot, Tommy." One, then several more Germans clambered out onto their parapet waving their hands. They found a gap in their wire fence and strolled out into no-man's land, coming to a halt about half-way. Some of our men went to meet them, and they were shaking hands and generally exchanging greetings as best they could.

177

Then, about nine o'clock, word came that a cease-fire had been arranged so both sides could bury their dead. (There were many bodies lying in the open.) Mass graves were dug and the dead were buried side by side with all their arms and equipment. Only identity discs and private papers were removed. A short burial service was held by a British and German chaplain.

On our front, the unofficial truce lasted until New Year's Day, 1915. Everybody walked about quite freely during the day, and at night there were quite a few clandestine meetings. At one of these meetings, we were able to swap a sandbag full of bully beef and jam for two long-handled wire cutters and an earth auger. They thought we were better fed; we thought they had much better tools. Such is war at its most absurd.

Lieutenant-Colonel C.A. Luckin
Beaconsfield, Quebec

✉ Grandma was a silver-haired lady. Although beginning to look a bit frail in her eighty-third year, her smile still lit up her face, and her stories delighted me for hours on end.

She had moved from the home in which she and grandpa had raised my mother and her brothers and sisters to one of those cold-looking senior-citizens' apartment complexes. As my sister and I entered her little apartment, I could see that she had been busy preparing for Christmas.

There was Christmas music on the record player. Ornaments adorned the tables in her living room. In the corner, on a beautiful old dresser, stood her little table-top tree, glimmering with lights.

I was puzzled to see it decorated, because it had become a tradition for my younger brother to devote an afternoon to decorating the tree with her. Grandma seemed almost apologetic when she explained that for some reason she could not wait this year.

She brought in an armful of boxes of various shapes and sizes, gifts from "the girls" – her daughters. She winked as she told us she was not supposed to open them until Christmas morning, but she reasoned that there might be something that didn't fit and needed to be exchanged.

There was a neatly wrapped package of jams, preserves, and cheeses; a lovely blouse; a pretty dress, and some "ladies things," which she concealed from me, but displayed to Cindy. She appeared proud as she held up each item for us to see.

We stayed for lunch; then it was time to go. We said our good-byes and for a moment I stood there looking at Grandma, wanting to hug her. I chose not to, and I always will regret that decision. The next day my grandmother died. It would not be a very joy-filled Christmas in our home.

After a while, though, I realized how fortunate we were. Christmas was not to take place on December twenty-fifth, but had happened for Cindy, Grandma, and me that night, in her apartment, with her newly decorated tree sparkling on the table top.

John O'Keefe
Halifax

✉ My Christmas story begins fourteen years ago, when our son, Brian, was five years old and his sisters Lisa and Lori were eight and seven. That year, we wanted to teach the kids the importance of giving.

We planned a shopping trip and discussed the amounts each child should spend, then trudged off to our neighbourhood department store, three little people in tow, with magnificent and unselfish plans in their heads.

I cannot remember what gifts Lisa or Lori bought that year, but as long as I live I won't forget Brian's first Christmas shopping spree.

He had looked at many gifts, suitable for sisters, or dads, or moms, but a wonderful Fort Apache, with its Indians, horses, and cowboys, was too strong a temptation for this little self-indulgent personality. Today, Brian is a wonderful, warm, generous, impulsive nineteen-year-old, always full of surprises.

Life is never dull around him, but neither his sisters nor his parents will ever let him forget the Christmas he spent the contents of his piggy bank exclusively on himself.

Sharon Sutcliffe
Cobourg, Ontario

✉ For as long as I could remember, my dad had played hockey on Saturday mornings. Sometimes his alarm would wake me and I'd hear him tiptoe down the hall to the stairs. I would wait for the door to lock behind him, then listen for the crunch of footsteps on frozen pavement. The hurried steps would grow fainter; I would pull the covers tight against myself and fall back to sleep.

I was gone by the time he returned at noon to kiss my mom good morning and hang up his damp underwear. I was playing road hockey with friends of my own. But some Saturday mornings in grade eleven I'd have to curtail my outdoor enthusiasm for an assignment due on Monday.

On one such Saturday I was working on a history assignment on the Neanderthal Man. The phone rang down the hall from my bedroom. I moved after the second ring, but my mom had already picked up the receiver.

"Hello," she said. Then the house went unusually quiet several seconds. I became concerned, opened my door, and headed down the hallway to the living-room, where my mom stood with her back to me. She turned, her eyes filled with tears.

My dad had suffered a heart attack. They had rushed him from the arena to a nearby hospital in the hope of preventing a second coronary. The doctors were still working on him. They didn't know if he would make it.

I thought of my dad. I thought of my mom. I thought of Christmas, only fourteen days away.

One of my dad's hockey buddies came to drive my mom to the hospital. She bundled herself against a constant shiver, told me to get supper for my younger brother and sister and to stay close to the phone, and left.

The late-afternoon sun disappeared behind the old two-storey house across the street; then Christmas lights were turned on in nearby homes. We ate supper, then I reminded my sister and brother of their chores before bed. As I went into the kitchen to do the dishes, I paused to look at some of the festive decorations my mom had begun to sprinkle throughout the house – cards hung up, an advent wreath on the dining-room table, and my grade-one Santa Claus, with a cotton beard, balanced on top of the bookshelf.

I'm the oldest, I thought. If something happens to my dad it's up to me to provide for the family. I said the Our Father over and over.

My dad lived. Three days before Christmas he came home. In all the rush, we had not bought many presents. But it was the best Christmas ever.

Michael Hamp
Toronto

✉ At Christmas in 1971, I was separated from my husband, whom I had sworn to love until death. I was dead, but no one had had the good grace to bury me. Steeped in self-pity, I cared for my three-year-old daughter and nine-month-old son. As I struggled to decorate a tree, write Christmas cards, and get through the ordeal, no one could convince me that there was any joy in the season. After all, my Santa Claus had left me and gone to Mexico with another woman. Worse yet, he had taken our support payments with him.

A week before Christmas, an envelope arrived in the mail. In it was a food voucher for twenty-five dollars, from the Salvation Army. My hands shook and my cheeks burned with the humiliation. How had they got my name? The time might come when I had to stand in welfare lines, but it hadn't happened yet. I wanted to rip the damn thing up – where did they get the right to offer me help? But I couldn't, not while I knew I had barely enough to pay next month's rent. With a sick lump in my stomach, I put the voucher away so it couldn't be seen.

Christmas Day would be spent at my parents', and I looked forward to not being alone. If I could get through the hours after putting the kids to bed on Christmas Eve and playing solitary Santa, I would be fine.

Early on the day before Christmas, I heard on the radio: "The Salvation Army announced today that they still have two hundred and twenty-one families who have not received their Christmas food gift. They are appealing to the public for donations to provide Christmas dinner for those less fortunate than themselves. Donations may be dropped off in person at Salvation Army Headquarters . . ."

The words made my cheeks burn. The voucher was still tucked in my purse. If they hadn't sent out so many unwanted vouchers they wouldn't be in trouble, I thought. It was 9:30 A.M. and the food stores closed at 6:00 P.M. I picked up the phone.

"Salvation Army." I stumbled to give my name and explained that I had heard their radio plea.

"Would you care to give a donation, sister?" The brotherly love in his voice irritated me rather than soothed.

"No, I can't give a donation – I don't have any money. You people sent me a voucher. How did you get my name?" The rude tone of my voice contrasted sharply with his tone.

"I'm sorry, but we don't discuss our gift lists unless you wish to give us the name of someone you know who also needs help."

"But you already are short!" Why was he willing to take another name when they desperately needed money?

"Well, I'm glad we were able to help you and I'd like to wish you a very Merry Christmas."

"You don't understand. I don't need it. I have my parents and my mother is cooking a huge turkey." I described our family's Christmas day. "I'll send the voucher back to you."

"Oh, thank you." His voice brightened. "Your gift will make someone else's Christmas brighter."

"But I'm not giving you anything. I'll just return it."

"Oh, don't bother doing that. We'll just put your name down for a gift to a less fortunate family. God bless you, sister, and have a lovely Christmas."

Somehow I had been elevated from recipient to donor. Somehow I felt generous beyond words. I had helped someone else. Yet I kept reminding myself that I had done nothing. His words and his genuine gratitude circled around in my mind, accompanied by visions of single people alone and desperate families. The baby pulled on my housecoat and I picked him up, hugging him tightly. Slowly we waltzed around the kitchen to the radio's caroling.

"Mommy, I want to dance, too!" I picked up my daughter, balancing one child on each hip. I had more than pink flamingos in Mexico. I had my children and my family. I had love and it was Christmas.

L.J. Christiansen
Maple Creek, Saskatchewan

✉ In 1944, I was stationed with the Air Force in the south of England. I spent my Christmas leave with an aunt who lived in a small market town in the fen country near Cambridge. On the train the one topic of conversation was the German breakthrough on the Continent. But my aunt, no military strategist, spoke of Christmas kitchen matters. The local butcher, hearing that she was to have a Canadian nephew for the holidays, had obtained the unobtainable – an honest-to-goodness peace-time turkey. And the baker's wife had made an iced Christmas cake.

Living with my aunt was a little girl named Babs, who had been evacuated from London at the outbreak of war. She was excited. There was not only the wonder of the turkey and the iced cake, but her parents, her older brother, and a cousin were all coming to my aunt's for Christmas. They would arrive on the twenty-fourth.

The twenty-fourth began as badly as it could. A thick fog shrouded the countryside. Babs and I groped our way into town to meet her family at the station, only to learn that the train would be hours late and might not come at all. I can remember Babs crying as no child should cry on Christmas Eve. But her folks did arrive, and the Christmas spirit prevailed that night.

Overnight, there was a sudden cold snap. When we woke up on Christmas morning, the sun was trying to break through. My aunt shooed us out of the tiny house to take a walk so she could prepare dinner in peace. On that walk, a small Christmas miracle occurred as we crossed the old stone bridge spanning a river. The cold snap had condensed the fog. Every blade of grass was coated with silver. Every twig, every branch of every tree had a crystal coating. The sky was mother-of-pearl; the metallic sheen of the river glowed through a misty veil. On the bank, below the bridge, stood two fishermen, and even they wore a kind of silvery nimbus. One of them threw his line into the water, and in the stillness there was a loud plop as his float hit the surface. For one moment, there was absolute silence. In that moment, the whole silvery scene was engraved upon my memory so that I have never forgotten it.

Fred C. Farr
Thornhill, Ontario

✉ My mother told me about one Christmas during the depression that was the happiest of all.

My father was fresh out of law school and just beginning to build up a practice. On Christmas Eve morning, my mother and he had a bitter argument. There was no money. The house was cold. There was no hope at all of buying a chicken or a turkey for Christmas dinner, and nothing for presents for us three small children. There was not even a Christmas tree. Mother said she felt guilty afterwards for scolding him, because he *did* work hard. He *did* have clients, but he was always too ashamed to press for his fees if the clients didn't pay up willingly. And, times being what they were, most people had trouble paying bills.

My father stormed out of the house and went to the office, partly to get away, partly hoping that perhaps one of his clients had sent in a cheque, which he could cash at the corner grocery store. But there was nothing. As he left his office he saw something on the floor – a ten-dollar bill. In those days, when a nickel could buy a loaf of bread, ten dollars was a fortune. Mother said he came home that afternoon with a Christmas tree, a load of wood for the stove, a turkey, and money for her to spend on gifts for us all.

Our childhood Christmases were always rich with love and music, crayons and books, pads of colored paper, jigsaw puzzles.

That particular Christmas was as wonderful as always, but my mother says it was the Christmas she began to believe in miracles.

Amalia Lindal-Webb
Toronto

✉ When I was a kid, we had a battery radio, but I cannot remember it making more than the feeblest sound.

One Christmas morning my brother and I discovered a big brown carton under the Christmas tree. All the other gifts were carefully wrapped in red or green or white tissue paper, and each bore a tag. The big brown box was a mystery to us: there was no clue at all as to who had put it there or who it was for.

We ate our breakfast with great haste, then helped Dad clean up the dishes while Mother got the goose into the oven. Then we rushed back to our speculations in the parlour, dying of curiosity about that box. It was too heavy to be a piece of coal. It must be something important, we decided.

At last we heard the kitchen door open and knew that our grandparents had come down the hill and we could start opening the gifts. Dad always made us wait until each present was opened before the next one was given out. This made the whole drama last longer and created an incredible curiosity about that big package.

Finally, there was only one thing left under that tree. Dad picked the brown box up and carried it to the other side of the room. Slowly he opened the top and gently pulled out a beautiful table radio and set it on the buffet. We all admired the walnut wood with the lattice opening backed by brown-and-gold cloth where the speaker was. We were especially impressed by the discreet little plate that bore the magical name "Marconi."

While we were examining it, Dad disappeared downstairs and returned with a long piece of wire, which he carefully strung around the room and attached to the stove-pipe. He fastened the other end to the back of the new radio and plugged the electrical cord into the wall outlet. We all crowded round, to get as close to the set as we could, so that we would be able to hear. Dad moved the dial to the right spot, then turned the radio on. The sound came out so loud you could hear it from the other side of the room. It was King George V with his Christmas message to the Empire.

Mother and Grandmother went back to their chairs, laughing nervously at how loud the sound was. Dad stood, self-satisfied and triumphant beside the buffet, grinning at everyone's astonishment, because he had known what to expect, but had wanted to surprise us all. Grandfather, an Englishman and a royalist to the core, returned to his chair with great dignity and sat rigidly at attention, knowing that he was in the very presence of the monarch himself. My brother and I knew it was an important moment, for we were listening to a person talking from the other side of the Atlantic.

I can take television for granted, but for me the wonder of the radio has never been lost to this day.

Fred Habermehl
Niagara Falls, Ontario

✉ Christmas Day in Israel arrived grey and cold in 1972. I lay in my cot, snuggled deep in my blankets.

The Israelis had been greatly amused as we, the volunteers, had argued about what makes Christmas Christmas. We came from many different countries and cultures. Just deciding on what day to celebrate had been a problem. The Danes wanted St. Nicholas Day, the eleventh; the French wanted Christmas Eve; the Americans, Australians, and Canadian (me) had voted for Christmas Day.

Then there had been the food. Jill couldn't believe we wanted to cook a hot dinner. But then in Australia it was usually a hundred degrees and Jill's idea of Christmas dinner was salad served around the pool. Turkey seemed to be a scarce commodity in Israel. We finally settled for stuffed chicken.

When we spoke of cutting down a tree for Christmas, the idea died rather quickly. My kibbutz father, Hagai, explained in great detail how twenty-one years ago these orchards had been desert. All of this resulted in a paper Christmas tree, which the Israelis thought was beautiful.

The day passed slowly. We were glad when it came time to begin preparations for dinner and our party. I spent most of the afternoon in the kitchen making shortbread and laughing while Marika and Pia tried to make plum pudding with orange sauce.

I had left Canada in September for the kibbutz and I was feeling homesick. The Christmas preparations made me think of real Christmas trees, and snow, and my brothers back home. I wondered who was decorating our tree this year, since it had always been my job.

At five minutes to six the operator put my call through to my family. By this time the whole kibbutz was gathered in the dining room, waiting for their dinner, and the roar was deafening. My connection was barely audible, and I had to shout to my brother. I was passed to another brother and to my grandmother until someone at the kibbutz finally realized I was shouting long-distance to Canada and yelled for everyone to shut up.

"Where's Dad?" I screamed into the bad connection. There was silence on the other end. "Hello!" I shouted. "Hello! Is there anyone there? Hello?" Finally I heard my mother's quiet voice on the other end of the line. "Where's Dad?" I was still yelling into the phone, completely oblivious to the fact that two hundred people were listening to me. "Gone? What do you mean gone? Gone where?" They had separated. Even over the bad line I could hear my mother crying. I could barely talk. My throat felt as if it had a band of steel wrapped around it.

I hung up the phone and stood staring at it until I began to notice the silence all around me. Everyone must have heard me shouting into the damned phone. I wiped my eyes with the back of my sleeve, brushed my hair out of my eyes, and turned to face everyone.

They made no attempt to cover the awkward moment. As I walked by each table, hands reached out to touch me. I reached my own table and sat down numbly. Slowly the dining room returned to its normal bustle and some of the Christmas we had felt resurfaced. By the end of the meal I was talking normally; I even joined in some of the singing. The phone call seemed unreal.

Later I looked up at the sky. It was overcast but light grey. "Snow!" I said.

"You're nuts in the head," Hagai said as he pushed the door open. "It has not snowed in Dvir for more than twenty years."

"Hagai," I said, "those are definitely snow clouds. Besides, what's Christmas without snow?"

"In Israel," Hagai answered, "usual."

"Normal, Hagai," I said. "You mean normal."

"No, I mean usual. Nothing is normal."

Later that night, at our Christmas party, someone came yelling down the stairs.

"Snow!" he yelled. "It's snowing."

We all rushed to see the snow in the desert. The ground was covered with beautiful white powder, and the air was filled with it. We made snowballs and laughed and ran wild. I lay in the snow feeling a million years older than the day before.

Slowly I began to move my arms over my head then down to my sides, and to open and close my legs, pushing the snow and making my imprint.

I stood up carefully and surveyed my snow angel. I knew it would be gone tomorrow, but in some way it drew a line for me, a connecting line, which reached out across the miles and across the years to other angels in the snow. Angels made always with a little hope, knowing that even though each would melt, another could be made.

Jean Teillet
Toronto

✉ When I was a little girl we lived in northern Wales, where the landscape is dominated by mountain peaks. When I was about five, I shared a bedroom with my older sister in an ancient house we were convinced was haunted. There was a wide fireplace in our room, which was never used. On a ledge half-way up, we stashed the horrible, bitter chocolate-covered herbal pills mother dosed us with every week, and which we only pretended to take. Would Santa descend in a shower of laxatives and expose our shameful secret?

I had been warned that if I were naughty, my Christmas stocking might only contain a lump of coal. It was a special joy to discover forgiveness in the form of a Jaffa orange, a shiny red apple, chocolate money, sticky sweets, jelly babies.

Our gifts were few and simple. Grandmother always sent us each a ten-shilling note, immediately confiscated for what father described as a "rainy day." We never could understand this: it rained almost every day in Wales.

On Christmas afternoon, the women tired, the men sleepy after the festive meal, they were glad to see us children leave the house for a lantern lecture at the church hall. The curate had a habit of showing half the slides upside down. I always thought of the Holy Land as a country of curiously reversible palm trees and camels who, in the heat of the day, rested comfortably on their humps, legs straight up in the air.

The best part of Christmas was the evening, when mother played the piano and the rest of us gathered around to sing.

When mother sang, she cast a spell over the whole room. She sang a song about three little girls, Dulcie, Daisy, and Dorothy May. The last line, "Blue eyes were weeping and so were the gray for angels had taken dear Dorothy May," always reduced me to tears. My loud sobs were interpreted as a sure sign that it was past my bedtime.

Gwyneth Shirley
Cochrane, Ontario

✉ In Czechoslovakia, Santa Claus came on Christmas Eve, right after the traditional Christmas dinner: fish soup, fried fish, and a delicious vegetable salad. Dessert was usually something made of marzipan – except one year, when my parents' English friends sent us a plum pudding. With it came instructions: douse the pudding with brandy and set a match to it, then serve as soon as the flames die down.

It all sounded rather adventurous and exotic. As soon as the main course was finished and the dishes were cleared, my mother poured a bottle of French cognac over the pudding and set it on fire. It burned for the longest time, and when the flame finally died down, the charred remains were totally inedible. "Oh, well," my mother said, "just one more proof that the English are peculiar people."

Sonja Sinclair
Toronto

POINTS OF THE COMPASS

Like the spoken essays of Stuart McLean (or those of
Margaret Visser, I suppose, the "archeologist of everyday life" who has since blossomed into authorship), or
the exchanges between listeners and host in the form
of contests, or the personal revelations inspired by
drama, or even, come to think of it, the making of
books from what is written to and for a radio program, the letter from abroad has become a uniquely
Morningside form of expression. With rare exceptions –
Carol Bishop, for instance, whose communiqué from
Moscow I've included here, is married to the CBC's
Soviet correspondent and has been a producer herself –
these writers are not professional journalists. But they
are not casual travellers, either: Bob Cosbey, who is in
his seventies, teaches English at the University of
Regina and goes to China to share his wisdom there;
Silvia Schriever is a physician whose work took her
to the Sudan in the summer of 1986 (she is also the sister of *Morningside*'s Beatrice Schriever, although that's

not why she wrote); Chris Burrows and her husband were social workers in Winnipeg before they decided to drive their van – the Great Canadian Canary, they used to call it, before they discovered that yellow was the colour of police cars – to Nicaragua and see what they could contribute. Others do other things; Nettie Wild, for example, is an actress when she's at home in Vancouver. Insofar as it's possible to generalize, I'd say they're just Canadians with unusually active curiosities and a common desire to share what they discover elsewhere.

Again with rare exceptions, they don't write about current events – or not the kind that makes headlines. They write about what they see, and what they think about it, and occasionally (although you may have to read between the lines to find it) how those discoveries illuminate their understanding of things at home. Like so many other people in this book, they are simply writers of letters, foreign correspondents, I suppose, in a more literal sense than that phrase usually conveys. Here are some letters some of them sent us during the two years of broadcasting this collection spans.

Wad E Heleau, The Sudan

✉ Midday lethargy. Today we are blessed with a fine haze and a light breeze. The *haboub* season is coming to an end. Soon the dense swirls of brown sand that engulf and blind us will be replaced by rain. I sit peacefully in the "white man's compound" where six of us live enclosed, cut off, neighbours to thirteen thousand Ethiopian refugees. Our beehive-shaped grass huts are surrounded by a wall of straw mats. But of late the need for privacy has been contorted into a sense of concern; the local police insist on providing us with an armed guard around the clock. Today one of the guards will not shake my hand in greeting when I meet him in the camp. And we hear that they smoke the local bong on the job. Volatile young men with semi-automatics: I can't tell whether I am being protected or kept in.

Ambiguity hangs heavy in the air. The two weeks since the American bombing of Libya have been confusing. Twice we have anticipated evacuation, packed our bags, and headed for the nearest town. Twice we have regained our calm and turned back. And between times I am the only doctor for these thirteen thousand people.

I want to tell you about my hospital. "Hospital"! What a word! Well, it is at least a place where the very sick stay, a long hallway with grass walls and roof, and a dirt floor littered with wrappers from syringes, with uneaten food, with mats and people. And the patients, oh, the patients. They lie stoic, uncomplaining on their crooked rope-strung beds. Their medical histories and physical findings would be the delight of any eager medical student still fascinated by matching clues with textbook descriptions. But for me, when I allow myself, they are symbols of despair. Mostly, I do not allow myself. By day I help the refugee attendants decide how best to care for them. By night I try to teach myself the intricacies of tropical medicine; as we have virtually no lab facilities, the textbooks only tantalize me with what I *could* do if only we were somewhere else.

And so I take refuge, refuge in the smiling faces of small children playing in the dirt, in the teaching of my medical knowledge to the attendants, in cooking a curry with some stale curry powder left here by some long-gone predecessor, in watching a train of camels lope across the horizon, in sleeping out under the stars, seeing the moon wax and wane, in learning Arabic (or at least enough to get by), in listening to the chanting and drumming drifting through the air at all times of night and day. The dogs barking, the donkeys braying.

As the sun begins its descent, I pack my camera into a wicker basket and flip-flop off across the brown sandy canyons towards a small line of green in the distance. Giggling children pass by on their donkeys. Those returning to the camp have slung large canvas bladders, now full of water, over their beasts' backs. There is cause for joy. Only two weeks ago, the Atbara River was parched. Now, the rains have come in Ethiopia, at the source, and the waters flow. I look up to see a turquoise and violet Abyssinian roller perched on a nearby bush. It bursts into flight, a dance of fertile blue in a barren land. A buzzing attracts my attention and I am surrounded by grasshoppers. I sneak up on them with my zoom lens but they are elusive. Two children delight at my photographer's pose. Later they approach me with their hands outstretched. They each have one of the lime-green and orange insects resting quietly on their chocolate-brown hands. I blush to realize how well I wear the name *khawaja*, white woman, which echoes around me wherever I go.

Down at the river, water containers get filled, and the air rings with laughter. I show three reserved young men what my zoom lens can do. They are enthralled; no longer aloof, they jump and exclaim and discuss this wonder. Me, I inhale the smell of wetness, wiggle my toes in the mud, imprint on my mind the pristine white-ness of the egrets as they wander through the green, green reeds, and carry these images back to camp across the dry, the barren, the bleak. Another day is drawing to a close.

Silvia Schriever

Kunming, China

✉ Walking around the streets here in Kunming, I've been asking myself why I *like* China so much. I can spend days looking and listening – just looking at the people. Well, one reason became clear to me today.

I was watching some little kids playing in a public park. Some of their games are familiar – London Bridge, hopscotch, scissors-stone-paper, hawk-and-chicken, marbles. The children look so lean and healthy, with clear complexions and good teeth, their clothes bright and clean, their hair neatly brushed. They walk or skip or

194

run through the crowds of grown-ups without even looking at them, but if they come face to face with me, they are both startled and delighted.

The street scenes I walk through now are not at all what they were on these same streets forty years ago and more. I know a woman, now in her early seventies, who has bound feet and who remembers being sold in the market-place at the age of seven. In those days, disease was endemic, famine was commonplace, and there were bandits and war-lords raiding the towns and cities. There was still slavery in the Yunnan Mountains. All over China, girl-children were so looked down on they weren't even counted when you asked a man how many children he had.

But since Liberation, China has laid the base for peace and health for the great mass of its people. This is not to say China is a Utopia. You can find beggars in China if you look for them. And I passed a billboard today that outlined the crimes of a rapist, the leader of a gang of thieves, and a drunk driver who killed two pedestrians. There are aspects of life that would not look like prosperity to Canadians. Housing, for example. A lot of people live in housing that a welfare client in Canada would refuse. The average amount of floor space per person in Chinese cities is six square metres. That's three steps forward and two steps to the side. There's a plan to have eight square metres per person by the year 2000, with a kitchen and bathroom for each family – that's what they are *aiming* at.

Yet everyone *has* housing, clothing, food, and public security. And they don't have the problems that affluence has brought to the West.

There are different reasons, too, that I like China. I see things here I don't see in Regina. For instance, today in downtown Kunming I came across a little park in which about fifteen blind people make a living by giving massages to passers-by. Each stands by a chair waiting for customers. You pick one out and tell him your trouble – a stiff back perhaps, or a sore arm – and he goes to work on you. And on a hill above Youth Street is a park in which long rows of flowering plum trees are in full blossom. Temporary platforms have been built so people can stand up among the blooms and have their pictures taken. There are line-ups behind each tree.

Then there are all the graceful young women . . . but at my age I'm not supposed to notice such things.

Bob Cosbey

Mindanao, Philippines

✉ Camp is a mud pit. The unit has been here for two weeks, and it shows. Laundry hangs from all the bushes, the floor near the cook pot and wash basin is slippery with mud. *Doyens*, hammocks sewn from rice sacks, hang from every available tree and weave a web under the shelter extending out from a farmer's house. A labour meeting is in full session and is scheduled to continue for three more days. Seventeen organizers working in the labour sector from around the island stare intently at a blackboard. They're a serious bunch, always meeting until late in the evening.

There are no hammocks to spare to sleep in outside. Inside the house, I find my place on the floor next to the farmer, his wife, and three children. This family, and others like them, are the people for whom this revolution is being fought. They are farmers whose land was expropriated by presidential decree. Their land was then granted to big landowners, many of whom are ex-military or friends or relatives of President Marcos. They're "cronies," as they're called. Working as tenants on their own land, the farmers tilled giant single-crop plantations. "For Export Only" was firmly stamped across the fruit and the economy. The New People's Army began to organize barrio after barrio of farmers to fight back. The military was brought in or, in some cases, private armies were hired. It's a brutal and inevitable cycle. Now, the farmers feed and house the guerrilla army.

Tonight, inside the farmhouse, a yellow gas lamp throws a warm

196

light on more than twenty guerrilla soldiers and organizers sleeping in the two-roomed bamboo house. Arms and legs dangle down from the *doyens*. Faces peer up from the carpet of people on the floor. The light is extinguished, and the house sleeps. One of the farmer's children, a two-year-old, has whooping cough. She struggles to pull wet breaths from her soggy lungs all night long. Every hour there's a changing of the guard. A figure appears at the door, an armalite rifle completing the silhouette against the moonlight.

The next morning I wake to feel the two-year-old snuggled against my stomach. Her mother sits looking out the window at the morning breakfast scene as fifty members of the New People's Army line up for rice and dried fish. The labour meeting is threatening to start. The armed unit has just finished exercises. The woman is living in a war zone, and it's in her back yard.

Six o'clock in the evening. Heads turn towards a man who has just walked into camp. He's barefoot and wears a straw hat. His features are strong in the light and the shadows. First, the commanding officer, Solo, talks to the newcomer. He listens attentively to the man, who speaks in the low, unhurried tones of the local dialect. Gradually a circle of people builds up around the man. He has spotted the military in the next barrio to ours, six and a half kilometres away. One squad on foot is travelling in a direction that would eventually bring them within one and a half kilometres of where we are.

Eight o'clock. A security briefing session is called for everyone in camp. We group around the blackboard. The crowd of organizers and red fighters are draped over the rafters and the makeshift tables and benches, leaning into the bright, white light of the petrol lamp. We are told we number sixty, with forty non-combatants. Solo stands at the blackboard and divides us into two basic teams. If the military attacks we are to, (1) relax (easier said than done, I thought); (2) gather our packs; and (3) find our group, assemble in the centre of camp, and wait for the command.

Solo draws a map on the blackboard. There's the highway. Towns are pin-pointed, the river, our camp, the enemy. He divides the map into four: twelve o'clock, three, six and nine o'clock, indicating the directions of our escape routes. We are told to sleep fully dressed, to be ready to go at a moment's notice, and everyone must take a guard duty tonight. My shift is two to three in the morning. The shift change wakes me out of the sleep of nightmares. I jump when she touches my shoulder. I am told to report to any member of the command if I see anything unusual. I sit with a woman from the labour group and we stare out into the wall of oversized house plants and whirring crickets that is the jungle.

It is the first time in my life I have stood guard against anything, let alone an enemy. The shelter behind me is filled with hammocks full of people who stand watch every day of their lives. Their snores mingle with the night sounds. One man sleeps fitfully, calling out incoherent half-thoughts. Solo, working late, reads a letter, which he then burns in the gas light. The flames from the letter light his face and then die. We sit in silence and listen to the jungle, knowing that a ring of guns is pointing out from the central spoke of camp as the red fighters swing in their hammocks at their out-posts, cradling their M-16 rifles. But farther out in the mountains, a larger noose of guns fights the dark and the mud, and searches for us.

✉ A woman carrying a shopping bag has just walked into camp. Her city pants and running shoes are caked with mud. She wears glasses and looks like she would be more at home in a library than in a jungle headquarters of the New People's Army. In fact, hers is one of the most strategic jobs of the underground. She is a courier, and she brings with her the life-blood of a guerrilla war: informa-tion. She carries letters folded into half-inch squares, which she hides in the folds of her clothes – letters small enough to eat, if she has to.

The woman has just come from a white area, as the urban centres are called. To get here she has had to travel by bus on the national highway, passing through military road-blocks. She gets off the bus in the nearby village, walks down the highway until there are few houses and a minimum of curious faces, and then turns off onto a path leading to a small bamboo house. This is one of her many drop points, and a guide, usually a farmer, will then lead her to the latest position of the floating headquarters. The courier, and others like her, provide the links for the underground. When a courier is captured, torture is inevitable, and code names and locations of the underground change as fast as a bullet drops into its chamber. And the underground waits, hoping the precious information dies with its messenger. But today the courier has arrived safely. She reports directly to the commanding officer of the unit, giving him the all-important squares of information.

Solo, the commanding officer, stands staring out the window, his back silhouetted against the light and greens of the jungle. He has been there a long time, holding the creased pages of one of the courier's letters. Bad news. There has been an informer at work at a regional level, and the military has been able to piece together sensitive information. A member of Solo's personal collective and a close friend knew the informer personally. The friend was expected to report to camp on the fifteenth of the month. It's now the twentieth and he still hasn't arrived. I think something may have happened to him, mumbles Solo, staring at the jungle, adjusting to the bad news, accepting it.

It's night. Solo, Robert, the propaganda officer, and Myong, a priest turned revolutionary, sit on the porch. The discussion turns to more news. The Americans have confirmed that the U.S. bases here house nuclear warheads. There is speculation that the province of Bukidnon hides another secret nuclear base as well. Solo sits on a bucket, his knees pulled close to his chest. If there is a nuclear war, he says, the Philippines will be a prime target of any first strike, and all the suffering we have gone through over all the years will be for nothing. We will have fought a revolution for nothing. The sound of the crickets closes in on the three revolutionaries on the porch.

The next day, Robert struggles with rewriting a propaganda directive from Manila, which arrived with the courier. The underground is to support local elections the opposition stands a chance of winning, and to boycott the presidential election, where rampant fraud in the past has guaranteed the president his palace. The position paper is in English, the only language common to the many dialects in the country. Robert paces the floor. Give me another word for *onus*, he demands. Someone gives him a sentence. Just one word. *Bastila*. Robert sweats through the rhetoric from the capital city until, finding a solution, he pounds out his translation on the typewriter, the clatter of the keys travelling out over the cleared meadow, mingling with the hoots of the jungle birds.

More letters arrive in camp. Another fat square of information from Manila for the propaganda officer, one for Myong, who reads that his former parish thinks that he's dead, and one for Solo. More bad news. Four partisans in a town two hours away are dead, the result of a military raid. The region-wide informer has started to wreak his havoc.

The following morning Solo and the courier sit face to face on a mat on the floor upstairs. A hand gun lies between them. The morning sun lights the room in bars and glints off the gun barrel. The two are deep in discussion, Solo carefully cleaning the gun as he speaks. The courier is leaving the floating headquarters this morning, and last-minute instructions and discussions are necessary. I recognize only a few words as the conversation occasionally slips from the dialect into English. Gun, enemy, national highway. She nods and mutters back. Robert is typing up the early-morning letter to go with her. Myong handwrites another. The letters are many pages long, single-spaced on thin, onion-skin paper, and then are folded, taped closed, and labelled with a code name. The courier is ready. She is barefoot, with her pants rolled up past her knees. Her running shoes are washed and dry and hang around her neck. When she nears the national highway, she'll wash the mud off her legs in a stream, roll down her pants, put on her clean shoes, and walk out onto the road without a trace of the mountain mud on her.

Solo hands her the now familiar half-inch-square letters. Carefully the mail of the underground is tucked into place and the courier pads off into the jungle.

Nettie Wild

Managua, Nicaragua

✉ We recently had a pleasant outing at our neighbour's family farm, or *finca*. We set out before lunch on a Sunday, eight of us in our jeep. There was our neighbour, Dona Adelfa, her three daughters, Sel, Dylan, and Dylan's best friend, Guillermo. The *finca* was about forty kilometres away, near the town of Mastepe. We spent an hour roaming around the ten-acre farm, sampling the oranges, lemons, grapefruit, mandarins, and bananas that grew there. We ate our lunch sitting on tree trunks, cut to appropriate heights, but had to share it with three large hogs, a dog, and half a dozen chickens. The pigs were particularly partial to the plantains, which had been skinned, rolled in salt, and baked in the ashes of our fire.

On the way home we stopped in Mastepe to meet Dona Adelfa's family – she's one of thirteen children. Adelfa's father and mother still live in the family home, a huge, rambling collection of buildings with high ceilings, surrounding a large patio area occupied by a beautiful white horse and several cats, chickens, and ducks.

Although Adelfa's parents live in the same house, they don't really live together. Father lives in certain rooms and Mother lives in others. The estrangement is political.

Father is a rotund, brusque man in his eighties who was a magistrate in the regime of the former dictator, Anastasio Somoza. He more or less abandoned the family to work on the Atlantic Coast, returning periodically, as Adelfa remarks bitterly, "to father another child." He sent none of his pay home.

Mother is in her late sixties. She looks worn out, but radiates warmth and concern. She spent her whole life in Mastepe with her ever-increasing brood and ran a small store and the *finca*, too.

And over the years she and her children became involved with the Sandinista movement. By the time the revolution came, they were giving shelter to "comrades on the run" at the farm. Many of her children were beaten by Somoza's National Guard, and others had to go into hiding. After Somoza's downfall, Father came home, and has remained blatantly and outspokenly opposed to the Sandinistas.

Later we moved on to a sister's home, where we met nieces, nephews, and cousins. We spent some time chatting with one sister, who is vice-dean of humanities at the university, about education in Canada. As we left, I mentioned to Adelfa how interesting I had found her sister. "Oh, yes," she replied offhandedly, "Ana Maria used to run guns for the National Liberation Front."

These are the realities of modern Nicaragua – nice, middle-aged ladies in polyester pant suits who used to run guns for the revolution, and families split asunder by political differences. Another reality is the Voice of America, which recently informed us of the great attack by the Contras on Managua. Sometimes its anti-Sandinista propaganda is so blatant it is hilariously funny. The other day it announced the Contras had blown up the tower that supplies electricity to the city. We listened, but we couldn't understand why there was still power – why we weren't in the dark. The next day, both papers published a picture of the damage: a couple of struts on one leg of a pylon had been bent. It's hard to believe this is what the Contras are doing with the $100 million sent them by the United States. My friends and I could have done as much damage with a ten-dollar box of firecrackers.

Chris Burrows

Suva, Fiji

✉ It is a steamy evening after a cooker of a day. The palm trees are rattling in the welcome breeze and the insects are making what my three-year-old calls the "snithery" noise. Between my fingers is a delightfully tasty morsel, made even more tasty by a distinct bout of homesickness. I'm eating maple sugar.

The taste sends me into a time warp, back about twenty years to when, as a kid, I went to Elmira, Ontario, during a sugaring season. We watched as the buckets of sap were dumped into the vats to be boiled off and saw – or rather, smelled – each stage of a process whose climax was a plate of pancakes crowned with golden maple syrup. Strange to be remembering all that here in Suva, the capital city of the Fiji Islands.

One of the odd things about leaving the northern hemisphere for the southern is that it takes a while to turn around the clock of the seasons. In Canada you are coming into spring, with all its hoopla of melting snow, budding trees, crocuses and tulips poking through the frosty earth . . . and maple sugar. Here it's summer and everyone waits for the relief of winter. There are no shoulder seasons of spring and autumn – just hot and not so hot. Our relationship with the seasons is an aspect of being Canadian I had, until now, with this taste of maple sugar in Fiji, never fully recognized.

Pat Cameron

Moscow, USSR

✉ It is one thing to realize intellectually there is a schism between the way of life in the Western and Communist worlds. It is quite another to be straddled over the two; living in the Soviet Union but privy to information from the West.

While the most serious accident in the history of nuclear power plants was occurring approximately four hundred and fifty miles away from Moscow, Moscovites were given only the briefest details. Life continued as normal here. While the Western community lived in a state of anxiety, their Soviet neighbours prepared for the May Day holidays.

Before the accident occurred, on April 26, the main concern for many members of the Canadian community living in the USSR was whether the Canadian hockey team would finish with the bronze or silver medal in the World Hockey Championships, which were being played in Moscow. After the final game, we began to receive fragmented queries and reports from Western media sources about a possible problem with one of the nuclear reactors at Chernobyl. Although I had been living in the Soviet Union for three months, I had never heard of Chernobyl.

Even in the Western community, it took a while for the magnitude of the accident to sink in. Only Western correspondents and diplomats were truly aware of the potential for disaster. Then three days later, a number of Western families left the country to take advantage of the four-day school holiday. While these families were away, they began to read in foreign newspapers about the catastrophe.

Then I flew to London. As I sat in a pub reading the English papers, the ramifications of the accident sank in. A large radioactive cloud had passed directly over the major dairy and grain-producing areas in the Soviet Union and its East Bloc neighbours. My six-year-old son will be living in Moscow for the next two years. Where will our dairy and grain products be coming from? Before going back to Moscow, I raced around London stocking up on dried milk powder and other foodstuffs.

I returned to Moscow: on the evening newscasts, I could see pictures of cows grazing peacefully in the fields near Kiev, children gambolling, and tulips waving in the air, while an announcer soothingly explained that life was as normal in Kiev. But embassies here in Moscow have advised their countrymen not to drink local dairy products, and to wash any fresh produce they buy. The Soviets have not made such recommendations to their own people, as the queues at the milk stores can attest.

May ninth was Victory Day in the Soviet Union, and a holiday. A ten o'clock in the evening, the sky over Moscow was ablaze with spectacular fireworks and the streets were crowded. As I stood among the celebrating Moscovites, my sense of dislocation was acute.

Life is slowly returning to normal in the Western community in Moscow. But, except for those in the immediate vicinity of the accident, life for most Soviets has been completely normal throughout the entire crisis.

Carol Bishop

Osaka, Japan

✉ I've been living in Japan for about four months now. Even though I'm over most of my initial disorientation, there are still many things Japanese to which I'm not yet accustomed; I doubt I ever will be. Although the language is difficult enough, it's really the crowds that continue to bother me. I never imagined there could be so many people sharing such limited space.

Japan is a small country. Its land area is roughly comparable to Newfoundland's, but almost three-quarters of the country is mountainous. Japan's population is about one hundred million, and eighty per cent of these people live in the stretch of land from Osaka to Tokyo, a nearly unbroken metropolis of eighty million people. The competition for space is intense, as is the competition for many things Canadians take for granted.

I live with a friend in Umeda, the district that forms the core of Osaka, Japan's second-largest city. Osaka is a sprawling metropolis of eight million souls. Its downtown is unexceptional, little more than a congestion of traffic and a tortuous web of train lines and freeways. Umeda is also home to dowdy office buildings, a few major hotels, and lots of bars, pachinko parlours, and love hotels.

The lack of room and the competition for it first struck me when I saw my new apartment. You could spit across it. It consists of two small rooms and a bathroom that would be at home in the space shuttle. Each room measures about ten feet by twelve feet. The rent for the apartment is $475 a month.

I share this apartment with only one other person. The crowds begin outside. Traffic is continuous. A local paper, The *Mainichi Daily* (literally, the daily daily), reported that there is one car for every twenty metres of road in Japan, cities and highways included. There is so little room for cars that they park on the sidewalks, two wheels on the road, two not.

Pedestrians share the sidewalks with the parked cars, and with bicyclists, too. The streets are usually so crowded the pedestrians have to sidestep the cyclists, who ring their bells clamorously and brake with ear-piercing squeals. This hubbub is accepted matter-of-factly by the Japanese, although I've adjusted to it only with difficulty.

There is no respite in the shopping malls, of which there are many, some more than a kilometre in length. The crowds are even thicker and the cyclists just as numerous. People ride their bicycles through the shopping arcades, weaving around the pedestrians or ringing their bells to clear a path.

Of course one *does* adapt. I've learned to walk with the flow. Like fish in a school, the Japanese crowds move naturally in currents. One side of the mall is for those people walking north or east, the other side for those going south or west. If you want to cross to a store on the far side of the mall, it's just like crossing a stream. You walk diagonally with the current.

Life in Japanese cities is predicated around the trains. Almost everybody commutes. It's in the train stations that the crowds are at their finest. During rush hour I have waited to get into the station, then waited to get on the train. In the station, a train rumbles in, its windows fogged with perspiration. The doors open and a crowd bursts out. Then the waiting crowd squeezes in, packed like mandarin oranges in a box. The addition of one more person is felt throughout the entire car. By the time we arrive at the next stop, we're all sweating profusely, though everyone seems to accept the crowding with equanimity. Times like these make me say, "Gee, it's nice in Vancouver."

Greg Fjetland

Near Lomé, Togo

✉ "I want to tell you a story," said Théophile, as he poured his guests another round of *sodabee*, a potent palm liquor of the West African coast. Behind him were his wife and three children, working around a fire, preparing a midnight meal of *foofoo*, a corn paste served with pepper sauce. The children took turns wielding the wooden pestle, as heavy as a sledge-hammer, pounding the corn meal in a knee-high wooden cylinder. The thudding hits the stillness of the night like a distant bass drum. A few insects crack into the glass of the kerosene lamp. Mosquitoes suck blood from the exposed ankles underneath the table. Just another sultry Saturday night in a village on the Togolese coast, a night rich with the pungent scents of tropical foliage, wood smoke, and warm bodies.

Off in the distance, rising out of the pale aura of light over the capital city, Lomé's only skyscraper, the fifty-two-floor hotel called the Second of February, pierces the horizon like the beacon of another century. So close – but still far from Théophile's home in the village.

Théophile, educated as a theologian in France and trained as an orator and philosopher in the tradition of his village, belongs to the coastal Ebé tribe. Were his president, General Eyademé, a member of the same ethnic group, it is likely that Théophile would have risen high in the Togolese government. But he's from the wrong tribe and his politics are at odds with President Eyademé's regime, in which money and power are closely guarded by the oligarchy. So Théophile keeps a low profile, teaching French to foreign-development workers. Tonight he's invited a few old African friends and some new European ones to his modest home. And, away from government ears, he begins his story.

"There is a village not far from here," he says. "One of my former students, a German nurse, treats lepers there. A month ago she came to me, very upset. She said I had to help her. Some children had been playing, or fighting, and they pushed a seven-year-old boy into a fire, upsetting a cauldron of boiling sauce. He was burned over eighty per cent of his body. His parents took him into their hut and laid him out on a straw mattress. The medicine man came and performed healing acts with bones and fetishes but everyone knew the boy had been laid down to die. My German friend got angry. Why had no one taken the boy to Lomé, to a doctor, to be treated, to be saved? The villagers simply refused – so she came to me.

"The people of the village are my brothers, my tribesmen, the Ebé. She thought I could convince them to do something, so I went. I talked to the boy's father, the boy's mother, then the village chief. At first I sided with the German woman, and the Christian morality I've been taught. At first I also thought the boy should be saved."

Théophile leaned forward. His face gleamed in the lamplight and his eyes glistened. Someone began to say something but he held up his hand for silence. He continued the story. "The longer I talked with the villagers, the more I realized I'd been changed by European values, the more I began to see the burned boy through African eyes. To treat the boy, to restore him to some kind of health would cost as much or more as they had to feed and clothe the rest of the family for years. But a new child would be free.

"We have a saying in our language," he said. "When one pot is broken you replace it by making a new one. There is no use in that village for a broken pot. There was no room in that family for a scarred, sickly, and maimed child. Africans face reality and they accept it. They accepted the death of that boy. That's what they told me, and that's what they told the German woman. She wouldn't accept it, but I could. In my heart, I'm still African."

Then the Europeans began to argue. One said that such fatalism both caused and perpetuated suffering and poverty in Africa. Suddenly the arguments became heated, fuelled by the *sodabee* and the conviction on the Europeans' side that the villagers were wrong, and by Théophile's calm assertion that, in their reality, the villagers were right. Soon, the *foofoo* forgotten, the story of the burned boy had grown and become an allegory for the whole story of Africa, with the whites on one side saying how the Africans ought to behave and Théophile on the other saying Africans should solve their own problems their own way.

By four in the morning the *sodabee* was gone and the sun was a promise on the horizon. It was a sultry Sunday morning. Nothing had been decided. Sometimes nothing is.

Joan Baxter

Plymouth, Montserrat, British West Indies

✉ Life on a tiny island is a fascinating experience. Montserrat is only thirty-nine square miles. Our closest neighbour is Antigua, a fifteen-minute flight. Our airport can't land anything larger than a twenty-seater. We have a population of twelve thousand. About two hundred expatriates live here year-round. There is little tourism, no pollution, no crowded beaches, no hurry.

We have very little money – enough to last two years if we are frugal. We have none of the amenities of North American life. Food is in constant shortage on the island, the phones go out regularly, the women at the market refuse to sell me tomatoes unless I buy cucumbers as well. I've never been happier.

We're struggling to find ways to stretch our stay in Montserrat. I work as a secretary for an eighty-one-year-old expatriate who claims to have worked for the CIA. My husband is painting the house we live in in exchange for rent. We have three vegetable gardens. We're learning that what we honestly work for means more than what can be bought easily. We've also discovered a new pride in being Canadian. This was demonstrated, in its basest form, when the Grey Cup was being played.

My husband is one of the true football fans of all time. Life in Montserrat precludes Canadian football but we had to see the Grey Cup. First attempts to get someone to mail us a videotape failed. A former boss of mine offered to bring a tape with him on his winter vacation to Guadalope. We could fly over for a drink and pick up the tape, he said. The island is a $200 plane ride away. Expensive drink. Out of the question.

By December, despair had set in. Even our fellow Canadians in Montserrat were beginning to talk about the Superbowl. They had forgotten. We couldn't. Finally, two friends told us they were coming to see us in January. Was there anything they could bring?

Not trusting the mail, we called them. Bring newspapers. Bring magazines. Bring ground coffee. Bring the Grey Cup tape!

We drew up Grey Cup party invitations and mailed them before either the friends or the tape had arrived. We invited a mix of Canadian and American expatriates, football fanatics, and people we knew would be thrilled to watch real North American television commercials. Liquor for the party was easy to obtain: it's one of the few things that isn't in perpetual shortage. Rye bread and cold cuts were too expensive. We begged, hoarded, and stockpiled the requisite junk food. The final menu was freshly made coconut chips, a can of Pringles of questionable age, and a wild-rice casserole made from a box of rice sent by my mother.

January twenty-first was game day. The rains started early, as they do at this time of year. We didn't mind. We knew that no one would be trapped in a blizzard on the way to the party. By five o'clock, when the first guests arrived, the sun was shining, the temperature was a balmy eighty-three degrees, and all was right with the world.

We had pre-game drinks on the gallery overlooking the ocean. The conversation ranged from favourite quarterbacks to the right time to pick bananas. At five-thirty we gathered to watch the sunset.

Game time was six-thirty. I made pompoms out of construction paper for each guest, with the name of the team they were to cheer for on the handle. At the playing of "O Canada," all the Canadians and several Americans stood. There were tears welling in the eyes of those who hadn't seen their country of birth for several years.

The game was a *mélange* of Americans trying to figure out what happened to the fourth down; Canadians explaining the rules; talk about the good old days when favourite players were still active.

A majority of guests switched allegiances with every point scored.

Next year we'll get the tape earlier. Maybe we can get some goldeye shipped in. Next year, we'll all still be homesick for Canada and grateful for something that takes us home for three hours, that makes us ache in a pleasant way for what we left behind.

Lindor Heuvel

Ouagadougou, Burkina Faso

✉ There was an odd mood in the Palace of Justice. People had crammed into the chamber by the hundreds. There were students and women standing on tiptoe with babies slumbering on their backs. There were soldiers dressed and armed for jungle warfare. Even a former president was there. There were also a few of us – curious white intruders.

We were packed into a room strangely reminiscent of a Protestant church hall somewhere in rural Canada. We would have been more comfortable had there been, say, two or three hundred fewer of us. It was difficult to breathe. The temperature outside in the blazing sun was in the mid-forties Celsius, and somewhat higher on the wooden pews inside.

But no one seemed to mind the heat or the pushing. They clearly considered themselves fortunate to have gained entry for the scheduled drama. Throughout the city of Ouagadougou, and across the dust-swept plain that is the impoverished and obscure country of Burkina Faso, people were gathered close to radios to listen to the proceedings.

This was the first sitting of the Peoples' Commission to Prevent Corruption. At 11:15, the ten-member commission filed in. They were as solemn as any jury as they took their places behind the bar. They called on Captain Thomas Sankara to take the stand, and to state without omission the extent of his personal wealth both inside and outside the country.

At this, the crowd whooped with delight. Thomas Sankara, a

charismatic thirty-seven-year-old army captain, is president of Burkina Faso.

He rose to face the commission. Dressed in combat fatigues, he stood with his bare arms crossed behind his back. Only once did he turn to acknowledge the audience, and then only long enough to flash a mischievous grin, much like a schoolboy summoned before the principal.

"Comrade Zongo," he began, addressing the president of the anti-corruption commission. "I begin with a list of my furnishings. First of all, I own a refrigerator, which I wish to note is not working." There were squeals of mirth.

His testimony continued. He possesses two televisions: one at home and one in his office; and three radios, which he specified were to keep track of world news. He said he bought a villa in Ouagadougou in 1976, seven years before he took power in a military coup, and he still owes two thousand dollars on it. He listed two racing bicycles, as well as one bike for his wife and two for his children. He said he has three dried and cracked guitars, to which he attaches great value. He and his wife have gold wedding rings, but other jewellery is mostly imitation, and not worth much.

The spectators could hardly contain themselves. Since when is it honourable *not* to be rich?

But the sombre commission demanded silence. Sankara was asked to state his finances. As captain in the army, he said, he receives 138,736 francs a month – that's about $400 American. His presidential salary, about $600 a month, goes to his wife to provide for children, in-laws, parents, and other hangers-on.

All told, he said, he had about $1,400 in local banks. But in three and a half years as president, he has received gifts totalling $2.5 million.

This drew catcalls and cries of outrage. Sankara paused before delivering the punch line. That money, as well as the Alpha-Romeo and BMW he was given, have all gone directly to the state. The audience applauded.

When Sankara finished, the commission informed him that all of his statements, and those of all ministers, bank managers, civil servants – of anyone summoned before them, would be investigated and verified. If anyone in the country knew of any falsehood, they were invited to write directly to the commission, which would be changed frequently, so that it would not be immune to investigation.

Not a word or a nuance of these proceedings is lost on the public. These are wary and wise people on a continent rife with corruption on a huge scale, a continent where presidents often have, in the form of custom-made cars, palaces, and foreign bank holdings, more billions of dollars than the national debts of their poverty-stricken countries.

Burkina Faso, called Upper Volta before Sankara's "revolution," underwent four military takeovers between 1974 and 1983, with each successive regime siphoning off untold millions of dollars from a desperately poor country where the average annual income is about $180. Under Sankara, things have changed. Radically. Corruption and illicit wealth are no longer sanctioned, no longer a laughing matter. Sankara and his council of young, idealistic, and surprisingly frank ministers insist that old rules must be broken if the country – and the continent – is going to make it. And that, in the end, is what this theatrical and brilliant performance in the Palace of Justice was all about.

Joan Baxter

Lima, Peru

✉ Last Thursday I went to visit a friend in a *pueblo joven*, one of the many "young towns" that have sprung up all around Lima – suburbs formed by squatters who have come in from the mountain regions looking for a better life in the city. My friend is a social worker who tries to help these people cope with the catastrophic changes they have faced.

"Many miss the beauty of their old surroundings," she says.

I can believe it. Lima lies in the vast coastal desert of Peru.

213

Nothing grows here without irrigation. Bare, brown, rocky hills rise up from dusty tawny plains. It never rains, although a perpetual grey mist, called "garua," hangs over the city all the winter months. It is now summer; one hot, sunny day follows another without a break. The pueblo bakes in desiccated dreariness. Children, some neat and clean, others with scanty clothing, kick up small whirl-winds of dust as they chase one another through the unpaved streets.

We called on Maria, one of the community's leaders. She is a mixture of Indian, Spanish, and black, and has a dynamic quality that some of her quiet Indian neighbours lack. Her stocky body threatens the seams of her short tight dress, and her big smile of welcome reveals several missing teeth. She kisses us warmly.

"El agua!" she exults. "Isn't it wonderful to have water at last!"

For six years this pueblo has been petitioning the municipal government to provide water and sewage facilities for its several thousand residents. Maria herself carried a banner right into down-town Lima, to the governor's palace, a march of twenty kilometres. Twice they marched in 1982, once in 1983, and again in 1985 to get the work restarted. Each time they were confronted by the army in riot gear.

"We were scared," she says. "But we needed water. Our signs said 'Water is a Right, Not a Privilege!'"

Just this week the work was completed, the taps at last turned on.

"My Indian neighbour told me it was coming twenty minutes before it reached us," said my friend. "With her keen hearing, she had become aware of an unfamiliar noise – the rushing of the water in the underground pipes."

"What a day it was!" said Maria, chuckling hugely. "And that one," she said, pointing to her bright-eyed, eight-year-old Carlos. "He knew it was carnival time, when everyone threw water on their friends. We were all drenched. It was so good!"

Maria, Juan, and their three children, Carlos, an older girl, Emilia, and baby Ignacio, live in one dark room. From his meagre wages as a city street sweeper, Juan scrimped to buy four woven bamboo mats, which, set up in a square, formed their first shelter.

Gradually he has been able to afford some bricks and, bit by bit, over the years, the house walls have taken shape. They still have a woven bamboo roof; it is airy but leakproof. The inside of the brick wall is plastered over; one day it will be brightened with paint. Already Carlos is contributing to the family income by going into Lima with his father and watching over parked cars, from whose owners he receives a few coins. But only at holiday time. Maria makes sure both older children go to school every day.

"Three-quarters of the children here attend regularly," our friend says. "It's one of the reasons their parents are here – because they feel their children will get a better education in Lima." What about the other quarter, we asked.

"Well, some of them must look after younger children, some must go out to work, some cannot afford pencils and paper."

Here we were interrupted by a pretty young girl, Pilar, a high-school student. Her parents come from the war-torn Ayacucho region, where a Maoist terrorist organization has been battling with the army for at least ten years. Pilar's mother barely supports the family as a *vendedora*, a street seller of chocolate bars and other snacks.

In a period of chaos in Ayacucho, her father lost his papers. Now, without them, he cannot get a job. Worse, he could be thrown in jail. Pilar anxiously asks if the social worker has had any news from the authorities. My friend shakes her head.

"Not yet," she says. "Have patience. Remember, it took six years to get the water."

Donalda Badone

Brikama, The Gambia

✉ This past January, I closed my pottery workshop in Vernon, British Columbia, and began preparations for a new job in West Africa. I had been asked by CUSO to work with a UN project engaged in designing improved cookstoves. I arrived in the Gambia in February and from touchdown at Yundum Airport I began adapting to the dry Harmattan season. It has rained one day since my arrival, and that, I'm told, is the only rain since last September.

The Gambia is a tiny country almost completely surrounded by Senegal. It is little more than a narrow strip of flat land on either side of the Gambia River. I had hoped to see more of the river, but the only passenger boat, the *Lady Chelal*, sank two years ago. My orientation with the improved-cookstoves project has taken me to many parts of the country already.

Travelling through villages, it is hard not to be shocked by the poverty and at the same time to realize that I have arrived at the most abundant time of year, just after the harvest. Relief aid is a way of life. There are surprising numbers of international-agency vehicles on the main road: Christian Childrens Fund, Save the Children, Peace Corp, Unicef, Action Aid. And it is not uncommon to hear stories of two agencies working in the same village, unknown to one another. This is called "overlap."

I am settling into my house in Brikama, a small town about thirty-five kilometres south of Banjul, the capital. My landlord's family live next door, and our houses share a walled compound. Just on the other side of this wall is a small road, which to my Western eyes first seemed like a very quiet back lane. It is travelled by motorcycles, horse carts, donkeys, small herds of sheep, and vendors selling everything from underwear to bonga fish.

Since the evening is cool, Gambians tend to go out later and many parties or dances will start after ten. In spite of this I was unprepared for one man who has awakened me on several occasions by angrily yelling up and down our street at five in the morning. Finally, I had enough. I jumped out of bed, ran out into the compound, and loudly hushed him. Quite startled, he left. I went back to bed, only to hear him come back a few minutes later. It took a lot of self-control to not leap out of bed again. The next morning I took my righteous indignation to my landlady, Tulie. She carefully explained that the man in question was, in fact, a holy man, calling the faithful to prayer at the mosque.

Well, it takes a while to change one's sensibilities.

Burt Cohen

216

MARGARET LAURENCE AND ELIZABETH SMART

Among the saddest events of the years of radio this book commemorates were the deaths, in February 1986 and January 1987, of two important Canadian woman novelists. Each had been a guest on *Morningside* over the years, and each had left her mark on us in other ways. They had on our listeners, as well. The eloquent remembrance of Margaret Laurence that opens this brief chapter of tribute was commissioned by us, and I can still remember Timothy Findley arriving grimly to record it the morning after she died. With Hal Wake producing, he recorded it in one studio while we broadcast the first portion of the program from another. It would have been difficult to do live.

But the other three pieces here – and there were others that came in – were unsolicited by us. The two people who wrote about Margaret Laurence – Sylvia Markle-Craine had in fact written what she sent to us while Margaret Laurence was still alive, but had kept it – and the one who wrote about Elizabeth Smart simply found *Morningside* an appropriate place to express their grief.

✉ Mind must be the firmer,
   Heart the more fierce,
   Courage the greater
   As our strength diminishes.

These are lines from an old English poem that was cherished by Margaret Laurence – cherished, rehearsed over time, and implemented. Wherever she found these words – whenever it was they first refused to go away and leave her alone – that moment must be counted as one of the most important in all the sixty years of her life. As words, as articulation, they became a corner-stone of her resources. They inform not only her writing: they also inform whatever we know of how she lived and how she died.

Margaret Laurence was a great believer in simplicity. She was also one of its greatest practitioners. This is where the *firmness* came in. Firmness, for Margaret Laurence, was one of simplicity's most important synonyms. "I will" and "I won't" were two of her absolutes. She would not and could not tolerate anything less than her full capacity to make words work on paper. Nor would she tolerate anything less than her full capacity to stand for what she believed in.

As time progressed and her capacities expanded, she also progressed from *firm* to *firmer*. If you knew Margaret Laurence, you had to contend with this sometimes difficult part of her will. And if you knew her well, you wished, in a way, you could protect her from it. Part of her firmness and, of course, an extremely potent part of her will was her rejection – which was total – of any kind of safety: personal, intellectual, or physical. She struggled thirty years and more at her table to produce on the page an account of

218

what was in her mind – and that, as any serious writer knows, is a struggle utterly without the benefit of self-preservation. The onslaught of fictional men and women, ideas, and events – all of whom and all of which can achieve their existence only if the writer succeeds at giving them articulation – has a strange, seductive power to suggest that articulation "cannot be achieved." Unless you are firm.

So Margaret Laurence stayed there at her table, no matter how long it took to get things right. And when she rose and when she handed over what she had written, she said: "This is it, the way it should be, the way it must be, the way it is and the way it will stay."

This is it: the way it will stay: *The Stone Angel, A Jest of God, The Fire Dwellers, A Bird in the House, The Diviners*: firm, firmer, firmest.

The fierceness in her was mighty.

Margaret Laurence had to contend with a body whose nervous system tended to betray her just when she needed it most to be strong. She shook. Her knees gave way. Her hands could be seen from almost any distance, reaching for the backs of chairs and the tops of tables – anything to hold her up and stop her from shaking. Rising to speak – choosing, against all odds, to rise at all – in order to tell what she believed – these were the harshest enemies she had whenever it came to speaking her mind. But speak her mind she must – and fiercely. She said something once that gave the essence of all her beliefs: her certainty that we, her beloved human-kind, were capable of wilful, self-determined sanity if only we would *try*. . . . Margaret Laurence believed, with a passion so pro-found it almost puts me to shame to think of it, that war and hatred must *and can* be put aside. And she devoted, even to the point of exhaustion, all the latter years of her life to activities supporting this belief. But her open espousal of peace through nuclear disarma-ment brought her, as it must, a host of enemies, name-callers, finger-pointers: people who called her a "fool," a "red," and the word that disturbed her most, "subversive." What Margaret Laurence said to these accusers was said with the kind of ferocity that only absolute certainty can justify. "If the quest for peace," she said, "is subversive, then what, in the name of God, is war?"

Fierce, fiercer, fiercest.

One day the word came that Margaret Laurence was going to die. No backing off, no second chance at survival, nothing to mitigate the certainty. Up to about a year before this day arrived, those of us who knew and loved her had been aware of her struggles to take up the pen again and write. Her last major piece of work had been published in 1974. This was her masterpiece, *The Diviners*. But since that year, her writer's output had been meagre: three books for children and one of essays written in the past. Her time was given over to anti-nuclear and peace activities. She was also – with great success and personal popularity – the chancellor of Trent University. But what she wanted – besides these things – was one more book. And it wouldn't come.

What very few people knew was that, during this time, Margaret Laurence was slowly going blind with cataracts. She couldn't properly wield the pen. She couldn't properly type, though both activities were still producing a vast outpouring of letters to students and fans and friends. And then there was a "miracle." A plastic lens was implanted in one of her eyes – and she began to write again. She could barely believe her good fortune. What she wrote, and what she completed, and what, in a not-too-distant future, will be published was a book devoted to the theme of motherhood: a memoir. She worked on this until the week before she died.

Brave, braver, bravest.

Euripides told us: "Never that which is shall die."

He didn't mean people, I guess. I guess what he meant was ideas and truths and things like that. I think he meant, too, that whatever goes into life – the whole of what is alive – is alive forever. Margaret Laurence is dead. But so – we are told – is Euripides. I'm sure you know exactly what I mean. Goodbye, Margaret Laurence. And thank you.

Timothy Findley
Cannington, Ontario

✉ Monday, January fifth, 1987. I'm driving home, late for dinner. I switch on the CBC and hear Margaret Atwood's voice talking about Margaret Laurence. I half listen. Then I suddenly realize that Margaret Atwood is saying "was" instead of "is." Later I go into my study to mourn Margaret Laurence, who was part of my inner life for twenty-two years. It amazes me that Margaret Laurence knew that innermost being and wrote about it. I look back at how much a part of my life she was. . . .

My sister, Betty Lambert, knows Margaret Laurence as a fellow writer.

"How did you meet? What's she like?" I ask.

"Well, I went to a party, knowing she'd be there and feeling quite intimidated. I looked for her and couldn't see her. Finally, I noticed a rather plain, frumpy-looking woman sitting in a corner in a beige pant suit, smoking. She was surrounded by young people. It was Laurence. I could never get near her all night. People seemed drawn to her, like so many moths to a flame. She looked so ordinary. I was rather disappointed."

In early 1983 Betty learns she has lung cancer. Shortly after that we learn that our mother also has cancer. Betty begins chemotherapy treatment. She asks me to go to the opening of her latest play in Toronto. We are determined to celebrate life amidst this onslaught of death. Somehow we make it. Betty goes from the hospital to the airport and I meet her there with my little mother-sucker, my nine-month-old son Daniel, along for the ride.

We fly from Vancouver to Toronto and stay with Adele Wiseman and her husband, Dmitry Stone. They have been Betty's close friends for years. "You can stay in Peggy's room," Adele says. "I'll just go and get some sheets."

I wonder idly who Peggy might be. The room is small and there are books everywhere. I put Danny on the floor to investigate his new surroundings and I leaf through the books. There are markers in the books saying "Please don't remove." They are signed "M.L." I hold one of the markers in my hand.

Adele returns, bearing sheets. "Who is Peggy?" I ask.

"Peggy? That's Margaret Laurence, Peggy to her friends. This is her room – she stays here when she's in Toronto."

Adele moves towards the bed. "Don't change the sheets!" I announce dramatically. "I want to sleep in Margaret Laurence's bed, dirty sheets and all." I fall onto the bed. "She's my favourite writer."

Adele laughs.

A few days later, I am packing to leave. A storm rages outside. Danny and I watch ancient trees fall gracefully over. Power lines break. I hear on the radio that it is the tip of a tornado. There is a knock at the door. I open it to find a windblown Margaret Laurence.

"Hi," she says. "You're Betty's sister, aren't you? God, what a ride!"

She comes in as I stand dumbfounded. It is the same marvellous face that has stared at me from book jackets for years, the face that Margaret Atwood once described as that of an "exotic Eskimo witch." But the face has a body and talks. I am totally unnerved. She's carrying a dishevelled old shopping bag. She plunks it down on a dining-room chair.

"Put the kettle on, will you, and do you mind if I change? These panty hose are killing me."

I put the kettle on and come back to find Margaret Laurence stripping off panty hose, prim blouse, tailored jacket, and skirt. She reaches into the shopping bag and produces grungy slacks and a beat-up sweater, which she quickly dons.

"Ah, that feels better. I hate dressing up."

We sit down to tea. "I'm sorry about Betty," she says, as she lights up the first of many cigarettes.

"Yes. It's lung cancer, from smoking."

She fixes me with her incredible brown gaze. "I know." She dares me to say anything to her about smoking. But I don't dare. But it's hard to go on acting as though someone is a Canadian literary legend when you've seen her in her underwear. We talk about children. My four sons, her son and daughter. I tell her about the sheets. She roars with laughter. "For God's sake, change them," she orders. "And don't lose my place in my books."

She talks of her work in the peace movement. "It's taking most of my time, but it's important," she says quietly, as she lights another cigarette. "And we *can* make a difference." She coughs. A smoker's cough. Betty's cough.

Adele and Betty appear in the doorway, very wet-looking. "It's mad out there," says Adele. "If we're going to make your flights we have to go. Right now!"

I am devastated. I want to stay, talk to Margaret Laurence. Tell her how much her work has meant to me, tell her how she's touched me and taught me. Instead I dash around, organizing everything. Adele and I finally get the suitcases in the car, struggling not to be blown away. My emotions are as wild as the weather. I go back in, clutching my camera.

"Just one photo, please, Adele," I beg. "I want to take Daniel surrounded by three of Canada's best writers. When will he ever have this chance again?"

Margaret Laurence grabs Daniel and sits in a chair. Daniel nuzzles her breast. "No, no," she says gently, moving his head away. "It's too late for that." Betty and Adele stand on either side of her.

"Scrunch down," I say to them. They scrunch closer.

"Okay, say sex."

"Not cheese?" asks Margaret.

"No, sex is better than cheese."

They laugh and I press the shutter. My camera jams.

"Oh, damn." I grab Betty's camera.

"Sex," they all say.

I take the shot just as Margaret jumps up, holding Daniel in front of her. "Oh, God, he's peed on me," she announces. She holds him out, grinning conspiratorially at me, woman to woman, somehow saying, isn't life wonderful and funny and surprising and worth it all.

Oh, Margaret Laurence. I thought you would be here forever. I feel real grief that you are gone. There will be no new novels from you about women and survival, about growing and loving, about being true to oneself. How I will miss that. But I will continue to love and to grow and survive and try to be true to myself, partly because of you.

Dorothy Beavington
White Rock, British Columbia

✉ I am sitting in my room where books are scattered like Gretel's crumbs, a trail that leads not home but away. In my hands is a book with your picture on the cover. You are sitting in front of a bookshelf, glasses in hand, wearing a good dust-jacket stare. I try to read the spine titles, and wonder if they are your books. Are they clues to who you are and how you came to be sitting here on this cover in my room? Do books marks us, leaving wounds? Do they heal us after the terrible rending from our bodies? Can we see the stitches where they have been removed, just under the heart?

There are so many things I want to ask you. I look at you and I see stories like fine, pale smoke drifting from your body. Some lie round your neck like garlands; people dance in your eyes. I want to write like you, forming and moulding, rounding and warming words into breathing flesh. Sometimes I want to be Morag and live in a woods where I seem to belong. My home wears an ancient druid face with its warm-womb rocks, gnarled driftwood and weeping trees scattered amongst the necessary things, like chairs and beds and mountains of books.

Do you have spaces that only words can fill? Do they secure you and smooth the hollows? Sometimes there is a choking feeling in my chest where words have caught going down. They spill out into poems or stories, changing the white pages to magic colours filled with movement. Is this how it's supposed to be?

Do you do this? Do you hold images in your head on photographic plates, acid-etched, until you need them? Do these images come fully formed? Or do they lie in their embryonic state waiting for your hand to bring them to life? A painful birthing that lives longer than ourselves.

Well, you are still here on this book cover and I am still trying to write. But I wanted to tell you how you have changed me, how you have enriched and broadened my life with your books, how things have not been the same since you let me into your world. The gift you give is given freely, with no strings, only bright promises and endless love. Thank you, Margaret Laurence, for sharing your life.

Sylvia Markle-Craine
Guelph, Ontario

✉ Before she took up the position of writer-in-residence at the University of Alberta in 1983, I read an article about Elizabeth Smart in the *Journal*. Later I heard an interview with her on *Morningside*. I had already bought, read, and reread *By Grand Central Station I Sat Down and Wept*. I had found it moving, almost overpowering at times. I knew that somehow I had to meet the author.

So how to go about it? One middle-aged, suburban nurse-housewife, with a level of self-esteem at that time that would have fit under a snake's belly, wanting to meet one illustrious, intelligent writer, esconced in the ivory tower of learning. Having never attended university, I was much in awe of those who did.

A free lecture and discussion was offered to the public. Elizabeth Smart was to be part of the panel. I'll see her at a distance, at least, I thought. I wanted so much to hear this woman whose strength, passion, and laser-like truth came through so beautifully in *By Grand Central Station*.

There were five authors on the panel. Elizabeth Smart was strangely quiet, I thought. Few questions were directed at her and when she answered in her cultured, husky voice she sounded almost apologetic. She was a diminutive figure, hunched over in her black clothes and wearing tennis shoes. She had a cigarette in one hand and with the other constantly pushed back the grey hair that fell over her eyes.

After the session, I asked her to autograph a copy of her book of poems, *A Bonus*. I wanted to say something that would make her notice me, but I was tongue-tied. I went home and wrote her a letter asking if it was true that anyone could visit the writer-in-residence, not just those enrolled in courses at the university. I also sent her a few poems of my own.

In early April, I received a reply and an invitation to phone. "I like your poems," she wrote. "They're fun. Keep it up. Forge ahead. I think the hardest thing is to believe in yourself. I've never handed anything to anyone without expecting them to hand it back saying, 'What's this rubbish?' Anyhow, I'm better at getting other people to believe in themselves, so I'll look forward to seeing you."

I met her in her room at the University of Alberta. Her room was quite high up, overlooking a bleak, snow-covered landscape, with colourless buildings belching white clouds of smoke into the cold, ice-blue sky. I thought it depressing. Maybe real writers rise above the view from their windows.

I read her some of my poems. She didn't say much. I think she found it hard to criticize others. I realized she was being kind.

The next time we met, she was not feeling very well, and was worried about an upcoming visit from her grandchildren. I thought she was tired, old, and very much alone. I don't think the academics really accepted her. She said that when she first arrived, she wondered if they had got her mixed up with someone else, as they did not seem to know who she was or what she had written. I don't know why I did not trust my instincts and befriend her – but I was afraid.

The last time I went to see her, a student was in her room when I arrived. The three of us made up poems together. Each person wrote a line and passed the paper on. We made up three or four and Elizabeth Smart put them in her drawer "to add to her collection." She talked about a recent reading tour of the Maritimes and the warmth and friendliness of the people, especially in Newfoundland. I had recently moved to this landlocked province from there, so I knew exactly what she was talking about.

She had been offered the first writer-in-residence post at Memorial University. She would have fitted in there; everyone would have loved her.

She left Edmonton for Toronto, and then I heard she had returned to England. I did not hear from her again. My memories are tinged with regret that I could not have thrown off the cloak of self-doubt when I was with her. I would have liked to have known her better.

Jennifer Huff
Spruce Grove, Alberta

MEMORABLE MEALS: A THIRD COURSE FROM ABROAD

This is a response not so much to *Morningside* (though that is where it all began, and all these stories were read in the season of 1986 to 1987) as to *The Morningside Papers* – the first edition. I received it from Sheree-Lee Powsey, a Canadian who had taken the first collection with her to China, where she, like Bob Cosbey, whose letter appears two chapters ago, was teaching English. Sheree-Lee had used the book in her classes, she wrote. Her students at the Southwest China Teachers University in Chengking had responded particularly to the two collections, or courses as I called them, of Memorable Meals. In response, they had written some stories of their own. She enclosed their letters. The actor Bill Johnston, himself of Chinese descent, read them on the radio. Here are some samples.

✉ In the spring of 1979, I had been a university student for a year. One day, during the winter holiday, I went to see my childhood nurse, a kind old woman. I hadn't seen her for two years. At that time she was over sixty years old and lived with her weak husband – a man who didn't work. With a little money she started up a small wine shop located at the northern part of a suburb of Chengdu, my home town. In her shop window there were several pieces of pot-stewed spareribs, half a salted pig's head, and several dishes of pickles, a fly circling around them. A few old men and women who seemed to be retired workers living in the neighbourhood were sitting around two old square tables, drinking and talking. My nurse had been an active middle-aged woman with a smiling face. But now, in the dim corner behind a dirty counter, I saw an exhausted granny with entirely white hair and a wrinkled, expressionless face. She hardly recognized me at first when I called to her. But when she knew who I was there was a flash of tears in her eyes.

Her hand trembling, she approached me with a tray full of dumplings . . . she had remembered what I liked best as a child. From 1959 to 1961, something went wrong in my country – a period known as the "difficult time of the Three Years." We had rationing of wheat, rice, and flour. I was always hungry and looked forward to Sundays and festivals, when my family could have an "affluent meal." That always meant dumplings with a little meat and lots of vegetables. My nurse could make this rough food seem very tasty. As I swallowed, she watched and smiled.

But now, on seeing her again, her dumplings tasted salty in my throat, although she sat behind me, full of joy, as if time had been turned back and I was a five-year-old boy sitting there greedily eating her meal.

Then, when the sun had set, I left her. I never saw her again. My brother came to see me and told me she had died of cancer and her small wine shop had been shut down.

All her life she had struggled with poverty. She never lived comfortably. She lacked everything – but love.

He Xiao-Bing

✉ I grew up in an old farm. I was the last son of my parents. I have two elder brothers and two elder sisters. Even though I have been away from my old home for more than ten years, I can remember everything about my family well.

My father is in the countryside far from the city. Around our house there are several kinds of trees and bamboo. They are green even in winter. In front of our house there is a river in which the water is very clear all the year. It flows quietly and slowly.

My father is a very hard man. He never allowed me to do anything before I was six. How I wanted to try everything with my elder brothers and sisters! But they, and my father, always thought of me as a little boy. When they introduced me to my relatives they always said I couldn't do anything because I was very young. I wanted to disagree with their opinions but I didn't know how.

I was happy when I played in the river with my friends. Of course my father was unhappy about it but I did it in secret. One very nice summer day my friends and I went to the river. Suddenly I was bit by something. I looked – and saw a crab gripping my leg with its pincers. It was big and brown. It hurt, but I didn't cry. Then my friends came to pull it away from me and we caught it. Then we began searching for other crabs. Just then my sister came to call me and told me that my father was angry and ordered me to come back at once. So we returned with our war booty – ten crabs in all. My sister promised to cook them.

That day was my most memorable day. I had done a valuable thing. When my sister cooked the crabs we all smelled the smell and wanted them very much. When I told them how I got them they were worried about my leg so I pointed to it with a smile and said don't worry. And my father finally learned that to really love a child is to trust him and know him. So all my family from then on let me try everything I wanted to do. Sometimes it is not easy to get freedom – sometimes you have to pay for it.

Ou Wen-fu

✉ My most memorable meal came at the time I was about to graduate from university. It was a Sunday and a group of us left the university on a picnic outing. I volunteered to be cook and bravely said: "I am good at making soup and the soup I make will delight your appetites."

So they put me in charge of the soup. I put in some onions, eggs, garlic, tomatoes, and soya-bean sauce, and stirred it well. It smelled delicious and I was very pleased with myself. But since it was watery I added some flour to thicken it.

When the soup was cooked I poured it into a large dish and took a spoonful to taste. To my surprise it was thick as glue and I had also added too much soya sauce. It was also salty. It tasted awful.

But we were hungry and we had to enjoy it – there was no choice.

Chen Huai-xin

✉ When I came to this university I was sixteen years old. This was when I first left my home town. Everything felt very unfamiliar. I often thought of my home town and my parents, and I often shed tears.

One cool morning I was ill. I lay in bed, heard the cool wind blowing, and saw falling leaves out the window. My heart was full of sadness.

Suddenly the door opened. A man came in, someone I knew. He smiled and came near my bed, then looked at me and said: "Cheer up, Lily, don't worry, you'll get over this very quickly. When you have recovered I want to invite you to have dinner with me. Would you?" I nodded that, yes, I would.

He was a handsome young man and older than I. We first met each other at the library and several times since then at the university. I always felt happy when he was there.

Soon I got over my sickness and I waited for him to invite me for dinner. I imagined that dinner many times in my heart. I was full of hope and I studied hard every day.

Now time has passed. He never invited me. We hardly ever met because he was about to graduate and had many things to do. Then he left and we never met again.

This is my secret – the memorable meal I never had. I don't dare hope that I ever will have it. But just remembering is a kind of meeting.

Lin Ping

✉ My childhood was always filled with innocence and fancy and I have many memories. I remember I was a boy of twelve when one day my friends and I went to Hong Huang Mountain to have fun. In fact, we indulged ourselves and forgot to go home. The day was becoming dark and we lost our way. After the sun had set we didn't know what to do. We had not eaten anything for twelve hours. We felt very hungry, cold, and frightened. There was no food to eat and no place to sleep on the mountain, and that night I spent the hardest night of my life. Finally day broke. Our hunger got worse and we marched on without any objective. By two o'clock we were too hungry to walk. I thought I would die of hunger.

Suddenly I saw an old farmer. I was very pleased. He was walking toward us, as if he was finding us. We told him we had lost our way and had not eaten anything for two days. Then the old farmer led us to his home and gave every one of us three potatoes. Food was never so appetizing. The potatoes were delicious and sweet, better than dainties of any kind. My stomach was full.

Next day, with the help of the old farmer, we returned home. Many years have passed, but those three potatoes have become the memory of my life.

Zheng Jia-fei

✉ At 3:15 on July fifth of this year my youngest brother died in a traffic accident. When I heard the news it seemed to make me lose my mind. My younger brother had been both friendly and clever – everyone he ever met still talks about him. The last time I saw him was on June first – just a month earlier. At noon that day he came to my room from Jiangbei. We were to have a family meal. Since we didn't know he was coming we hadn't prepared a rich meal for him. After lunch there was something that required him to return to Jiangbei immediately. He left, saying goodbye to my son. We thought it was just another goodbye.

But it was the last goodbye and that ordinary lunch was the last meal he would have with us. This is my most memorable meal.

Duan Ze-Yong

✉ In 1969 I worked as a peasant on an army farm in a county of Szechuan province. I and my companions came there from every part of the country, all graduates from universities and colleges. We couldn't go on to professional jobs and use what we had learned in school because it was the time of the Cultural Revolution.

We did all kinds of farm work in those years. The group I was in grew vegetables. One day we planned a trip to a mountain to cut some bamboo as supports for vine-growing vegetables. We got up early that day and walked fast but with a good feeling of enjoying nature. We had put some noodles in a basket for our lunch. We also brought some oil, soy sauce, vinegar, chili powder and other seasonings in a bag.

Halfway to our destination we had a short break. We sat on stones and put the basket and the bag of seasonings on the ground. There was a great feeling of quiet – there was nothing in the world but us in that forest so thick we couldn't see the sky.

It was nearly noon when we got to a bamboo field. In a short time we had all the bamboo we needed and began to prepare our meal. We made a fire of dry branches and put clean spring water on to boil. Everything was just right but after we put the noodles in the boiling water we couldn't find our bag of seasonings. We guessed we had lost it on the ground when we had our break. So we ate the noodles without any seasoning, without even a little salt.

This story happened over twenty years ago. There are no longer army farms. But that meal of noodles without salt and seasoning has always reminded me of that time in my life.

Chen Zefu

FISH STORIES, MANY OF THEM TRUE

W.O. Mitchell, the author and fisherman, and Franklin Arbuckle, the artist and fisherman, were on the radio one day and they started exchanging fish stories. Mitchell – his friends call him Bill – told a story about a dog he'd known that had been trained to retrieve fish. Later, Arbuckle thought about that, and wrote to clarify the matter, and started a whole new kettle of *Morningside* yarns. Honestly, this is true.

So it is true that one day a young man from Calgary wrote to *Morningside* about jigging for squid off the shore of his native Cape Breton, and his brother heard me read the letter on the air and wrote a kind of you-think-that's-something response.

Honestly.

✉ I know Bill Mitchell is a kind man and would never expose an animal to the hazard of a fish-hook in its mouth.

The idea of a dog retrieving a fish, however, has some substance. My dad, as a boy, had a dog that used to leap into the Moira River, which runs north of Belleville near the old homestead, and retrieve a fish by paddling backwards up close to the fish. By giving his tail a couple of quick flips, he would wrap it around the line and then jump to shore with the fish trailing behind. One thing Dad's dog could not conceivably do, as Bill alleges his trained dog did, is carry the fish to a stranger.

Anyway, here are two true stories my dad passed on to me. In one he and another boy, each about ten in 1872, while fishing with a string and a live frog for bait on the Moira River, hooked a monster sturgeon. They did not have the strength to haul the big fish into their punt, and that fish pulled them for miles up and downstream all day. About nightfall they managed to drag their catch half its length up the bank. Unfortunately, that great fish was not weighed, but it is said that eight large families on the Thomasburg line feasted on its meat for about a week. Actually, they had caught two fish, for the monster had apparently, while towing the punt, gobbled up a two-foot fish, which was still in perfect condition.

The other true adventure my dad told me happened in about 1895, near Alliston, Ontario, where he was living at the time. He was fishing with a friend one June afternoon when they had to take refuge from a fierce thunderstorm in a farmer's house. The farmer and my dad and friend sat down around the kitchen stove while the farmer's dog rested underneath. The catch of two trout had been thrown on top of the stove, which was not lit. Suddenly a lightning bolt hit the stove by way of the chimney and scattered stove-pipes and stove lids all over the place. When the three collected themselves and wiped some of the soot and ashes off their faces, they found they were pretty deaf – but unhurt. Sadly, the dog was quite dead. But the fish were still on the stove – *perfectly fried*! All they did was add a dab of butter and a little salt.

Franklin Arbuckle
Toronto

✉ I was fishing for mackerel in Bar Harbor, Maine, from some rocks ten feet above the water. I used nothing more than a lead jig and a spinning rod. Every cast brought in a one-pound mackerel.

I stored them in a rock pool, where they wiggled and splashed. This action attracted the seagulls, ever-ready for an easy meal.

On what was *not* intended to be my final cast of the day, I could feel that there was a good-sized mackerel hooked. The fish on the line broke the surface and was promptly gulped by a marauding gull. What I didn't know at this point was that the fish the gull stole had swallowed the jig, which had, in turn, emerged through the gill opening, leaving the mackerel "strung" on the line. As the gull gained altitude, the jig, with another, larger mackerel, broke surface. I was then in the unique position of catching two fish and one gull on one cast. However, the gull and the fish were tethered to my rod and were flying in a thirty-foot circle around my head.

I did the only humane thing. I cut the line. The weight of the mackerel on the jig pulled the line free from the seagull's mackerel. One mackerel went back to school. One seagull finished its lunch. And I finished fishing for the day.

Alan Indge
Souris, Prince Edward Island

✉ In the summer of 1912, when I was ten, my family went out on a chartered deep-sea fishing boat off the coast of Bay View, Maine. The sea was fairly choppy and my dad was seasick for the first time in his life. Two of the fishermen on board got their lines tangled in one fish. When finally the big cod was landed on deck, its very large mouth, or maw, or whatever you call it, contained my dad's upper denture – which believe it or not was then retrieved!

Dorothy Pfeiffer
Burlington, Ontario

237

✉ Nothing really prepared us for our exceptional moment on the secluded banks of the Yakoun River on Graham Island of the Queen Charlottes.

The sight of the locally famed Sitka spruce, fifty metres high, three hundred years old, ever-golden rather than evergreen, was in itself worth a pilgrim's journey.

My secondary intention was to try my luck casting for steelhead trout. But the narrow river was almost literally bridged by a steady parade of Chum salmon. Angling for the tasty giants in the fresh-water portion of their spawning run is, of course, strictly forbidden. Witnessing the mysterious cyclic event in such volume was a genuine thrill.

Perched on a high branch of a tree near our vantage point was a beautiful bald eagle. Unfettered by human fishing regulations, the eagle chose his moment and plummeted down to try his talons on a choice specimen. The third portion of our triple-play spectacle was set in motion, and an unexpected drama ensued.

Either through greed or over-confidence, the monarch of the air tangled with more than his match. The weighty salmon's thrashing caught the eagle off balance and a thorough dunking resulted. Injured pride was soon accompanied by panic as drenched wings lost their effectiveness. The bird struggled to release its grasp, only to find its claws caught in the bony flesh. Locked in combat, the pair seemed doomed to destroy one another.

Quickly I reached for my fishing rod. Praying for an accurate cast, I arched the rod back and flung out the line. The salmon leaped for the hook as if it sensed it to be a lifeline. As I reeled in, the fish seemed to race toward me eagerly.

Apparently realizing my mercy mission, the two kings co-operated completely. Seizing the legs of the eagle, I was able to extricate the talons with a swift twist and launch the bird to freedom. By chance, my fishing hook almost shook itself free, and the wounded but wriggling salmon gratefully re-entered the river.

Harold Sharlow
Calgary

⊠ Three years ago, on the Big Sevogle River, a branch of the North-West Miramichi deep in the New Brunswick wilderness, a group of us were astounded to see what was obviously a seeing-eye grilse. This teenage salmon, on his way upriver for his first spawning after a year in the ocean, actually nudged a blind adult salmon of about twelve pounds away from rock ledges and other obstructions.

We were standing on the river bank in front of the camp looking down on the great brown pool at about noon, trying to spot some salmon, when a member of the group pointed downwards and said, "Look at that – a salmon and a grilse over near that rock."

As the salmon moved slowly about the pool, the grilse seemed to be tormenting the larger fish by bunting it, particularly when the salmon headed towards an obstruction. We watched for some time, puzzled by the behaviour of the grilse. One of the fishermen, with keener sight than mine, slid down the bank a few yards and watched the fish closely. The sun was almost directly overhead and when the fish turned towards us they were clearly visible. Suddenly the fisherman closer to the water shouted, "That salmon is blind – look at his eyes, they're opaque. He must have cataracts." We all moved down the bank for a closer look, and without a doubt, the larger fish was sightless.

And even stranger, the grilse continued to steer his companion away from rocks, ledges, and other obstructions by gently nudging his side and moving him in the proper direction.

Charles A. Pope
Ottawa

⊠ Alberta is rightfully noted for its big jackfish. American anglers call them Great Northern Pike, but most native Albertans refer to them as slough sharks. "How big are they?" you ask. Well, sir, my buddy and I went ice fishing in Raseberry Lake near Fox Creek last winter.

239

He hollered, "I got one! Feels like a good one, but he just keeps going around in big circles under the ice."

I knew what that fish was up to, but my friend didn't hear me when I shouted for him to cut the line. No, sir, it was too late! The big jack had used his dorsal fin to inscribe a circle around both Pat and his pick-up truck, which we'd parked out on the ice. On the third time around the sharp dorsal fin cut through the ice. Fortunately, I was able to help Pat get out of the water, but we're going to have to wait for the spring breakup before we can have his pick-up towed out.

Will Reese
Edmonton

✉ I live near Kootenay Lake in British Columbia. The area is a paradise and the lake has great fishing. Regularly, catches of ten- or twelve-kilo trout are noted in our local paper. But in ten years of living here I've only been fishing once, and at that I only caught a couple of small kokanee.

There was one night in a different place, though, that I did catch something big.

Some years ago I was helping out with a mission organization in north-western Brazil. Our base was thirty-five hundred kilometres from the mouth of the Amazon, on one of its tributaries called the Madeira. I'd been there a couple of months and fished a number of times with fellow workers and had even made my own fishing "rod," a lathe-turned piece of hardwood a foot or so long, with a whole lot of sixty-kilo test line on it. Completing the outfit was a steel leader (for the piranhas), a big hunk of lead, and a hook the size of my thumb. One night, carrying my fishing gear in one hand and my flashlight in the other, I made my way on the jungle path down to the river.

Now for a boy from the arid British Columbia interior, the jungle was sensory overload. It was like a green ocean, wavy on top and seething with life through to its bottom. I'd heard all the stories

240

about jaguars, alligators, the big black ants with paralyzing stingers, tarantula spiders, stinging caterpillars, and countless other creatures, such as the bushmaster snake and all his crawling relatives. Visions of these denizens were bad enough, and coupled with the sounds of the night, it was pretty eerie. "Sensurround" was not invented by Hollywood: it came from the tropical rain forest, where sound is everywhere – a cacophony of noise from far away and inside your head, as interminable and irritating as a kid practising a recalcitrant violin, yet vibrant and throbbing with nocturnal life.

Not totally comfortable in those surroundings, I nonetheless made it to the river and slipped my way down the muddy bank to try fishing.

The river was another world. I spun my weighted and baited line about my head and cast it upstream. The Madeira was a kilometre wide and had a relentless, warm, murky current. As my hook drifted downstream I thought about the creatures I'd seen pulled from its depths: an electric eel that I had sense enough not to touch; a dogfish with a mouth one-third its length full of ragged teeth that looked as if they could shred flesh about as effectively as a chainsaw; a catfish eighty kilograms in weight caught on half-inch nylon rope tied to a tree; a metre-long piraracu with scales as big and hard as serving spoons, and prized tasty flesh; and piranhas – big muscles controlling big jaws. The locals didn't fear the piranhas, but they did fear the fresh-water porpoises. Any river death was blamed on the large mammals. The night I went fishing I could distinctly hear the porpoises breathing about the surface as I repeatedly cast.

A lightning storm began in the distance. I felt small and alone in the tropical blackness as I flung my hook one more time. I waited for it to drift downstream and then slowly coiled my line. It became apparent that something was attached. Each second, the line became tougher to reel in and the catch grew in my imagination. Nothing jumped or splashed, it just pulled on the line with a steady resistance. As the seconds passed I sensed something directly in front of me, something big enough to block out the lightning storm, some creature I'd never heard of or seen before. I fumbled for my flashlight and with heart accelerating, turned it on. Not a metre away from my nose was a propeller, and further investigation revealed wings and a tail. A plane! I'd caught our Mission Cessna 206. I'd hooked the far wing and pulled the whole craft towards me. After regaining my composure, and disengaging my sixty-kilogram test from the wing, I grabbed my legitimate catch and headed up the jungle path to home and bed.

John Penner
Nelson, British Columbia

✉ When I was really short, my family lived at 31 Main Street, Galt, in an apartment above my father's store. The building was old, built in 1853. It had two-foot-thick stone walls, high ceilings, and long, narrow rooms. In the spring the Grand River, two blocks away, would rise with the ice and run-off, and so would all the store stock. We started on the first of March, walking all the merchandise out of the cellar, into the store. After the aisles got too narrow and the spaces behind the showcases were filled, the apartment halls, dining-room, and living-room became temporary warehousing. Wooden crates, barrels, cardboard boxes, piles of stuff in excelsior, tissue paper, or newsprint always seemed in the way. I remember small piles on every step from the cellar up to the store, then up to the apartment. "Always bring something up when you come, but let Dad put it away – he might have to find it to sell."

Sometime in mid-March, a policeman would call around to warn us of ice movement on the river, but we'd already know. The Grand River was backing up though the cellar drain. Every night after supper, Dad had to go down and bank up the coal furnace. The start of the flood was indicated by his choice of footwear. First toe rubbers over his store shoes, then floppy galoshes, followed by serious red-bottom rubber boots and finally garter-belt hip-waders. My brother and I would go down to watch Dad move through the excelsior floating in the coffee-coloured water to the furnace. He had to keep banking the cinders inside the furnace to keep the fire above the flooding. When he was done, he'd ask for his fishing rod.

This had been standing in the turn of the stairs beside the coal shovel for two weeks, all set to go. And there was my dad, standing in a flooded basement, lit by one sixty-watt bulb, in his shirt and tie, store pants and hip-waders, fishing in the far end with a spinning rod.

My brother and I sat on the rough-sawn steps, trying not to snag our pyjamas, and learned how to fish; learned how to drop a plug just beside the packing case floating thirty feet away in the dark, how to flip the bait around the stone pillar in the middle, how to delicately lift it over a soggy island of paper while retrieving, how to cast when there isn't quite four feet of headroom and nowhere to swing. My father showed off in a casual way, putting the plug just where he wanted it.

Then he'd go still, quiet, a kind of cat-alert quality. He would pause and slowly retrieve, watching – pause – turn his rod away – pause – retrieve – pause – flick the rod tip, retrieve, suddenly against something zipping the brown fantastic!

We caught seven different kinds of fish – suckers, baby carp, sunfish, catfish, and trout. There were a couple of true double-uglies we never identified. My brother and I would carry kitchen pans of brown cellar water up through the dark store to home to show Mom. We filled a flat-sided round aquarium and watched it until bedtime.

The season lasted a week and then the water retreated. Our summer began when the water disappeared and we cleaned out the debris. The store stuff went back downstairs and after the flooding had extinguished the furnace, the fire wasn't rebuilt until the next fall.

Steve Howard
Toronto

✉ My mother and I were making a trip from our home in Windsor to our cottage on the Big Rideau Lake with an overnight stop at my grandfather's farm in Ayr. My beloved goldfish was in a jar on the dashboard. The exit at Drumbo appeared suddenly out of the dark. While we and the car made the turn safely, the goldfish was not quite so lucky. The jar slid off the dashboard and smashed on the steering column. The front seat was covered with water and glass and the goldfish was flopping on the floor. My mother was relieved to find that my tears were not for myself but for the dying goldfish. She promised to save my fish. I, with a child's logic, decided to supply the fish with whatever moisture possible. I therefore proceeded to spit on the poor fish. We pulled in at the first farmhouse with lights shining. It was now near midnight. The woman opened her door to two wet, bedraggled individuals begging for water for a goldfish. My mother explained what had happened as I continued to spit on the fish. The woman stared with horror at my mother's leg. A shard of glass had cut it, fortunately not badly, but she did have blood running down the length of her calf, which neither of us had noticed. The woman bandaged my mother's leg while I got water for my fish.

A new pet was added to the family's menagerie that summer: a small grey kitten. The kitten and the goldfish were left together one day while the family was out. When we got back, only the kitten was left. She lived to be eighteen years old.

Laurie Maus
Picton, Ontario

✉ A friend of mine belongs to an old, well-established, traditional Toronto family that owns a vacation retreat on one of Ontario's many lakes. Every summer they celebrate the opening of their cottage by inviting friends and relatives up for a big fish fry, and it is considered to be the highlight of the early-summer social calendar.

On this particular occasion they purchased two fat and juicy whitefish, which they laid out on the kitchen table. The job of preparing these fish was made even more difficult thanks to the family's old cat, who used every trick in his feline book to snatch a piece of the fish for himself.

Later that evening, after the guests had devoured the first of those tasty fish, the hostess went into the kitchen to fetch the second. Much to her dismay, the fish had disappeared. Quickly, though, she put two and two together and concluded that the cat had at last been successful in his attempts at stealing that delectable morsel. The hostess ducked out the kitchen door, following a trail of condiments and fish scales, and found the old cat very dead in the laneway. She concluded that the fish was tainted and that the cat, having eaten it, had died of food poisoning.

You can imagine her dilemma as she looked down at the poisoned cat and out at her unsuspecting guests, milling about on the front lawn. How was she going to break the news to them? How was she going to treat them for food poisoning? How was this going to look on the society pages? She tried quietly informing some of her closest and most trusted friends, hoping they might offer some quick advice. But, human nature being what it is, when they heard that they had just been poisoned, they did what anyone else in the same situation might: they panicked!

The word spread rapidly and soon everyone piled into cars en route to the nearest doctor, an elderly man who ran a small clinic in an even smaller town. He was completely unprepared for that evening's onslaught of panic-stricken socialites. He did what he could to calm those waiting in his outer office while in his tiny, cramped examination room he and his beleaguered assistant pumped each and every stomach.

Weak and weary, the guests and their embarrassed but relieved hosts dragged themselves back to the cottage. As everyone fell into the place looking for a soft chair or even a bed on which to sit, the host remembered the poor cat, whose determination to have some fish had cost him his life but by whose death the rest had been saved. Thinking that he would bury the poor creature in a special spot overlooking the lake, he went out to where it still lay in the back laneway. He knelt down, only to discover that the cat his wife had figured had been poisoned by the stolen fish had in fact died of a badly crushed skull, the result of its being run over by a passing truck.

He scooped up the old thief and put him in a garbage can in the garage, deciding that he would wait until the next morning to tell his guests.

William MacLean
Toronto

✉ For eight years, I worked as the education co-ordinator at the Vancouver aquarium. The fish I found most awe-inspiring, even admirable, was a rather large common mottled grey ling cod – not even a true cod, a fish most abundant in British Columbia waters and quite highly represented at the aquarium. Let me say that my ling cod was not just any ling cod. It was a *particular* ling cod, female, and most affectionately called Lucy. Lucy, as it turns out, was anything but affectionate in my mind, but who is to question the mysterious sexual foreplay of the ling cod?

Anyway, Lucy did what every female ling cod of age does in the spring. She became enormously gravid, or laden with eggs. Now, just a quick review of fish biology. Female fish produce eggs all by themselves, then get them fertilized later, externally, by an obliging, seldom monogamous, male fish. It is a system that works rather well for them. Lucy was a huge ling cod – I estimate forty pounds or more. But when egg-bound, she grew enormously, grotesquely. Weeks would go by and she seemed to stretch herself almost so that you could imagine giant taut seams forming along her belly. Having been pregnant and overdue myself, I can fully appreciate how uncomfortable and irritable Lucy must have been.

Patrons of the aquarium would often ask if we could put Lucy out of her apparent misery by squeezing out a few eggs or giving her a more comfortable rock on which she might perch her massive bulk. But there was no comforting Lucy. Nature would have to take its course.

It wasn't as if there weren't any obliging male ling cods ready and waiting to rush to Lucy's aid when the time came. In her very large tank, there were several possible suitors – all considerably smaller than Lucy, as nature would have it. The real problem with

Lucy and her men was that the anxious males couldn't quite determine just when Lucy was ready. Obviously her signals were a little vague or misleading, for when an overzealous fellow would finally muster the courage and make a pass at Lucy, she would, in quite a matter-of-fact but oh-so-effective way, eat the male, whole, in one gulp, with her gaping mouth. She remained egg-bound. You can imagine the effect on the remaining suitors.

After a month or more in this state, late at night, Lucy "blew" her eggs. The tank became opaque-white with eggs, literally thousands of eggs. The carnivorous and perpetually voracious starfish, sea anemones, and crabs feasted on the scattered egg mass. The rest were siphoned off and unceremoniously dumped. When the white cloud cleared, Lucy was back to her pregravid, normal state, apparently totally unaffected by the experience. The males were still perched far way from Lucy, and occasionally another brave suitor would be found missing, presumed consumed in his effort to fulfil his natural urges.

This annual event went on for four or five years until it was decided that the ever-growing, ever-voracious Lucy had to go. It was simply too costly to keep replacing the men in Lucy's life – or stomach, as the case may be. But where to send Lucy? I believe, although it bears confirmation, that it was my friend and aquarium biologist Stefani Hewlett who finally decided Lucy's fate – to return from where she came: the ocean. There, I hope, she has discovered there are more fish in the sea.

Postscript: And what of the male lings? They remain in their now spacious tank, decidedly more relaxed, and if I'm not mistaken, with recognizable smiles on their faces.

Kathy Butler
Kelowna, British Columbia

✉ One afternoon, my husband, brother-in-law and I accompanied my dad fishing in his boat. The fact that I was included amazed and delighted me, for I knew nothing about fishing, never having been taken before.

Off we went, first to one favourite spot, then to another, farther up the lake, until we were in an isolated spot called the Outlet, and Dad called for the anchor to be dropped just feet away from some rocks that were barely submerged beneath the water, almost in the middle of the channel. "Nobody comes in here," said Dad; "they're afraid of these rocks."

It was very quiet after we cut the motor. There were no other boats around anywhere. Conditions were perfect and we settled in to fish. First, though, Dad lit up a big cigar, and happily chomped on it while he selected a fat minnow and attached it to his hook. My husband did the same for me and showed me how to lower my line and reel it back until the bait hovered just over the bottom. The bass lurked in the depths off those big rocks.

My husband and brother-in-law now had their lines in the water, too, and my father was relaxed against the gunwale, legs stretched out, cigar between the fingers of one hand, the other hand holding onto his fishing rod. Quiet conversation flowed easily as we sat in the gently rocking boat. I felt excited at being out fishing with the men, an afternoon away from the children. We were content just to sit there.

Suddenly, a rod bent sharply and my husband became alert. He began reeling his prize in. The fish fought furiously. At last it was brought to the side of the boat, where my brother-in-law held the net. But before the fish could be guided into the net, my brother-in-law's pole bent over; he had a bite. He handed my father the net while he worked his line. No sooner had Dad manoeuvred the net into position than *his* pole went over! Dad dropped the net and handed me his cigar to hold. Within seconds, I got a strike and excitedly began to reel in. There we were, all four of us intent on landing our fish at the same time.

Finally, they were all in the boat safely. I just sat there, wide-eyed. Suddenly I realized that the men were all laughing at me. I had needed two hands to reel in my fish – and I had put the stogie in my mouth.

Dorothy Anderson
Thornbury, Ontario

✉ I flexed my golden rod and silver spilled out, and drew a graceful arc over the mirror of blue to a spot from which shimmering rings grew to escape the bonds of the pool. The rings cast gold about my feet and I heard a gentle voice sing out. From the locus where my lure broke the stillness, two golden eyes appeared. A magic form rose above the water slowly. Giant gill plates sent silver flashes out, lighting the pines about the pool. Not scales, but myriad paisley shapes in pinks and purples and brilliant orange and yellow glistened. Their rays touched my face and we were one.

Submerged, we flew over forests of luxuriant green kelp and red and gold coral in formation with shimmering legions of strange fishes. Faster and faster we sailed, through magic caves and hollows, meeting graceful squid and rays and dolphins and seals. An aquatic symphony.

Another pull at my toe, and my eyes opened to brilliant bands of setting sunlight passing through pines – the same pines, the same pond, the same rocky stool – the same old snag! Somehow the wieners I cooked for dinner lacked that same old taste of failure. Who likes fish anyway?

Thomas Brawn
Ottawa

✉ In many ways I often thought that Howard and I were living out the old fable of "The Ant and the Grasshopper," except that Howard's string was not on a fiddle, but on a fishing reel. During the hot summer days, I worked putting away hay and grain for the winter, while Howard fished. Howard loved fishing, and each season found him at a different spot looking for a different species. The hazy hot days of summer were reserved for Norton Creek.

The creek once had been a fairly formidable stream, but ambitious and sometimes ill-advised drainage projects had changed all that. Deprived of the swamps that had acted like giant sponges and given it a steady flow all year long, the creek was now little more than a glorified and twisty drainage canal. Spring run off would cause it to rush over its banks for a week or so; then summer would find the creek's tea-coloured waters wandering through the farmlands, sluggish and weedy at its edges.

Howard seemed much like the creek. He was the sole survivor of a well-to-do family, but a series of misadventures had left him rather down-at-the-heels. Odd jobs looked after his needs and gave him plenty of time for fishing. He was slow and meandering, lacking direction and ambition – a bit weedy at the edges.

On those summer days he spent at the creek, he would put his old green rowboat into the water above our place and let it drift with the current. For the next four or five hours, the time it took him to travel about a half mile down the creek, the fly would sail out into the water, and the line would sing through the reel.

Now Howard wasn't after just any kind of fish. He was after a muskie. And he wasn't after just any muskie, but one particularly sly old fellow that Howard had met many times on that stretch of creek. Howard figured that fish must have weighed more than thirty pounds, and was maybe forty years old, or more.

Many times they had fought each other, each of them using a lifetime's supply of skills. Each time the old muskie would get in around the cat's-tails, breaking Howard's line. Again and again they would court each other, and the dance would begin anew.

I don't know if Howard ever did catch that old muskie. I don't think he really wanted to. This was Howard's last major goal, and I think he realized his life was tied to that old fish. Howard was in his early sixties when he died one winter, about a decade ago. I've often wondered if that old muskie looked for him on the next hot summer's day.

Wayne McKell
St. Chrysostome, Quebec

✉ A few years ago while attending Mount Allison University, I returned home to Louisbourg, Cape Breton, for a long weekend. Even though I arrived late in the day, my brother, a lobster fisherman, complied with my request that we go squid-jiggin'. We were on the water some time after the sun had set. It was a cloudy night that promised rain, and sure enough, just as we approached the harbour mouth, we felt the first droplets on our faces. The wind had picked up and came in from the south-east, making the water quite choppy over a slight swell. It was then that I had my first glimpse of phosphorescence in the ocean. The bow would cut into the waves and a great spray was set up. As the water hit the boat, it would suddenly flash and glow in a beautiful blue-green light. The water looked like a curtain of pastel turquoise lace as it was flung to the left and right. Then, while standing behind the cabin, I noticed that as the water was churned up by the boat's propeller, it also became possessed of the magic light. For a short distance behind us, you could make out exactly where the boat had been by tracing the glowing trail.

Finally, we stopped just outside the harbour mouth and turned off the engine. There were only two lights visible in the darkness – the beacon of the nearby lighthouse flashing its warning for rocks you couldn't see, and the sixty-watt bulb in the open cabin of the boat, up to which my brother held two jigs. If you haven't seen a jig, it's a nasty-looking hook that looks remarkably similar to the scolex of a tapeworm. (Clear as mud, right? My undergraduate degree was in biology.) In answer to my curious glances, my brother turned off the light and held up the jigs. All I could see was the blue-green glow from the jigs' phosphorescent plastic shafts. He'd held them to the bulb to infuse them with light, presumably to make them more enticing to the squid.

It was well past prime squid-jiggin' time (at dusk when they came to the surface to feed), but we put our lines out anyway. We let them fall quite a few fathoms before we started the regular pull, let out, pull, let out, pull, let out, of jigging. Just when I thought my arm was about to fall off, I felt a definite tug on the line. There is a certain thrill mixed with trepidation knowing that you have something on the line down there in the inky blackness. Not knowing what to expect, never having seen a live squid before, I started pulling up the line. After what seemed an eternity, I peered over the edge. A few fathoms down, I could discern a vague glowing blob. Just as the jig broke the surface, several things happened in close succession. First, I had a brief glimpse of a squid, its tentacles clinging to the jig, outlined in the phosphorescent glow of the water. Second, I heard a rather rude-sounding squelching noise, which was immediately followed by my face being doused with sea water. Third, I let go of the jig line. And then my brother began to laugh.

Once I'd cleaned my glasses so that I could see again, I realized what had happened. As the squid was being pulled up through the water, the disturbance set off a bioluminescent glow around the animal. When it broke the surface, it quickly contracted its mantle. In the open ocean, this would have quickly propelled it away. But in this case it only managed to fill my face with briny ocean water – at the same time emitting a sound that can best be described as the sound of a whoopee cushion. The trick to avoid this come-uppance, according to my brother, is to avert your eyes and face just before the squid reaches the surface. Grabbing the jig and flicking it over your shoulder, providing your aim is accurate, lands the squid at your feet behind you and not into the depths whence it has been removed.

Before the weather got too bad (and my stomach became too queasy), we headed back in with a small load of fifty or sixty squids. And all the way back, we were cacophonously lambasted with some of the rudest noises imaginable from our recently collected company.

Gerry Lunn
Calgary

✉ First let me introduce myself. My name is Carlton Lunn and I am the fisherman brother of Gerry Lunn, whose fish story you read recently. Hearing my brother's story inspired me, though (nothing like brotherly love, eh?) and remembering that incident made me want to tell you one of my own fishing experiences. So here's my story.

252

On a fairly uneventful-looking morning, I motored my way down the shore with the sun readying itself to begin its climb into the heavens. A radiant golden-red fan of colour made up my horizon, promising warmth and clarity for the day ahead. As with every other day of lobster fishing, I had to check my bait nets for fresh fish before I began to haul my string of traps. The mackerel were running quite heavily at the time and I had hopes of getting a good catch from three nets. I was not disappointed. My first net had about eight hundred pounds of mackerel. I decided to haul it aboard and pick the mackerel out inside the boat.

As I hauled the net with its slippery cargo over the rail, I happened to look out to sea and noticed a pod of blackfish about a quarter-mile off the starboard side. Blackfish are small whales, also called "potheads," that frequent our shore, travelling in small pods as they chase the schools of mackerel hither and yon.

Shutting down my engine, I started to work cleaning my net, letting my boat drift with the tide. A gentle wind picked at the collar of my oil jacket. After perhaps fifteen minutes, I glanced towards the area where I had first seen the whales, and my heartbeat quickened when I saw that they were only a few hundred yards away, and heading straight for me.

Abandoning my work, I arose and sat on the rail of my boat watching as about a dozen black backs alternately appeared and vanished amidst small plumes of diminishing spray emanating from their blowholes. I became mesmerized by the only sound available to my ears: the gentle lapping of water against the sides of my boat mixed with the "whoosh!" as blowholes were cleared.

Twenty feet from the boat, five whales on either side of the pod split to go around the alternate ends of my vessel, while two in the centre submerged without a whisper, gliding under my keel, turning belly to brilliant white belly as they slid below, every mark visible in the crystal-clear water. I rushed to the opposite side in time to catch the completion of this slow barrel roll; they emerged as if being born from the bowels of my boat.

There was a brief regrouping and, I swear, a taking of turns as two more broke from the pod and headed towards me again. I was ecstatic: a repeat performance! Time became non-existent for me as I was repeatedly treated to the peaceful play of creatures almost equalling the thirty-foot length of my boat. Not being satisfied with going under the boat (no doubt seeing who could come closest to my keel without touching), they decided to expose themselves, running from stern to bow, watching me with one great eye as they rolled, probably noticing the idiot grin of pleasure stuck on my face. This went on so long that I was able to tell the various members of the pod apart by the markings on their bodies.

Unfortunately the time came when I realized that the performance was over and as I looked across my boat, I saw to my astonishment a great head stuck out of the water on a forty-five-degree angle not ten feet from me! "Hello, old boy," I croaked, and in reply received a great side-to-side swish of goodbye. Then, ever so slowly, the head slipped beneath the surface, breaking the spell.

Carlton Lunn
Cape Breton, Nova Scotia

SHORT SHORT STORIES: PART TWO

Further demonstrations of the abilities of *Morningside*'s listeners' abilities to compose complete works of fiction on one typewritten page or less. This batch, by the way (there are some more later on), is just a little heavier in tone than those that first arrived.

✉ There are three main characters: the janitor sloshing his way through the usual routine, the old man who has been through it all many, many times and who never tires of it, and the young girl fresh from the country where the snow stays white in the fields between storms.

The janitor has given up all thought of love. It has failed him (and he, it) so consistently that he no longer notices the rare glances that come his way from the tenants, but rather keeps his eyes on the fine gleam that the water from his mop brings out in the old marble floor. For him, there remain only special moments in that hour before dawn when his eyes soften into the darkness and, from the sickbed of his childhood, he can hear the other children playing outdoors. This lifts him into his work clothes as the city wakes up around him.

The old man has weathered every possible opinion of him with uncanny grace, and has survived a full life devoid of meaning. The bloom of his adult years was devoted to a gloriously social alcoholic trance from which he miraculously awoke to discover that it was too late for him. His life had become a screen in front of his eyes with no depth, no future, no past. He has been consumed in an inferno, and now sits motionless, simply watching what happens.

The young girl was raped by her older brother on a brilliant summer afternoon in the same shadows of the barn where he had been savagely whipped by their father a few years earlier. None of them were ever the same. She became a demon of competitiveness, voted class queen, most likely to succeed. She moved to the city and rented a room from the janitor, glancing down at the marble floor in his lobby. Her room was next to the old man's.

These three gradually became each other's family. Their story, intermingled with a thousand other stories in the city, has already been told many times. It has the usual more or less happy ending.

Tim Crawford
Montreal

✉ "Shall I send her away, Timothy?"

"I don't know, Mother."

"I think it's best dear, don't you?"

"I suppose so, Mother. Whatever you say."

"Why, Timothy, you're thirty years old. Surely it's not a question of what *I* say, is it? If you want to see that girl it's entirely up to you. I don't care one way or the other. Although I must admit, I don't really see the point. You two never had much in common that I could see. But it's your life, dear."

The doorbell chimed again and Timothy imagined Marcie waiting patiently outside. The bright sun would highlight the gold strands in her auburn hair and add just a touch of shine to her soft, tanned skin. Marcie's large, gentle, inquisitive brown eyes would seek him out – *Tim, it's been so long. I was afraid you'd forgotten me. Why did you leave so suddenly, without a word?*

"Well, Timothy? What will you do?" His mother's voice startled him. "Having visitors today may not be a very good idea. And besides, you need your rest, dear. But if you want to make yourself sick, that's up to you. You'd better decide soon, though, because I don't want that girl hovering out there all day."

Timothy closed his eyes. "Send her away, Mother," he heard himself whisper.

By the time he reached the window and raised the blind, Marcie was walking away. Timothy watched until she disappeared from view. Outside, the bleak winter landscape framed an image of his own pale, ghostly form reflected in the glass – empty eyes, sunken chest, and vague lingerings of the elusive shadow of who he might have been. And then his mother's image loomed behind his own – tall, strong, and enveloping.

Nancy Kilpatrick
Toronto

✉ I don't remember much of the way I was before but everyone says I've changed so I guess it must be true.

I know I used to drive a truck but they took away my licence and Mary's started hiding our car keys. I don't think it's fair to say I can't drive any more after only one accident. And I didn't even hit anybody. The police car hit me.

And now everything is different. Mary makes me sleep in a room by myself. I told her I was lonely but she said I couldn't sleep with her, it would be like sleeping with a child. And that's silly. I'm bigger than the kids.

She bought me a teddy bear so I wouldn't be so lonely. I call it Ben.

But I don't like to be alone all day. Joey goes to school. Amanda's at her sitter's. I told Mary I'd go there, too. I like Mrs. Eakin. But she said Mrs. Eakin doesn't want me.

I know my wife has to work so we can have money for things. I got fired because of the accident but I wouldn't mind getting another job. But Mary says truck driving was all I knew how to do and now I can't drive. She says I've changed too much to learn anything else. But I learned our new telephone number, no problem. I just didn't think to use it last time I got lost.

It's boring being alone in the house all day. That's why I go out so much. And most times I do remember my coat if it's cold. Just some days are sunny and don't look cold.

Yesterday I tried to visit Mr. Johnson next door. I used to stay with him every day until the time I borrowed that money from him. I wanted to explain I was only going to use it to buy a bottle of wine for him and me to share. Mary doesn't leave any money in the house ever since I gave fifty dollars to an Indian I met at the bar in the King George Hotel. He needed it to buy winter coats for his six kids. I saw the kids and they didn't have any coats, but she wouldn't listen.

Mr. Johnson wouldn't listen, either. He told me to go away. So I thought I'd visit Joey in school. Mary went to see his teacher last week, so I figured it was my turn. It took me a while to find his class and then he yelled at me in front of everybody, "Go away, Dad! Go home! Get out of here!"

The teacher took me to the office and phoned Mary. She came

from work and drove me home. She didn't say anything but I figured I was in trouble again.

Last night her mother came to see her. They thought I was
watching TV but I heard everything they said.

"I don't know why you don't put him in a home," Mary's mother
said.

"You know they won't take him unless the tests show something
actually wrong with him. And the tests say he's normal."

"That's ridiculous. He's a grown man with the mind of a child.
It's too much of a burden on you."

"Well," Mary said, "I can't just turn him out on the street the
way he is. I wish they'd take him into a home."

And that's silly. I already have a home.

Amber Hayward
Hinton, Alberta

✉ I was very conspicuous. . . . Blue eyes, light hair, tanned skin.
I dabbed the sweat off my upper lip. "I wish it would rain," I
commented to the girl walking with me.

"Yes, ma'am," she said.

Manila's Pasay market was packed. Carcasses swarming with
flies, bamboo-crated chickens, brilliantly coloured fish. People pushing and laughing. Pairs of women arm in arm, loitering youths,
unemployed men.

I was too tall. I was sweating great circles to my waist. They
were all watching me. I longed to blot the river running down my
front.

"I like the look of those mangoes," I told my companion. "They
look just right."

"Yes, ma'am," she said.

She thinks I'm crazy, I thought. I should shop at Rustan's like
the other ma'ams and not drag her here and embarrass her. I
shouldn't come to her market.

"I'm going to buy some," I said as I pointed to the mangoes, and started in on my memorized phrases. The vendor talked loudly, praising the fruit. I bought them for fifteen pesos after offers and counter-offers. I felt triumphant.

"What do you think?" I asked her. "They're beauties and I got a bargain."

"Yes, ma'am," she said. She hesitated, and said, "They are worth only *nine* pesos."

We stood together, dark and tiny next to tall and fair.

It was hot and smelly and moist. I took a deep breath. The driver was waiting with the car. I was careful to avoid its hot metal as he helped me into its solitary back seat.

Mary Norris
Victoria, British Columbia

✉ The two Canadian university students, having just arrived in China, stopped in front of a store. "Look, they're selling dogs and cats for food," said the girl. "Can you believe that? Let's go in." The boy followed her into a store teeming with yelping dogs and meowing cats. In one corner cowered a small orange kitten. The girl bent down and stroked the kitten. It purred. The girl turned to her companion. "I'm not going to let this kitten be sold for food. I'm going to smuggle it back to Canada. I'm going to save this kitten." She asked the storekeeper the price of the kitten. She paid him. The storekeeper picked up the kitten and, with a deft touch, broke the kitten's neck, put it in a paper bag, and handed it to the young Canadian university student.

F. Stewart Fisher
Campbellville, Ontario

✉ Rain glittered down around the sides of the covered archway where we, members of the high-school band, had drifted for shelter. In a few minutes we would be on the field, marching in from an end zone to perform our ten-minute half-time show. It was a big effort for us teenagers. I clutched my saxophone and pulled at an ill-fitting uniform, feeling every inch the too-tall, awkward, tongue-tied fifteen-year-old. Never anywhere near the sports and cheer-leader "in" crowd, the band and its uniformed anonymity was a good hiding place for me in 1958.

Janice stood a little way off, thin and small, narrow-faced, dark, plain. We hardly knew each other. She played the clarinet, and was always on the opposite side of the band. We had not spoken outside of band functions. The band members shuffled around keep-ing warm and dry, and soon Janice and I were next to one another. After lots of silence and some comments on the rain, she asked if I would be at the school dance in a week's time. I was just too uncomfortable for dances. I made some excuse. In those days, a good many of us made excuses and stayed away. Pretty soon the bandmaster gave his signal and we formed up.

Later that year, as winter was biting in, Janice shot herself. She just loaded her father's hunting rifle, went into the family kitchen, and killed herself. We all heard what happened, of course, but the authorities hushed it up. In a few days, Janice was forgotten in our school.

I haven't thought of these incidents for twenty-nine years. Her death couldn't have had anything to do with me. I hardly knew her. Only lately have I wondered. Was I part of the failure and anguish that killed Janice? She left a note. It said she was friendless and that she disliked school. It didn't mention the band. I was a shy and naïve kid, and for years after, it never occurred to me that I could have been a part of Janice's life and death.

William Skidmore
Hyde Park, Ontario

✉ The night before, the party at the rooming house had turned into a shouting match in the kitchen. Grabbing a couple of beers, he had retired to his bedroom. She had been invited by a girlfriend, who had abandoned her sometime during the evening. With no money for a cab home, she had scrounged a blanket and found refuge curled up on the couch.

It's morning and now he stands in the kitchen surveying the wasteland of empty bottles and overflowing ashtrays. He heads towards the front door. Passing the living-room, he sees her head emerging from beneath the blanket.

"Coffee?" he asks.

"You coming back with it?" she says throwing the blanket aside and sitting up.

"Wasn't planning to," he says.

Standing, she picks up the sweater and purse she had used as a pillow. He holds the door open for her.

But the restaurant is full. So with Styrofoam cups in hand they walk to a nearby park. At the first bench he hands her his cup and, digging a newspaper out of a nearby waste container, spreads it across the seat to cover the dew. They remove the tops, take a steaming sip, and sigh.

From her purse she takes out a hairbrush and sets it on her lap. Taking the bobby-pins from her hair, she places them on the bench between them. After a few tugs, the brush begins to move smoothly through her hair. Her calm seeps into him.

Reaching for the bobby-pins, she finds they're gone. They are in his hand. One by one he presents them to her, until her hair is in place.

"Buy you breakfast?" he offers.

"Sure," she says.

Gathering up the newspaper and cups, they drop them into the container. Walking off they bump and brush, and words come easier.

Ray Button
Ottawa

CHRIS'S LIFE

Chris is Chris Czajkowski, pronounced "Tchaikovsky," as she wrote in her introductory letter to me in the fall of 1985, and her life is alone and remote and, as her regular listeners will know, rich. She introduced herself to me by mail, and I responded by asking her to keep writing, and we have stayed in touch that way ever since. If the description of her location in that first sentence sounds familiar, it is because Jim Handman, who has produced almost all the broadcasts of her correspondence – Lorna Jackson has done most of the reading – picked it up as a kind of catch-phrase.

August

✉ I live seventy-five miles from a store, and twenty-five miles from a road. I built my house with logs from the forest, and it sits in the bottom of a deep, narrow valley, close by the Atnarko River. A mountain rears high above the valley rim, and from its summit the homestead is a pale smudge in a vast coniferous sea, seven thousand feet below. Beyond it, a chaos of rock and ice stretches west to Bella Coola, and three hundred miles south to Vancouver.

Jack and Trudy Turner pre-empted the property thirty years ago, and they still farm it, keeping horses for the heavy work, and growing their own vegetables, and meat, and hay to feed their livestock. Since they came, the boundaries of the Tweedsmuir Provincial Park have enclosed the surrounding wilderness, and we have no close neighbours.

I had never built a house before, nor felled a tree, and had had very little experience with a chain-saw. First, the land had to be cleared. Trees deprived of their fellows in this ancient, virgin forest cannot stand violent winds; so everything that might fall onto the house had to be removed. Most of them were Douglas fir, many a hundred feet tall and four feet thick at the butt. The bar on the saw could not reach through them. It was nerve-wracking to stand at the foot of these giants, and devastating to watch them crash to the ground in clouds of red dust and a welter of broken branches. It was not pleasant to see four hundred years of majestic growth reduced so quickly to a dismembered carcass, the limbs laboriously piled for burning in the fall.

Most fell where I had expected them to, but a few kept me guessing or pinched tight on the saw, and one pirouetted on its stump like a ballet dancer and toppled in a totally different direction. Some got well and truly hung on their craggy armed neighbours, and some were cut through but still stood there and waited for the wind to push them over. Many were too big for house logs. I would use them later for lumber. Meanwhile, I had to scour the property for trees of the right thickness. It seemed incredible that such dense forest could yield so few straight trees.

But at last, they were all down, and pale and sticky with sap where the bark had been stripped off with an axe, and the Turners and their horses took time out from hay-making to help me haul them. It was an exciting day when the foundations were rolled onto their rocks, and the first of the wall logs was notched into place.

That fall, I had been living in a tent, but was advised to move within the safety of my house walls. There was no floor; the door hole and two window holes gaped emptily; and only half the roof was on. The day I moved, it poured with rain. I laid a few boards on the floor joists in the corner, and moved my camp, including a protesting cat, by wheelbarrow. I sat in the dry section and watched water dripping through the unfinished part of the ceiling.

That evening, as the storm cleared and the twilight gathered, the alders by the river were suddenly shaken. Next thing, a large grizzly ambled unconcernedly towards the house on a route he and his ancestors had no doubt used for generations. My window hole seemed far too big. The dog barked. The bear stopped and stared, and a puzzled expression appeared on his face. Surely this wasn't here last year? He turned and walked with dignity back into the forest.

I saw many grizzlies that fall. Poor eyesight and bad hearing gave them all a puzzled look, but as soon as they smelt me they were off in a great crashing gallop through the brush.

Finally, by the end of October, the floor was laid, the door hung, and all the windows in. I hurriedly built an insulated, grizzly-proof hen-house, dug a large hole in the rocky ground for an outhouse, and hauled my firewood, which was already under eight inches of wet snow. I had run out of money and nails, and made temporary furniture of poles tied up with bale string, and prepared to face my first winter.

After the initial fall, there was very little snow. A few thaws followed by cold spells reduced the country to glare ice, which made travel very difficult without spiked boots. I soon discovered the inadequacy of my floor insulation: the more the stove roared, the more the wind howled between the cracks in the boards, and everything more than a few feet from the stove was frozen solid. During one cold snap, I did not remove my outdoor clothes for a week!

But I enjoyed the winter, and began to explore my surroundings, travelling up and down the lakes on the ice. I continued to make mail trips approximately once a month, as I had done through the summer, although it sometimes took two days to journey each way.

Then a cold, dry spring was followed by a very hot, dry summer. The garden was so slow, even the weeds wouldn't grow, but now at last, I have peas, carrots, potatoes, broccoli, and beans all ready at once. Several quarts of round green peas and chunks of pale yellow wax beans rub shoulders with the dust-shrouded jars of meat I canned last March.

Most of the hay crop is in; the asters are a purple mist along the fences; and the bunchberries glow like embers where the sunlight reaches through the forest. The days are shorter, and the mornings, at least, are cooler. Soon the salmon will come, and the first frosts, and we must be prepared for another winter.

Yours,
Chris

September

✉ The journey to Bella Coola follows the river, and may take anything from eight hours to two days. Before the advent of the float-plane base at Nimpo, everything had to be horse-packed up here. Good trails were built, but in two places there are lakes on which the early settlers used rafts, and so the trails around them are either poor or non-existent.

Lonesome Lake is seven miles long, a sinuous sheet of water that zigzags between interlocking spurs. The sides are a series of bluffs and rock slides, which plunge below the surface to unmeasured depths. The river has pushed a long bank of willows into the head of the lake, almost cutting off the first mile and creating a shallow lagoon. I keep a canoe here; I had it flown in at the beginning of my first summer.

266

I waited at the wharf with mixed feelings, that May morning, for I had not canoed before. A sudden roar, and the orange Beaver hopped over the eastern mountain and spiralled down between the valley walls. Under its wing, a flash of teal green showed that the canoe had been strapped to a float.

The pilot taxied to the wharf, untied the boat, and flipped it into the water with a smack. It was second-hand, scraped and patched, and on land had been heavy and awkward, but when I took hold of the rope, it seemed alive, and it was amazing how lightly and easily it rode the water. The smallest of tugs brought it docilely to my feet.

A brisk wind sprang up, and when the rest of the freight had been unloaded and the plane had roared away, the little craft was jigging like a mayfly. Now how does one get in without tipping it over?

I pulled it against the wharf and tentatively stretched a foot into the bottom. Immediately, a large gap widened between my legs and I leapt back onto solid land. I tried again, with the same result. Perhaps it was the wind. With a guilty feeling of cowardice, I pulled the canoe out of the water and hiked home.

The next morning was a gem of spring willow green and dew-shine, and the lagoon was glassy. The canoe lay obediently by the wharf, and I cautiously extended my weight into it and settled onto my knees, like an illustration I'd seen in a book. I shoved myself away, and upon severing that tie with the land, I was born into a new world, which has never lost its magic.

A flick of the paddle sent the canoe sliding over the water. It was like flying; like hang-gliding over the plummeting depths of the reflections. My pea-green boat hung between the real and the upside-down world. Patches of weed swam up to meet me, and in the shadows of their forests lurked needle-sharp squaw fish and thick-scaled suckers with downward-facing mouths like gulping vacuum cleaners. A breeze blanked out the mirror world. Trembling sun flickers quivered over the sandy bottom, and wavelets tinkled against the thin hull. My dog, upon being allowed into the bow, promptly went to sleep – what a soulless companion to have at a time like that.

At the outlet of Lonesome Lake, the river is joined by Hunlen Creek. It has run through another series of lakes, and flows gently to the rim, where it leaps unbroken for a thousand feet, then atom-izes into spray at the bottom of a sunless canyon. Tons of rock have fallen into the canyon and have been spewed out as a massive boulder fan, which sprawls across the valley. After every flood, the creek cuts new channels through the wedge of pale granite, and at high water, the crossing can be dangerous.

Below it, a good trail plunges through a dark stretch of cedar swamp, an Emily Carr landscape of green and gloom, a prime place for mosquitoes in the summer and grizzlies in the fall. Huge cot-tonwoods send vast corrugated trunks into the canopy, and Devil's Clubs writhe like spiny snakes beside the boggy creeks.

After about an hour, the country opens out into the second lake, the Stillwater. This was created by a creek within living memory, and the bleached bones of the drowned forest still stand in the shallows, providing homes for tree swallows in spring and perches for eagles when the salmon run. Until recently, I had fought the swamps and the wild-rose thickets and scrambled over rock slides to reach the far end, but this summer I acquired a second canoe.

From the Stillwater to the highway is ten miles. Only three are trail, the other seven being a rough tote road, which can be driven in summer, so I thought I would portage the canoe.

I propped it up, crawled underneath it, and settled the makeshift yoke onto my shoulders. It balanced well, and I set off confidently up the trail. Within yards, my shoulders were in agony, and I searched frantically for a branch on which to hang the bow. The trail climbs twice over rocky bluffs, and the worst was going down, for I had to tip the canoe sharply forward, keep my body back, and still try to look down at the insecure footing. The river boiled at the foot of the bluffs, and the noise, trapped by the hull, boomed about my ears. The mosquitoes thought it was a great place for lunch. I rested at every available projection, and was never so thankful to reach the Stillwater.

On the last Wednesday in August, I left home when the first pink glow touched the bald rock at the top of the mountain. I carried a light camp in case I was benighted, and the dog at my heels packed, too. The lagoon was a still grey, and tendrils of mist rose like weeds. One of the greatest joys of canoeing is its silence, and I shot round a bunch of slough grass into a mob of geese, which rose in a thrashing of wings and a ringing clamour. Behind them, staring ghost-like through the shifting mist, was a large bull moose. Land animals seem bemused by a canoe, and don't seem to associate it with dreaded humans, and I paddled close to him, marvelling at his heavily muscled body and great rack of fuzzy antlers.

Low rafts of clouds gathered and lopped off the tops of the mountains, and a stiff north breeze had me working hard all down the lake. Hunlen Creek was nearly dry, and it was easy to pick a way over the ridges and gullies of the boulder fan. The wind had strengthened by the time I reached the Stillwater, and my new canoe was reluctant to co-operate.

There is too much risk of vandalism to leave my truck at the tote road. Friends often meet me, but on that day there was no one, and I walked the seven miles to the highway. That was not the end of the journey, for the first permanent resident with a telephone is at Stuie, a further ten miles. I stay here with friends who pick up my mail, and store my truck and my town clothes. In winter, traffic along the highway is scarce, but everything stops for a hitch-hiker. The summer tourists bring their prejudices into the valley with them, and for several miles, large, empty vehicles whizzed past before a tiny car squeezed me, my pack, and my dog onto a non-existent space on the back seat.

That weekend was the Bella Coola Fall Fair. To an outsider, this must be a drab spectacle. The building is an ugly asbestos arch, unlined and unadorned. The lighting is poor, the display space inadequate, and the standard of entries not always very good. I expect the PNE in Vancouver is visually more attractive, but I bet it is not half as much fun.

The Valley has a warm and lively community. In events such as these, everyone participates and no one is a stranger. On the Thursday, entries were brought in and people arrived with proud smiles clutching fat turnips, impossible cabbages, and baking and needlework and pickles. The heavy scent of flowers filled the building, and children scampered up and down with crafts and vegetable monsters.

Friday was judging day, and on the Saturday, everyone rushed in to see who had got the red cards, and who the blue. That the flowers had started to wilt and the baking looked a little dry did not matter. There was the parade, the fancy dress, the speeches, the tractor-drawn train rides for the kids, and home-made pies and hamburgers. In the afternoon, logging sports tested the skills of axe- and chain-saw-men. Our ladies' tug-of-war team could not compete with the superior weight of the girls from the Credit Union, and I am ashamed to say that in the ladies' nail-driving contest, I was not even placed.

I thoroughly enjoy my sporadic socializing, but would not do so if I lived with people all the time. I need to be alone, for it is only then that my senses are sharpened and my mind stretched. After a few days of trying to fit into the routine of others, it is always a pleasure to return to the wilderness. I seem to slide into its rhythms like a hand into an old glove. Even in a strange place, or when the weather piles on the hardships, the wild places seem comfortable to me, and in an artificial world of noise and confusion, the wilderness makes sense.

Although it rained at the fair, as it always does, we had none at home, for we receive much less precipitation than the coast. But a day or two after I had returned, the wind changed, the temperature crashed, and a wild storm drove snow well down the valley sides. As the clouds evaporated, the mountain shone in dazzling winter splendour, painted with porcelain-blue shadows. Hard frosts preserved the snow for three days while the sun shone from a cloudless sky and the blackflies tramped heavy-footed over face and arms in a frantic effort for a last feed. Their bites do not affect me much any more, but I can't get used to the crawling.

The garden was a blackened ruin, and we dug the potatoes and harvested the pea and bean vines, hanging them in the barn for cow feed. Green and orange tomatoes festoon every window sill, and our diet is suddenly full of apples as the windfalls thump relent-lessly to the ground. The weather has turned milder again, but the forest is a shimmer of colour. The pastel browns and burgundies of the sarsaparilla, the purple of the red willow, and the glowing embers of the bunchberries are scattered with the gold of the dis-carded birch trees, and the fall is upon us.

Regards,
Chris

December

✉ When the thermometer registered −32°C and I had to stoke the fire five times a night, when I had to confine my activities to within ten feet of the stove, and smash four inches of ice every day to haul water, I could feel little sympathy for the Vancouverites during their little cold snap in November. Mind you, I had no plumbing to freeze, nor driving to do, although my own progress home on the fragile new ice was slippery enough, and I was reduced to a cautious shuffle close to the shore of the lake. But at least I had no one else to bump into.

My floor insulation was still not adequate, although I was more comfortable than last year. There was no snow to bank the foun-dations, and the cold air still worked its way through the floor-boards.

The river had backed up again and solidified into amazing pat-terns of frozen swirls, each little ice ridge decorated with spiky crystals. An ice fall had built up just above the island, and water continued to spew upwards like molten rock from a volcano, and the green lava flowed and solidified down its sides. Wraiths of mist wafted from the hole and shone gold in the two brief hours of sunshine, which is all the narrow valley allows us this time of year.

My first water-hole was close to shore, but the ice grew so fast from the bottom of the river, there was soon no room for the bucket.

So I chopped another farther out over the main channel, and had to cut through fourteen inches of ice. As I broke through, water splashed everywhere and froze instantly into my clothes.

Doing the laundry was fun. I packed water to the stove for the wash, but most of my clothes are heavy wool and require a lot of rinsing, and this is easier to do in the river. I dunked each garment through the ice hole on the end of a long stick, then tossed it into a metal bucket. If left to drain on the ice, they would freeze and stick, and I have ripped clothes this way. The bucket was brought inside to thaw, and a couple of garments were dripped at a time before they could be put onto the drying rack.

A few degrees rise in temperatures took the river out. My newly chopped water-hole was swept away, and the great slabs of ice clunked and grated against each other. The water, strangely silent in its frozen prison, now made curious sucking sounds as it lapped under the jagged ice shelf.

Because of lack of feed in this rocky, rugged country, my neighbours must graze their horses in a natural swampy meadow fifteen miles upriver. This time of year, a trip to fetch them takes two days. We wanted to avoid sleeping out in − 30° weather if we could, but we were worried that a warm spell would bring rain and ice up the rocky trail, stranding the horses. So when it warmed to − 15°, and we heard of rain approaching Vancouver, we set off.

Three miles above us is Tenas Lake, a pretty oval rimmed with birch and backed by the seamed rock faces and the broken summits of Mount Ada. Above it, the river is tangled amongst a monstrous mess of windfall cedars and spruce. Three more miles brought us to Rainbow Lake, which is almost as long as Lonesome Lake. I had not been this far before, and as always was enthralled by the prospect of new country. The ice was good, with a thin crunchy surface of dry snow that hissed in the wind, and progress was excellent.

We dumped our gear where we would camp that night, then continued the short distance to Elbow Lake. The lake is deep and twisted, and the ice was unreliable, so we stayed on the trail, and eventually arrived at a windswept flat covered with curly orange slough grass and scrubby willow. It took a while, crashing through the brittle vegetation, before we heard the bells and found the animals. Black, chunky Star, fat, golden Nugget, and the two colts, Bess, with her inelegant black patches, and Tempest, with her neat Arab ears and a disposition to match her name. They were in excellent shape and dived towards our pockets for treats.

We led them back to the campsite. It was not a good one, for sleeping close to a trail in bear country is not advisable, but there was feed for the horses, and shelter amongst the trees from the wind, and the only place flat enough to lie on was the trail. The bear tracks we had seen had all been a few days old and were heading straight upriver so we hoped the cold weather had encouraged their makers to go to bed.

While we ate our stew, warmed by a great fir-bark fire, pellets of snow pattered onto our clothes. It was still quite cold, but all day we'd heard the west wind roaring over the tree-tops, and during the night the temperature rose dramatically to several degrees above freezing. It did not rain, but the warmth had licked the snow off the ice and we had to stay on the trails. In places, tiny creeks had oozed into huge cascades of ice that blocked the trail in all directions, and we had to cut a way round for the horses.

A few days before Christmas, I hiked back out to Stuie. It was cold again, and another skiff of snow provided excellent traction. Three weeks before there had still been open water, so I tested my route carefully, but nowhere was there less than eighteen inches of ice on the lake.

It is a strange sensation, standing in the middle of a frozen lake, knowing that you have only your own limited experience to rely on. You are very conscious of that thin skin, that tenuous membrane that separates you from a nasty experience. The apprehension is not helped by the noise – the terrifying pings, cracks, whines, groans, and subterranean grumbles that issue from beneath your feet like some monstrous flatulence.

There were fox and wolf tracks all over the lake, and even mice and squirrels. What were these small creatures doing so far from shore and the security of their regular haunts? Were they lost? What attracted them onto the ice in the first place?

Winter travel is rarely quiet. Snow squeaks or crunches, and once, last year, after successive rains had frozen thin layers above the main ice, I crashed along on crampons, each step a shattering discord of broken glass. Like seven miles of walking through cucumber frames.

Christmas at Stuie was great. There were all the usual Christ-massy things, a turkey, a pudding, a tree, and a five-year-old child, so we had a good excuse to make paper chains and hide secrets from each other. They had had rain, and the whole place was a skating rink. Dripping fog on the ice was especially slippery: once it was so bad that when the dog sneezed, she fell over.

I went to William's Lake to pick up my truck with its "new" second-hand motor. Everyone was Christmas shopping, but I had money only for art supplies, two hundred pounds of flour, fifty pounds of sugar, and a bucket of honey and another of molasses. I spent my last dollars on an extra layer of insulation for the floor. I filled the truck with supplies for my neighbours, and dropped everything off at Nimpo. It will be flown in to me tomorrow, weather permitting, and I can mail this letter.

The fog had cleared, and it was cold again by the time I set off for home. The mild spell had opened the channel in the Stillwater, and I was able to launch the canoe. But in one place, the river is sluggish and never free of the mountain shadow, and new ice had formed. At first, the canoe crunched through the leaf-patterned plates, but soon I came to a halt and had to ease back through the broken passage until I could drag the canoe onto the old shelf. I hauled it like a sledge for about half a mile until I could launch it again.

The sky was milky with mare's tails, and they turned pink as the sun dropped below the rim of the world. I was about three-quarters of the way up Lonesome Lake with at least two hours of travelling to do, so I hiked to a promontory and scratched around for the makings of a fire. I smashed lumps of ice with the axe, filled the billy, and crouched around the flames. Supper was soup, and tea, and turkey sandwiches.

It was a day past the full moon, and I waited an hour for it to rise. Large crystals had formed on the surface of the ice, some long like needles, some like delicate and intricate fans, and others a series of hexagonal plates. As the moon rose, they flashed like fairy fire, and the mountains sailed moon-white against the indigo sky. Surely few sights can be more beautiful.

Happy New Year,
Chris

February

✉ Lonesome Lake is famous for it trumpeter swans. A swan, with its snowy plumage and long neck, is a symbol of elegance. Have you ever wondered why a swan has a long neck? Because it grubs about underwater in the mud – hardly an elegant occupation by human standards, but as it feeds on the roots of water weeds, it is of great necessity to the swan.

The trumpeter is the world's largest waterfowl, which means it has one of the world's largest pairs of feet. In flight, they are flattened under the tail, and in the water, although very efficient as paddles and mud stirrers, they are hidden and do not mar the image of gracefulness. But on land, they are almost an embarrassment. They are black, webbed, as big as a side plate, and have claws on the toes to help the birds scramble clumsily out of the water. They turn inwards so that they often overlap, and support two short, leathery legs, slightly bowed. As the birds come in to land, these marvellous feet swing forward as brakes, and the birds slide like aircraft across the ice, colliding with any other birds unfortunate enough to be in the way. There is a great gabbling and tail-wagging while dignity is restored.

These swans used to exist all over North America, even as far south and east as Florida. Their quills were valued for pens, and their down for powder puffs, and the Hudson's Bay Company exported thousands of skins. Apart from a few attempts to reintroduce them into Ontario and Montana, they are now confined to the west coast.

They nest in Alaska, each pair requiring a large territory, but in winter, they gather in remote inlets along the Coast Range. By far the largest flock, between three and four hundred birds, comes to our valley.

They start arriving in small groups in October, and their strident honks ring against the valley walls. They work the weedy shallows on the lakes, but when these freeze, they congregate daily at Lonesome Lake, flying in long undulating ribbons of winking wings, where they receive a government-sponsored grain allowance to supplement their foraging. The feeding program was started in 1932 (at that time, this was the only known location of the swans, and their numbers had been reduced to thirty-five after a severe winter), and has been executed for the past forty-five years by my neighbour, Trudy Turner.

The swan-grain shed is at the far end of the lagoon, for there the river channel passes close to the shore. The birds have excellent eyesight, and as soon as we step onto the ice half a mile away, the chorus of trumpeting swells, and many of the birds take off to meet us. Squadrons of honking swans fly past at eye level, their wings whooshing and their pinions rattling.

It is quite something to stand in the middle of four hundred giant birds whose beaks are higher than our waists and only inches from our heads as we bend to scoop grain from the sack. The clamour becomes deafening, then suddenly muffled as the grain swishes into the water or patters onto the densely packed backs.

When the river is frozen, the swans must pick the grain off the ice, and they can do this only if the surface is firm. If it has snowed, the feedsack must be carried back and forth, honking swans in pursuit, until the snow has been sufficiently compressed by four hundred pairs of those wonderful black feet.

Despite their welfare status, these are still wild birds who spend much of their day hunting for their natural food. Sudden movements, loud noises, or a stranger in unfamiliar clothes will alarm

276

them, and when encountered away from the feeding grounds, they are very wary. Once I was hiking by the foot of the lake, several hundred yards from a flock supported by an inch of new ice. For a while, they were content to discuss my intrusion, but suddenly they panicked and took off. There was a tremendous roar as a hundred pairs of beating wings and pounding feet were amplified by the drum skin of the ice. Their shrill clamouring echoed against the valley wall long after they had disappeared from sight.

Feeding usually starts at the end of December and continues into March, when the swans begin to depart. Half a pound per bird per day means that ten to fourteen thousand pounds of grain must be brought in annually. It used to be horse-packed and rafted up the lakes, but now it is flown in from Nimpo.

Plane days can be the peak of frustration. Our problem is lack of communication. When I was last out, I had booked a plane for December thirtieth, to bring in the food I'd bought before Christ-mas. There was mail to go out, including my last letter to you. At the appointed time, ten o'clock, I was down at the lagoon. Cloud was low, so I lit a fire and waited. Four hours later, the cloud lifted, but still hung in wisps about the peaks, so it was possible that Nimpo was not clear. When the light deteriorated, I gave up and hiked home. The next day, the fog cleared around noon. Still no plane; so I left the mail, wrapped in plastic, under a tripod of poles decked with orange ribbons of survey tape. A week later, it still had not come. One night, a tremendous warm wind sprang up and beat the house with shuddering gusts. In the morning it was pour-ing with rain: the mail was still sitting on the ice. By noon it was snowing, huge white flakes tumbling thick and fast, each window a dazzling blur. At first it melted, but by evening, it was deepening, heavy wet stuff that bowed and broke the birches and slithered with solid thumps off the firs. By morning, there was fourteen inches, and it was raining again.

It rained for days, and packed the snow to icy slush and turned the surface of the lagoon to soup. On Sunday, January twelfth, the sky was clear, but the warm wind still roared, and mare's tails streamed across the mountain from the west. Several times, we heard planes of all sizes, for when the weather is bad on the coast, aircraft use our long north-south valley. The sun had left us, but still shone on the peaks, when a red Cessna flew low overhead and dipped towards the lake. I grabbed my pack and hiked down. The plane had carved a channel through the new ice on top of the soup, and beside it, shrouded in my blue tarp, was a small pile of freight. It was only half a load – no doubt the pilot had been worried about the poor conditions – so the insulation is still at Nimpo, where it will have to stay until finances permit another flight.

The next day was raining again, and the trail had become too icy for the horses. On the far side of the river was an old trail, little used, that would have to be brushed out after the recent snow. My two hundred pounds of flour, my sugar, the half-dozen boxes of groceries, and the hardware had to be loaded into the canoe and paddled upriver to the foot of the rapids. I hauled them out onto the ice shelf, then packed them onto the horses. My shopping had ridden in a truck, a plane, a canoe, and on horseback, and had taken a month to get home. Think of me when next you go to the corner store.

With regards,
Chris

March

✉ While I was house-sitting at Stuie, my dog presented me with eight puppies. I had to go through the miserable business of dispatching six, and when I wanted to return home, the other two were ten days old. They were a foot long, fat as marmots, with ineffectual legs not strong enough to lift their floppy bellies off the ground. How to carry them was the problem.

I had acquired their mother before I came to live here, and decided she would have to learn to pack to earn her keep. At first, she lagged behind, stopped in mute appeal at the slightest obstruction, and overbalanced repeatedly. She looked the picture of dejection with her tail tight between her legs, but gradually she became resigned to it, and a look back would show her tail stiffly horizontal and a most martyred expression on her face. It was over a year before she willingly accepted the pack, and although I still have to carry it for her on the steepest country and through the thickest bush, it is quite amazing to watch her think as she manoeuvres her extra bulk through windfalls and over other obstacles.

I had debated letting her take the puppies, but she sometimes bangs into rocks or falls through thin ice, so I gave her my coat and lunch, the tea billy, and other sundries, and carried the babies in the front of my shirt. The trip took eleven hours, for the trails were glazed with ice, and the shelf around the Stillwater had deteriorated, and was covered with a foot of half-frozen slush, which dragged on my legs and overflowed into my boots. The puppies travelled surprisingly well, wriggling and making little grunty noises the whole way. Every couple of hours they became more restless, and I laid my insulated sleeping mat on the ground and got the dog to feed them.

The icy remains of the snow were slow to depart. The sun was glorious at times, but the winds were brisk and cool, and the nights sharp with frost. The swans had left abruptly after the cold spell in February, and a few early migrants made an occasional attempt to sing. Big blackflies emerged from nowhere and began to buzz and batter against the sealed windows.

It is a restless time, usually too cold to sit out of doors, but too bright to stay in. The building debris in the yard was a shock as the snow receded, but nothing could be done until the surface of the ground unfroze. Gardening was out of the question, but I planted seeds of cabbages, onions, and tomatoes in plastic gallon chain-oil cans with their sides cut off. These unlovely containers crowd my sunniest window sills and I drool at the thought of fresh greens so many weeks away.

I brought twigs of alder and cottonwood inside; the alder catkins elongated immediately and shed pools of pollen over the table, and the cottonwood buds are opening slowly, filling the house with the heady scent of balsam.

Successive early winters and dry summers have seriously depleted hay reserves, and as soon as possible, my neighbours took their horses the fifteen miles upriver to Elbow Lake again. I stayed at home this time and looked after the cows. The black-and-white one is dry, and only brown-and-white Clarion needs milking. Her calf and the bull complete the herd. In summer, they are milked wherever they happen to be, but at present they are still shut up at night, and are milked in the barn.

It is a shadowy place, smelling of healthy manure and hay, and the uneven pole stanchions are dark with use. Cows are very much creatures of habit, and their routines must be strictly adhered to, to ensure co-operation. First, the loose hay, smelling of summer, is forked into the mangers. Then the cow is tied up, and the calf's muzzle removed so it can have first go. Clarion is tough to milk, and her back teats are particularly small and awkward, and so the calf is encouraged to tackle these. Meanwhile, the bull is fetched in from his day corral. He is a black, woolly Galloway, more like a bear than a bull, and is decidedly more boisterous than one would wish; so he has to be handled with great caution.

I do not milk often enough these days to keep in practice, and my hands invariably ache. My legs are too long for the stool, and my knees jam against the cow's belly. Her vast stomachs gurgle placidly close to my ear. But the cow is quiet, and the milk sings into the pail until the teats are flaccid and empty. As I leave the barn, I have a quick look around. Have I forgotten anything? But no, there is no irritated bawling, only the contented sound of munching.

Yours,
Chris

P HIL'S TOWN

If Chris Czajkowski was a familiar voice to regular *Morningside* listeners from 1986 to 1987 (well, Lorna Jackson's voice reading Chris's words), Phil Milner was, and remains, a stranger. The reason is straightforward: the letters presented here were never broadcast.

I've always regretted that. Phil Milner is a transplanted American who has settled happily into life in Antigonish, Nova Scotia. He asked us if we'd be interested in his literary observations. We said yes. He sent them in. I liked them very much. But a higher authority than I – I'm talking about Gloria Bishop, but since, as I've said earlier, our disagreements are so rare as to be insignificant, I don't want to say so in public – ruled that since he had chosen to write in a fictional format they didn't, as the old magazine rejection formula goes, "meet our needs." I still like them, and present them with pleasure here.

Oh, is Craigenputtock really Antigonish in disguise? I don't know, or care. It's somewhere in Canada.

October

✉ If you've ever driven to Cape Breton on the Trans-Canada Highway, you will remember Craigenputtock. There are two stop lights between Sydney, Cape Breton, and Moncton, New Brunswick, a distance of about five hundred kilometres, and I can see them both from my office in the high-rise. Forcing the transportation system to yield on its principle of limited access to boost the commerce of a town of five thousand people is testimony to our ability to choose cunning and effective politicians. So is the presence of the Philatelic Centre, that glass-and-stone structure, with its landscaped grounds and mercury vapour lights that appeared on St. Dunstable Street two years ago and is now our third-largest employer. So are the fine wharves in the fishing villages of Craigenputtock County, many of which were rebuilt shortly before the winds of reform blew the Liberals out of power, and our legendary MP, the Honourable John C. Cameron, into the Senate.

Like many of us with offices in the high-rise, I spend hours looking out the window. The maples are turning now, so the mountain is a different colour each day; on windy mornings a hundred seagulls and big crows huddle on the football field; in January there will be snow on the bare trees and the pulp trucks will edge up the Trans-Canada highway with their lights on; sometimes a funeral procession follows a long black Cadillac up the hill to the graveyard where I will one day be buried.

Leroy Oberlander and I were looking at that view from the coffee lounge once, and he told me this. "I looked at that highway and that cemetery for five years before it dawned on me that there are only two ways out of Craigenputtock, and I was looking at them both."

Look long enough and all sorts of things will dawn on you. Sometimes it occurs to young faculty that it is time to move on – that Craigenputtock isn't Toronto, St. Dunstable isn't the U. of T., and that the roar of traffic in the fast lane cannot even be heard in

Craigenputtock. Sometimes it dawns on people that they are trapped.

But if you keep looking, you will discover, after you have extracted all the pleasure that self-torture can offer, that the things Craigenputtock has to look at can lead you to an understanding of human limitation, mortality, and fate at a deeper level than people in more bustling places can ever know. You don't have to discover that, but you can.

The town office is in an old brick building on Main Street at the middle stop light. The big clock on the roof has Roman numerals. There is a surprisingly new sculpture of a Scottish farmer and his wife and horse on the sidewalk in front. The inscription on the plaque reads:

From the lone shieling on the misty island,
Mountains divide us and the waste of seas,
But still the blood is true, the heart is highland,
And in our dreams we see the Hebrides.

Wizened men make speeches about this longing on St. Andrew's Day and, again, at the opening ceremony of Highland Games week. I have played with the idea that my Scottish-Canadian neighbours long for Scotland the way that I, in quiet moments, long for an Indiana town that I wouldn't return to if I could.

The Pictou-Craigenputtock Regional Library uses the side entrance of the town office. It features one large room bulging with books, hissing radiators, a washroom that smells like mothballs, and Mrs. MacDougall, a librarian who loves books and can tell you about them. Through the picture window, you can see the Roma Restaurant, owned by Nick Papandropolis; and the office of the *Casket*, our weekly newspaper.

When a Winnebago is having a tough time making the tight left turn at the stop light into Mr. White's trailer court, we get a back-up. Otherwise, except for Highland Games week, the only traffic jams are after hockey matches at the arena and weekend masses at the cathedral. If you hear a horn honk in Craigenputtock, you assume that a tourist honked it.

Eighty per cent of Craigenputtock is Catholic; and we attend mass at St. Dunstable Cathedral. University students go to the chapel, where masses tend to be long on good feeling and short on sin. The United Church is at the stop light at Main and Church, and the Anglicans gather at a small but lovely place up the street beside the funeral home. The Baptists are wedged between the Highland Trailer Court and the Trans-Canada Highway. There are also two Mormon missionaries. Their faces change, but they are always clean-cut, about twenty years old, and dressed in Sunday clothes. Sometimes the Mormons knock on the doors of certain of my colleagues, who point out contradictions in Mormon thought to them. Except for arguing with the Mormons, we never discuss religion in Craigenputtock.

Until next time,
Phil

November

✉ I ate lobster for the first time in my life at a dinner party during my first year in Craigenputtock. My lobster was served up with a green salad, a pasta dish, rolls and butter, and dessert after. It was good; but somehow I had expected more. Later, I had lobster in Craigenputtock's finest restaurant, the Lobster Treat. Good, but the shell was hard; the meat was tough. I wondered what the fuss was all about. Then, one soft summer night after my third year here, a former student invited my wife and me to his cottage on the Mira River.

When you go to a lobster feed on the Mira, you go to eat lobster: no rolls and butter, no thoughtfully chosen side dishes. Also, no knives, forks, spoons, lobster shears, or nutcrackers. What there is, first, is men in ball caps. They run back and forth from the boiling pot and shout manic instructions at their wives, who are seated at a picnic table where they can admire the cuisine and compliment the chefs. On the Mira, men cook; women witness.

The picnic table is covered with copies of the *Cape Breton Post*, which serve as a tablecloth. In the centre there is a saucepan of melted butter, and a platter bulging with steaming lobsters; a bottle of Schooner beer sits beside each plate. Off to the side an inverted propane blow torch heats the lobster pot.

Here, I must tell you something that Maritime women keep from their husbands. *Anyone* can cook lobster well. If you follow this simple recipe, your lobster will be as well-cooked as anyone else's: fill a big pot half full of salt water (everyone agrees that the perfect salt water is ocean water). Once the water is boiling, drop the live lobster into the pot. Grab a lobster by the feeler every once in a while, and give the feeler a yank. When you are holding a feeler without a lobster attached, the lobster is cooked. The mystique of lobster has nothing to do with recipes.

While anyone can cook a lobster well, nobody except an expert can eat one properly. The art of the Mira lobster feed lies not in the cooking but in the eating.

First, you twist off the tail. Then, taking hold of the sides of the tail from behind, you place your thumbs against the shell on the back of tail, and push the thumbs down while you pull the front apart with your hands. It is not quite as hard to do as to describe, and if you do it right, the meat separates neatly from the shell. Then, you do something that is most impressive to those who have never seen it done. You tear off a claw, place it on the table, sharp side down, lay the palm of your left hand on top of the claw, and smash the top of your hand with your right fist. If you have done this properly, you have opened the claw, and may proceed to eat the meat. But this can be tricky. I have seen beer, shells, and butter go flying. Picnic tables, steady as they are, have shaken. If you hit the claw too hard, you embed smashed shell into the meat, and the back of your hand will sting. A good time to sip your Schooner is when someone else is smashing his lobster claw.

After you have finished the claws and the tail in this dramatic and satisfying way, you are ready to do the things that separate the Maritimer from the rest of us. You must have been born here to have the patience and the stomach to eat the legs, the tomalley (green stuff that looks as if it has been eaten before), and the roe (called "the red stuff," which tastes like crayons).

The non-Miran sits at the table, his four lobster bodies beside his plate bearing witness to his heroic eating. He wants no more lobster.

"How's she coming, b'y?" the Miran asks.

"Just fine."

"Good, eh?"

"Great," the non-Miran answers.

"Uh, what you going to do with those?" he finally asks, nodding towards the pile of bodies that sit, claws and tails removed, but otherwise shamefully untouched, in front of the non-Miran.

"I don't know," I say. "Would you like them?"

"You know, I might just pick at them a little," the Miran says.

If he gets the bodies at 9:30 P.M., he will still be picking at them at midnight. The lobster's eight legs are long and thinner than straws, but there is meat in them. So the Miran rips off a leg, sucks, bites, squeezes, and chews. Eight times. Then he turns to the green innards. The tomalley is not, contrary to what the non-Maritimer is told at a certain point in every lobster feed, the best part. When I eat the tomalley, I tell myself that soon this moment will be over and I will have passed another of life's small tests.

One topic of conversation at a lobster feed on the Mira is how to tell a male lobster from a female lobster. There are two ways. If you take a male lobster and place it on the table beside a female lobster, you discover that the female lobster has a broader tail. The other way is hard to explain but easy to demonstrate if you have a lobster in your hands. You pick up the lobster and turn it over so you can see the stomach. You will see a half dozen or so double finger-like protrusions. The uppermost protrusions are the genitals. If you flick them with your fingers, you will discover that on some lobsters they are hard and on others they are soft. If they are hard, the lobster is a male. After such knowledge, what forgiveness?

Until next time,
Phil

December

✉ I heard my first seagull at the age of thirty-two and spent my first August evening watching the sun set over the Atlantic in 1976.

I came to Craigenputtock for a job, and I wanted to belong. I set out to acquire Maritime diffidence and reticence, personality traits that I saw and admired here, and to eradicate the blunt directness that people here define, correctly I suppose, as American. I wanted to become the sort of person who had lived his life among seagulls, Scottish fiddles, salmon, and Don Messer's Jubilee.

When I came here from a land where a certain amount of posturing and pizzazz are viewed as a citizen's birthright, I was puzzled by the results of the October exams. Students for whom I could call up no faces whatsoever had written the best examination papers. They had obviously mastered the material, but they had not been moved to ask questions, to challenge my interpretations, to show me poems or short stories that they had written, or to do the other things that outstanding American students did when they took English classes. In class the next day, I singled out the faceless authors of these excellent tests. They seemed as embarrassed as they were pleased by the public attention that their accomplishments brought.

When I asked where they were from, they flashed smiles that were unique to this place. The smiles said this: "You probably won't care, but it is certainly nice of you to act interested." Then they'd say, "I'm a Caper," or "From East Bay" or "From Mabou," or St. Peters or Cheticamp or Glace Bay, and they would nod to the friends from the same place who stood in a half circle behind them, wearing identical hockey jackets and similar embarrassed smiles.

Only after I had lived here a few years did I realize that the smile also said something else: "Humble as I am, I might know a few things that a person like yourself hasn't thought of." But by the time I had figured that out, I was using the smile myself, and reacting with bemused tolerance to the airs of Ontarians and Englishmen and other Americans.

I have observed these deferential students in their candid moments – as guests in my home, in their senior seminars, in their cups at the Triangle Tavern or the Big D – and I can tell you that they understand their professors very well indeed. Nobody gets away with very much in this small place. Nobody will tell you that you are being pompous, complacent, obnoxious, or that you have a loud mouth.

"If you want to make a fool of yourself," a friend told me, "people in Craigenputtock will let you."

I am not a better person than I used to be, but I believe I am a less visibly aggressive person, a person who is more careful not to be caught posturing than my training and instincts prepared me to be. If I am, it is because I know that my pretensions, my moral failings, my affectations, and all the boasts that I do not deliver on will be noted and chuckled over by a lot of people who know me very well.

This familiarity cuts another way. When you live day in and day out with the same people, you learn that their virtues and their shortcomings are simply different spots on the same tapestry. The man who hogged the middle of the racquetball court and then smashed me in the small of the back with the ball on Wednesday brings my injured ten-year-old home from a softball game on Saturday, after he has spent three hours of his own time waiting in the out-patient room of the hospital because he couldn't get hold of me. The man who cut me off in the Jim's One Stop parking lot last Thursday is standing beside me at the eleven o'clock mass on Sunday. If I shook my fist at him in the parking lot, we would both dread the kiss of peace. I learn that the colleague who said such savage things about me at a dinner party, and whom I have been giving the cold shoulder to ever since I heard, has a daughter with leukemia; my frosty pride is revealed to me as the unworthy thing that it is. Everyone's virtues and vices are more or less public here. The lesson of small-town life is this: we are all in this together.

Craigenputtock, Nova Scotia, is an acquired taste. It is not grand, like the Rockies, or warm, like Bermuda, or bubbling with human energy, like New York City. The apples that grow on the trees in

Craigenputtock are small and hard as stones. But, if you eat enough of them, and then find yourself some place where they have only the flawless, big, juicy apples produced for the wised-up urban consumers, you miss them.

Until next time,
Phil

January

✉ One job I had during my first year at St. Dunstable was Friday afternoon ice-fetcher for the faculty bar. I would stop by Mr. White's house in front of his trailer park, knock on his door, and give the wealthiest man in town seventy-five cents. Mr. White was short; he wore gold-rimmed glasses, and his grey hair was styled in a closely cropped flat top. I would wait in his outer office while he disappeared into what looked like the kitchen and returned with my bag of ice. He'd hand me the ice, then he'd tell me some things about Craigenputtock. He told me about the Chisholms, who started with a pick-up truck and now own the Eastern Maritime Construction Company and the mall. He told me about Philburt Newell, who came here from Cape Breton, and started the Five to a Dollar; he worked hard, and now he owns houses all over town. He told me how Father Boyd transformed St. Dunstable into the major university that it is today.

Sometimes, one bag of ice wasn't enough, and I would return to Mr. White's house much later. On these occasions I would be glassy-eyed; and, standing in his heated outer office, I'd wonder if the beer on my breath was noticeable. Sometimes, on these second trips, instead of telling me about good Craigenputtockers who did well, Mr. White told me about other Craigenputtock men, men who did well for a while, but lost it. He told me about Johnny Higgins, who owned the most lucrative chicken farm in Craigenputtock County, but who reached the point where he'd just sit home and drink. When he died, there was hardly money to bury him. He told me about Louis's boys, some of them from good families; now they ride the bottle-exchange truck, and spend their evenings at the Triangle Tavern. Mr. White was a kind man, and if there was a lesson for me in these night-time stories, it was an oblique one. He told them as illustrations of the quirks of fate.

The next year, a newer faculty member took over my job as ice-fetcher, and I lost direct contact with Mr. White. I noted, however, and respected the steady improvement in his trailer court, campground, apartment-rental operation, and business headquarters. Some of my students rented from him, and I visited them in their well-heated, cleanly painted, unexploitive houses, trailers, and apartments. I met travellers who stayed all night in Craigenputtock at Mr. White's court and loved our town. Once I drank a beer with his son, quieter than Mr. White, but possessing the same confident purposefulness. I attended – another fold of my life – Chamber of Commerce meetings for a year. Mr. White spoke seldom, but when he did, everyone listened, and then hurried to implement his suggestion. He persuaded the chamber to print maps of Craigenputtock, so he could distribute them to people he met on his annual winter trip to Florida. The maps were eight-and-one-half-by-eleven-inch typing paper with black ink. They showed the Trans-Canada, Halifax, the Atlantic Ocean, Toronto, and a huge Craigenputtock. On the back, there was a list of Craigenputtock facts and virtues.

Eleven years after my days as ice man, my mother-in-law moved to town. She needed to store her furniture while she looked for a place to live. I recommended Mr. White. His storage unit turned out to be as good as I knew it would be, a room in a huge red barn for a reasonable price with excellent security, and no leaks.

When she found an apartment four months later my family took three evenings and helped her move her things. Each night I would go to Mr. White's house, knock on his door, ask for the key to his barn, and wait in the outer office while he fetched it.

He told me about the campaign to raise seven million dollars for a new hospital, about more hard-working and successful Craigenputtock families. He began to tell me about the growth of the university.

"I know about that," I said.

"*You* do," he said, the way people say it here.

"I work there."

"I see," he said.

"I've lived in Craigenputtock for eleven years," I said.

"Eleven years," he repeated.

"Eleven years used to seem like a long time to live in one place," I said.

Mr. White handed me the key to the red barn and the key to the inside storage room. He looked at me thoughtfully.

"Well, I hope you enjoy Craigenputtock," he said.

All the best,
Phil

Aspects of Living, Aspects of Death

This is tough stuff – six different writers on six different subjects, having in common only that they write about the darker side of the world. But this is part of *Morningside*, too. We deal with it as I think these letters deal with it: head on, looking for the meaning underneath.

In only a couple of cases do I know the specific incidents or stories on the radio that engendered these pieces. Facial disfigurement, which J.W. Norberg writes about from Winnipeg, had indeed been one of our subjects (I talked with a courageous woman from Ontario, and met her husband); children with Down's Syndrome, the topic Ingrid Connidis addresses so personally and eloquently, are a frequent theme; and Donna Martin, who has conquered her blindness, in fact wrote as part of the voluminous response to our series of women's panels. But Mark Leier, who had a very different kind of letter in the first *Morningside Papers*, just wrote the thoughts that open this collection because he had something he wanted to say, and so, I think, did the other writer here. Her letter is anonymous, for fairly obvious reasons, but the original was signed. In fact, as you can tell from its first sentence, it is from someone with whom I'd already exchanged letters on another subject. More proof, I suppose – if proof is needed – of how quietly common such situations are, and closer to us all than we might think.

✉ Six weeks ago, a friend of mine died. He was a man I have known since I was nine years old, and he died of AIDS. He was not quite thirty. I want to point out that I am not gay. Not to avoid any social stigma, but to emphasize that I do not have the same right to mourn him as his lover does. To emphasize that this disease strikes at all of us, gay or straight, monogamous or not. I was the only one of a circle of his straight friends who knew he was ill, and he made me promise not to tell the others.

He could always make me laugh. Not chuckle or smile, but laugh until I wept, until my stomach and cheek muscles hurt. Often we would see something and turn to each other and make the same funny retort. When I lost my virginity, I was given a lovely compliment: the woman said that she was disappointed that I hadn't saved myself for her. I replied that in fact I had, but I read a lot. When I told Randy the story, he beat me to the punch line. "Well, you do read a lot!" he said. That strange little bond is broken forever.

He told me he was sick nearly two years ago. He just announced it, then forbade any emotion or talk. I kept the promise not to tell, holding back the anger when people made gay jokes, steering the conversation away when old friends asked how Randy was or commented on how thin he looked. At the very end, he did not want to see me, largely, I believe, because he did not want to have to deal with any emotional displays. That made me angry with him, angry that gay friends had replaced me and our old circle, angry that I could not hold him and tell him I loved him, angry that he would dare to leave me like this. I wanted to lash out at his lover, who fought his own grief to tell me calmly and strongly that Randy's own preference was to not see me at the end. I wanted to shout that I had known Randy long before he had, long before Randy knew he was gay, and that I was entitled to be with him. Even as the adrenalin rushed through me, I was aware how foolish my reaction was. I knew Randy's lover was right, and, more painfully, that he knew far better than I did what Randy's needs were. Randy died that night.

Randy was not a saint. He was completely dependable: you could always depend on him to be an hour late, usually with a bizarre excuse. He would forget appointments and rendezvous. He could be hurtful, and his sarcasm could separate the layers of plywood.

I have only the dimmest idea of the torment he went through discovering, if that is the word, that he was gay in a small, tough working-class town that made heterosexual adolescence no picnic. He came out of the closet at university, and one close friend bolted. I know it hurt Randy, for certainly he needed his friends in those first years. Later, I had other glimpses of the toll being gay in this society exacts, but only glimpses, for Randy was a private man who learned to carry his own burdens without much help. We could still get together, laugh, even make the same smart-ass comments at the same time; then we'd go back to our different worlds. I was happy when Randy met a special man and fell in love, for he'd often joked about meeting a nice man and settling down and having kids. Then he learned that he had AIDS and had perhaps three years to live. He joked about that, even as he was deciding how he wanted to be buried and how we would divide up his possessions. He insisted I would get his Yma Sumac records, whether I wanted them or not.

I felt very much alone when he died. The people I am closest to now did not know Randy well, while the friends we shared from high school, with a few exceptions, are no longer friends of mine.

I could not talk with Randy's gay friends, for the terms of our mutual friendship were so different and separate. All his old friends could do was get together to note his passing. We purchased a print to hang in the lounge near the hospital bed where he died, and sent money to the AIDS support group. It is not nearly enough to do for a man who was an important part of my life, yet I can think of nothing that would be an adequate way of saying goodbye. AIDS does affect us all. Randy has paid the ultimate price of our ignorance; and all who knew him have paid, too.

Mark Leier
Burnaby, British Columbia

✉ I know the answers
    but I can't make them come.
    I am so tired
    but they won't let me sleep.
    Who's this now?
    Oh, yes, the physiotherapist.
    She's assessing the damage.
    Tomorrow she says she'll put my limbs,
    especially the left side,
    through all their normal range of motions.
    She can do what she wants –
    I don't care.

    I wish someone would put the tissue by my right hand.
    My mouth is drooling and needs wiping.
    My back is burning – I struggle to move off it.
    But in frustration
    I give up.
    I'll just try to doze until
    Someone will move me onto my side.
    Here's the nurse with another pill.
    I can't swallow it –
    I try again. Choke – cough –

breathless, but the pill is down. She's gone!
She didn't see the pleading in my eyes.
Where am I? Oh, Lord, now I remember –
I was just frightened out of my sleep.
There are hands reaching for me,
arms lifting me.
I am in a chair – oh, it's a wheelchair.
They're telling me it's good to have a change of
position –
They say it's good for my lungs.
My head is spinning and I feel faint.
They're brushing my hair
and fussing over me
telling me how nice I look
in my new floral housecoat
I've never seen it before.
Alice must have brought it and hung it in the closet –
The men would never have thought of that.

I guess I'm not going to faint after all
But they're pushing me down the hall
At breakneck speed –
the scream inside me won't come
but I can feel the tears
running over my right cheek.
I hear someone say, "Oh, no!"
Three or four nurses are suddenly gathered around me
They're angry at the young girl who was pushing my chair.
They're putting my left hand on my lap.
Where's the blood coming from?
I wish they'd tell me.
They're washing the hand off
And wrapping it in a bandage.
One nurse is telling another that my left hand
Was trailing beside the chair
As I was wheeled down the hall.

It was caught in the spokes of the wheel.
I couldn't help it. I didn't know.
I close my eyes.
When I look up I realize I'm sitting at a table.
It's a long table with a lot of other people sitting there.
They're all old.
Some are sleeping. Some are calling out.
A young girl in white is trying to quiet them.
There's another girl. What's she doing?
Putting bibs on the people –
Everyone one of these old people.
Bibs! She says it's dinner time.

I form the words
slowly
and carefully
in my mind.
I say them
over and over.
She's coming toward me.
"Here's your bib, Mrs. White, it's time to eat."
With my right hand
I grasp the wheelchair arm
tightly
and concentrate.
"I – do – *not* –
wear –
bibs!"
She stops short – hesitates
and looks at me.
I know she's seeing me
for the first time.
Her cheek touches mine –
And she hugs me.

Ruth Lee-Knight
Swift Current, Saskatchewan

✉ I am a university professor and I was thirty-three when Kari, my first child, was born. I had wanted a girl, in part because I already had two sons by marriage: they were my husband's children and became mine when we married. I was thrilled when our baby was born and was so obviously a lively little girl.

Within about ten minutes of her birth we were told that Kari had Down's Syndrome. Like many parents before us, we were taken off guard and were certain we had just heard bad news. But there was also a feeling of empathy for her, the sense that it was unfair for her to be met with disappointment after working so hard to arrive. It took several days to work through a range of emotions, but the attachment began despite them. By the second night she was staying in my room and I was getting to know her. My family, including my parents, sisters, and brothers were all falling in love with Kari.

When she was four days old, extensive tests were done and it was discovered that Kari had a hole in her heart – a ventricular septum defect – which would require surgery when she was about one. And then it didn't matter that she was retarded; all that mattered was keeping her healthy.

It takes time to adjust to having a handicapped child, no matter how much you love her. You initially mourn for the child you expected but didn't get, and then you mourn on your child's behalf for the things she will not be able to do and for her struggles. And then you think about the things your child *can* do, and how you can help her. It is a wonderful experience to make that transition, to experience life from your child's vantage point, one so different from yours, and to accept life on new terms.

New parents learn of facets of themselves they didn't dream about before. They also gain a wealth of information about raising babies and become preoccupied with their child, threatening to bore the closest of friends. I went through the same process, except more so. In addition to reading all the standard books about babies, there were also books about Down's Syndrome. When Kari was six weeks old we began the infant-stimulation program, run by the Children's Psychiatric and Research Institute in London. Once a week, our "home-worker" taught us how to help Kari develop. Kari did very well, with the exception of "gross motor skills" – feats like crawling and walking. It was suspected that her heart problems were slowing her down in this area.

I know now why children like Kari are called "special." I used to think it was patronizing, a way to make parents of handicapped children feel better. I now believe that it is the adjective that springs most naturally to mind after knowing and loving special children.

Kari was unique, partly because of the Down's Syndrome. Most people with Down's Syndrome have poor muscle tone and this makes them seem "floppy," especially when they are infants. This made Kari feel unusually cozy to hold, so relaxed, as though she comfortably moulded to fit your body. Other children felt very stiff. Retarded children are also inclined to be more placid. This meant that Kari, although very alert and sparkly, was exceptionally easy to please and make happy. Down's children tend also to be smaller than average. Kari was dainty, a nice complement to her quietly impish manner. It also made her seem precocious to strangers, who assumed she was younger than she actually was and advanced for her age.

As she grew, Kari went everywhere with me. We went shopping downtown. We joined the Mums, Pops, and Tots exercise and swim class at the Y when she was five months old. I took her to work to show her off. We went to England and Norway to visit relatives. She travelled by car, train, bus, plane, rowboat, backpack, carriage, stroller, and sleigh. It was great for her, I loved it, and she touched many strangers. Rarely did we go on an outing without someone stopping to say how lovely she was. I decided quite early on that in such cases I would let people know she had Down's Syndrome in the hope that perhaps the next time they met an older person with Down's Syndrome, they would remember the little girl who was so cute and respond more compassionately.

The sad thing about Down's Syndrome is not that you have a retarded child, but that the retardation is so often accompanied by a life-threatening physical problem. We were lucky because Kari's heart problem never seemed to cause her any suffering. She was a joyful child. We were unlucky because Kari died three days after the surgery she had to correct her heart problems.

I will never love another child as I loved Kari. In her thirteen months she showed me more about what is important in life than any person I know. Others helped me learn from her, but she was the teacher. We learned a lot about the ignorance we all have about Down's Syndrome. So much can be done, so much is possible.

It's very hard to lose a child; it's difficult to find meaning in the loss. But that her life had meaning is unquestionable. I try to focus on the joy Kari brought, especially to her family. When Kari died I lost my darling daughter, my little girl. But the lessons she taught me will be with me until I die. Kari made me grow. She taught us the limitations of intellect and the limitlessness of love and spirit; the joy of freely accepting the simplest pleasures and wonders of life; how great a parent's love can be; that what at first we may think is adversity can be the most precious of gifts. She taught us the uniqueness and importance of every life. I consider having had Kari my greatest blessing.

Ingrid Connidis
London, Ontario

✉ As a mother of four children under eleven, with a fifth child expected to join our family next August, I have been at home full-time since our first child was born. I can truthfully say that I have never felt guilty about being a career mother. I've always felt – even though, as a former teacher and psychologist, I know studies can be cited to the contrary – that the best and most critical nurturing and care-giving are usually the nurturing and care-giving that occur within the home. Rather, I have felt guilty about staying home because I am blind.

Blind since birth, I have always been made to feel that I must somehow set an example for other blind people. Oh, I have rebelled against having such a responsibility laid upon me. I believe – or say

300

I do – that everyone should be allowed to be who and what he or she can be. But I guess in a way I have accepted it, too. I attended public school at a time when blind children never went to public school. I collected two university degrees and was a thesis away from a third, and gathered enough honours and scholarships along the way to leave me without debts or any need for financial help from my family. In a world where the majority of blind persons were unemployed, I had a part-time job through graduate school and turned it into full-time employment. For the first year of marriage, I supported my university-student husband.

Then my husband took a teaching job in a small rural community. It was his first job and it was important to him. But there was no employment there for me as a blind person, regardless of what skills I had to offer. There was no public transportation, either, and my sense of independence and self-esteem took quite a tumble.

We started our family, and I gave up my dreams of being the world's greatest living psychologist and family counsellor, and, woefully untrained as a housekeeper or cook, launched my career as a full-time mother.

It hasn't been easy. I'll never be the type to sew and embroider, make jam, or grow a huge garden. Yet I love and treasure being a mother, being able to breastfeed, being able to be here when my children need me – and sometimes even when they don't.

Mothering is the most important job I'll ever do. I know that. And yet, to feel justified, I somehow have to do more. So I do mounds of community and church work, edit a province-wide church newsletter three times a year, write an occasional newspaper column, and sometimes teach adult-education courses. And in the past year or so I have been pleasantly surprised at the success I have enjoyed in public speaking. I hope I can gradually build another career possibility for myself.

These things are productive and fulfilling and fun, and I would not want to stop doing them any more than I would want to stop being a mother.

I sometimes think wistfully what a wonderful thing it would be to have a pay cheque I could wave around at the end of every month, not because of the extras it would buy, but because it would say, "Look at me. Look what I can do, I'm valuable." Why must I keep reminding myself that money is not a measure of our value in life?

Perhaps there will come a day when society, when all of us, man or woman, blind or sighted, rich or poor, will gain the confidence and courage to value ourselves, not in terms of what we do or how much we make, but in terms of who we are.

Donna C. Martin
Sedgewick, Alberta

✉ I am facially disfigured and have been so since birth. It is quite an experience to wake up and face each day and each situation of each day knowing you will have to deal with the ignorance and unfeeling behaviour of many of the people you will come in contact with. You pay a price for "being different."

There is no shame in having a disfigurement, any more than there is in being blonde, red-headed, short, or fat, or in having a beard or wearing glasses or a hearing aid, but strangers seem defensive. My disfigurement is a large birthmark affecting my left eyebrow and eyelid and people usually accuse me of having a black eye.

My wish in life has been to be the same as others so I will not be noticed. Whether I would have had a better life as Mr. Vanilla I am not sure, but I am sure it would have been less stressful.

Disfigured people must learn to deal with who they are as persons. They must learn to like themselves and have confidence in their values. Above all, they do not have to be light-years better than the next person to get along in this world – all they have to do is to be a *little* better *all the time*.

We must also learn to hold our heads high and meet each day secure in the knowledge that we are just as good as the next person. We do not have to apologize to anyone for how we look. If I could choose, I would ask for a life without a disfigurement. But that is only a starting point. Most people find some physical defect in themselves that they blame for all the failure in their life. It is what is inside a person that counts. Learn to realize what those strengths are and give yourself credit for them. Then you can take on any challenge.

J.W. Norberg
Winnipeg

✉ I am no longer living at my other address. I am in between a shelter and my own place. I had to leave very suddenly with no money and a purse filled with the most important documents: passport, marriage certificate, and all those cards with numbers that speak to computers in government offices. I am now, officially, poor. I do not feel any different. Once the decision was made to leave I was amazed at the social-welfare mechanism that started to move to help me.

This shelter allows a woman time to think over her situation. The rhythm of life here, the business of keeping the shelter clean and tidy is shared by all of us.

There is no doubt we cry. Last night, three of us sat down in various moods of down and compared the worst parts of our lives that brought us so abruptly to this place. Wife abuse in any form seems to be a human problem. Culture and religion have nothing to do with the problem. The accusations of mistrust, the inglorious put-downs are the same. The meanness that drives men to seek relief for their blackest moods is directed at the one "object" they consider their absolute right to treat as they see fit.

Some send flowers, chocolates, tearful promises of never again. "Will you seek help for this behavior?" "No. Isn't my promise good enough for you any more? Why are you leaving me?" "Because you beat me up. You say you love me in your own way – that is the saddest truth you have said to me."

The sad and tragic truth is that the men do love us in their own way. Perhaps we are all they have ever come close to loving. But they have a problem they don't want to discuss, and we don't have a lifetime to wait for them to change. It hurts, but we want to survive, too. We long for peace in our homes.

We hope, too. We laugh about our foibles, our false starts. No one talks about getting rich; instead, we speak of cleaning apartments, getting back together with scattered children. Right through the pain, we talk and even make plans without the men who have brought us to this place and this time.

Anonymous

FACING THE LAUGHTER

This is tough stuff, too. But it has a happy resolution, or at least the beginning of one. I am presenting Paul Lamphier's first letter the way he wrote it, beginning in his own awkward handwriting and then set in type with his original spelling. I wonder if you'll react as I did as you begin to work your way through this letter, and I wonder if it will slowly dawn on you, as it dawned on me, how remarkable his story really is.

A later letter from Paul, written on a word processor, is also set in type. There were a couple more in between, but I think the story, and its outcome, will be clear from this pair alone. Did the editors correct any spelling mistakes in the later letter? Maybe one or two. But we've done that in other letters as well, on other subjects.

Sept 23/88

Peter

This is a letter that was started last year, one that was put away as many times as it up brought out.

I am writing in response to your artical about talking books. They have become a passion of mine, I have always had or or atlest tried to read, ever chance I could get. But I must to my dismay reading has never been one of my strongest still skills.

As mention I started this letter last Noveber, what inspred me to write you then is in some way dealing with the talking books. Let me explane.

Last November on your Alberta report there was a artical about a 30 year old mother faced with being expelled from the university of Calgary for the lack of english skills.

The person you were talking with then proceded to read a paragraph by eith this same lady or another person, to show how bad the level of writer gram is.

There was one other thing that happen in an around the reading of that letter which I am sure noone even peck up on, either at begining or the end there was a (how can I express it) snicker or nervous laugh. I heard; an believe me thats all I heard, from that point on I swore to myself that I would face the laughter.

I am sure you are lost by all of this, I will try to explane it as briefly as possible.

The laughter I heard was not so much from the radio, but from within my memory of my school days. I was not one of the most outstanding student when it came to reading and writing. When ever it came time for someone to read out loud or read there work I would do anything to hide an the days I couldn't hide all I heard was laughter. Laughter I would never for get.

This is not a letter of a person hard done by I would be the last to complane about my situation. I am writing this letter on a num- ber of account.

First one being of thanks for the reminder of the laughter. I know this is a strange thing to be thankful for, but from that point on I have try to keep a promise to myself, one that I would hope at less try to under stand the use of the english gramer.

The second thing is on your new years day show you talk about making resolution an keeping them. We mine, (which was made to myself) was to go back to school (being univerty). Which I am pleased to say is what I am doing know.

The Therd is one of information on your part,

To say I am in university is not all that easy, the step take an information I have pick up has been remarkable for me.

The first step was to approach the university an ask about requirement need, then for the first in I admitted I have a problem with writing. So to make a long story short an I had to have a enalise do on me much to my surprise I found out I have a learning desabity, in regard to reading & writing.

This learning of the disabity was & is just the begen an of a long & hard strugle to achive the stander requid of university level.

One that is made much easy by the fact that I qualfy as some one take can get talking books from the public library as well as all my test on talking books. The world I only look at an strugled with is now open to me by these book my reading or leason to book has become one of great interest an satisfaction. In the it took me to read one book by sight I have read at less 8 tooking books.

The joy is shown all over my face.

Thanks to the kick in the but.
Paul Lamphier

✉ It has been a while since you have heard from me, there is so much that I would like to tell you about concerning my progression in learning to face the laughter. First things first. In my last letter I was highly critical of how little the university seemed to be doing with regards to disabled students. My intention might have been justified, but to be fair I was looking at it with a biased point of view. I was under the impression that this being a higher form of education they would recognize people with different habits of learning. But what I did not take into consideration was how much has been achieved in the past few years, being that, this is new ground for the educational system. What I am trying to say is that I was wrong in being so harsh, what I should have considered and had been thankful for was and is the progress that has been and continues to be made.

A part of that progress you are witnessing by this letter. No more hard to read handwritten letters, or more important essays. In the university's attempt to help the different habits of the students in a position much like my self, there are finally two word processors in the main library on campus. The machines are still rather new to me so I really can not say whether or not they will help my grades, but what I can tell you is the difference it has made in my ability to compose, without the aggravation of looking over my work and trying to read and understand what I was attempting to say. Now when I find I have misspelled a word or phrase, I can now add it without rewriting the whole page over, which was my biggest problem. Although I am just now able to start to recognize some of my mistakes, I am still having some problems. Slowing down my thoughts so I could write without losing what I was trying to say was and is one of them, another is stumbling on words I couldn't sound out properly. But they don't take the time or the energy to fix, as they did when I had to write it out by hand.

The excitement that these machines have created is really quite something to see. The people I have met when working with the processor are fellow students in somewhat the same position as myself. Although we have our troubles in different areas there is a sense of achievement, and what can only be described as a sigh of relief, that can be noticed around the campus. But there is a problem that is just now coming to light because of the machines. You see, Peter, the word processors are situated in little rooms that are not very soundproof. So when there are two or three people in one room at the same time, trying to learn how to work with the machines, there is excitement, and joy, which, in turn, leads to laughter. This time, Peter, the laughter is coming from within the rooms, and that is the problem that the university is having to deal with!

It feels good to be able to do this (write). For me it is the sole purpose in being here. The need to be able to put on paper the ideas and stories that are locked in my head is my greatest drive and incentive. The past year for me has been one of great joy and satisfaction, as well as failure and struggle. There were times when, like everyone else, I wonder what I am doing in this place. When everything at times seems to be going against me, it makes it hard to see the good in life.

What is really good is life itself, and the people I have met in my life. All have left their mark on me, as you have, Peter. I thank you for caring. There were times when I didn't think I could handle the work load and in some strange way what you did for me was just the thing to keep me going. From Room 222, in the midst of all the laughter, my deepest thanks.

Paul Lamphier
London, Ontario

THE BATTLE OF THE SEASONS

This *isn't* tough stuff. It jumps the gun a bit, if you're working your way through this book in order. (There's a chapter on winter at the end.) But I thought we could all use a little interlude here, and that you'd enjoy this dialogue in verse. I guess it's not unlike the exchange between me and Art Hister – oh, sorry, *Doctor* Art Hister – that appears earlier. Bruce Knapp is a former Beefeater who now lives in Peterborough, Ontario, from where, among other things, he publishes collections of his verse. He was on *Morningside* one day, and I asked him to read his epic about the cold. Marie Dorey must have heard it. Her response arrived two days later.

✉ I hate the blasted winter: to see the summer go:
I hate to see the freezing rain, I hate to see the snow.

I hate the blasted woollens, I hate the blasted skis.
I hate to see the grey geese go to where they'll *never* freeze!

I hate the blasted hockey. And I hate the curling, too.
I hate to shovel out my drive. I hate my frozen loo.

I hate the blasted whiteness. I hate the damn' gas bills.
I hate the bloody snowmobiles all roaring o'er the hills.

I hate the blasted snowploughs: I hate each whitened field;
I hate the blasted trucks which blind my blasted car's
    windshield!

I hate the damn' block heater, which gobbles up my dough.
I hate each blasted slip and skid as through the snow I go!

I hate the weather forecasts – a blasted wrong expression!
I hate each yuppy voice that warns of each new deep
    depression.

I hate the bloody Santas and their mercantile "Ho! Ho!"
I hate those Christmas carols on October's radio!

I hate the double glazing, which shuts out clean, fresh air.
I hate the bloody drafts, which blow despite my blasted
    care!

I hate the damned goose pimples, the runny nose I dread.
I hate each blasted red-cheeked kid. I hate each blasted sled.

I hate the blasted chilblains, which never seem to pass.
I hate to miss my footing and to sprawl upon my ass.

I hate that chilly feeling, the icicles that bunch:
I hate them dripping down my neck as through the snow I
    crunch.

I hate the blasted people – the richer they, the horrider! –
Who can afford the blasted trip to winter south in Florida!

For I'm a damned sun person who loves the long, warm
    days:
Sun-bathing in my garden in the torrid August haze.

I wish I were an ursus: that it could be my fate
To miss the whole damned winter scene and – happy! –
    hibernate.

Bruce Knapp
Peterborough, Ontario

✉ I hate to see the winter go
I hate the signs of spring
I hate the blasted blossoms
They only mean one thing:

Hornets' nests and insects
Ants upon the wing
Mosquitoes, blackflies, spiders
All manner of things that sting.

I hate the blasted pigeons
Upon my sill they sit
Hatching ugly, hawk-beaked babes
Mid filth and stench! Oh (dear).

I hate the blasted brown-eyed susans
Blowing in the breeze
And golden rod and milkweed pod
That make me gag and sneeze.

I hate the blasted summer
And planting all those flowers
Lawn mowers, slugs, and cold cuts
Kids screeching till all hours.

I'll miss my "Old Man Winter"
In his stark sterility
I dread the summer horning in
With false fragility.

I'll miss the swooshing of my skis
The taste of deep, cold powder
The laughter bouncing off the trees
The smell of steaming chowder.

I hate the blazing summer
And all her dirty tricks
Nettles, thorns, and ivy
Enough to make us sick.

I hate all those amusement parks
We go like mindless asses
Inverted on the loop-the-loop
I always lose my glasses.

I hate the loathsome house flies
That spread their germs so crudely
I hate the trillion dandelions
That poke their snouts up rudely.

I hate the blasted Blue Jay games
Balancing two beers
Is chilling, when some dolt climbs past
Spilling in my ears.

While sitting in the stadium
I hate those boorish guys
Who puff cigars and blow their smoke
Directly in my eyes.

"Go to hell," they smugly say
To me, "You're free to leave."
"With all this smoke I am in hell,"
I tell them with a sneeze.

I much prefer the wintertime
When all the bugs are dead
I love those peaceful, long, long nights
With children all in bed.

Marie Dorey
Toronto

PASSIONS FOR FOOD— AND HOW TO CONQUER THEM

So many of the responses to my appeal for people to share their private passions turned out to be about food that it was evident they deserved a chapter on their own. This is it, in which gourmets of everything from peanut butter to creamed salmon rhapsodize about their loves. To end it all: some notes on coping in the kitchen. First, though (and in case you're tempted), another matter that concerned *Morningside* listeners in the late 1980s: diets. And that, too, was started by some musings of my own.

✎ The news is not all bad. You may remember me beginning the billboards one winter morning – it was the day I was to talk to the curler Ed Werenich about how the pooh-bahs of his sport wanted *him* to lose weight – by saying, "I'm too fat." That was Friday, February sixth, and I was already four days into what I called "subsisting on bran and celery and milk with blue veins in it." I *was* too fat, too. I had seen myself on television, walking a beach with Mike Duffy, and it occurred to me Duff could hide behind me, in profile. In my television career, latest edition, I wore a lot of what I liked to think of as loose sweaters, but whenever I turned sideways you could see the bulging truth. The week before the world's most perfect grandchild arrived, my daughter, her mother, looked as if she'd inherited her figure from me. But she, my daughter, became thin again; I stayed rotund. Now, ten weeks after my public lament, I am no Evelyn Hart. But I can see my toes when I'm standing. I've taken five, count 'em five, notches in my belt. My pants are gathered at the waist, like the neck of an old marbles bag. Two separate people, moved by my wan appearance, have asked me solicitously if I'm feeling all right. And last night I got into a sports jacket I hadn't worn since 1978.

I am very boring about all this. It is not safe to ask me about vitamins, or whether there's sugar in yoghurt. I know more about which diet books are useful and which are not than you would care to hear, and I can put more self-righteousness into my order of a second mineral water or a coffee with, ahem, no sugar, than Jimmy Swaggert can inveigh in his summary of Tammy Faye Bakker's adventures with pills. A person's diet, I have come to realize, is about as interesting to his friends and colleagues as his back pain or his golf score.

That said, I now know that my recent adventures with my waistline have put me among the majority of adult Canadians of the 1980s. We have gone diet-whacky. On the plane that brought me back from Calgary, Air Canada circulated a note about what it calls "not a diet menu" – which means, of course, it is – but, and I quote, "a new concept of nutrition . . . carefully selected to meet nutritional requirements . . . less salt, fat and sugar . . . lower in calories," et cetera, et cetera. How did it taste? Still another thing I don't know. I was in the fourth row, and the light cuisine was all gone by the time the attendant was ready for my order. Since the last time I had butter, cream, white flour, sugar in my coffee, skin on my chicken, dessert with my dinner, or any of a whole lot of other things that were, or which I *thought* were, essential to my existence, it is now seventy-two days, one night and two and a half hours. Who's counting? *I'm* counting. I went on a diet after dinner – and what a dinner it was – on February 2, 1987. I stopped drinking wine or booze at that time as well, and the only reason they are not on the list I just recited is that a few evenings ago, at the end of the ninth week of my new regime, I had one glass of wine with my fish. The next night I had two glasses with my chicken salad – hold the mayo – and the night after that I had two Scotches with the first round of the Stanley Cup playoffs. The funny thing is, or funny if you know anything about my lifelong enchantment with drinking, I didn't enjoy any of those drinks very much. I may be on the wagon again. I don't know. I've actually come to *like* not drinking. Good heavens.

The thing you are supposed to announce after you have announced what I just did is how many pounds you have dropped. I don't know that, either. I know this is hard to believe. I ran into an old friend at a party the other night, someone I hadn't seen for months, and he said he'd heard I was shrinking and he wanted to know by how much.

"I don't know," I said.

"Of course you know," he replied.

"No, honestly," I said. "I don't want to *lift* myself, I just want to be . . . well, not fat any more."

"I'll bet you've lost at least ten pounds," he said.

"Ten?" I said. "More like thirty."

"See," he said, and he had me. But the truth is I haven't weighed myself since I started this plan. I stood on a bathroom scale in the hotel I was staying at in Calgary in February, but when the needle climbed past where I'd hoped it would stop I hopped off, like a guy bailing out of an airplane before it hits the mountain. I just didn't want to know. I still don't. Again, I don't know why. Maybe it's just that over the past few years I've come to associate standing on a scale with bad news, and among my failings (I am not alone in this, I know) is that one of the ways I handle bad news in my life is to refuse to take delivery of it. I don't fill in the last number on my tax form, either, until it's time to write the cheque.

✉ When I was a little girl I was always painfully thin. Like lots of kids, I was tall, gangly, all legs and elbows. My appetite, however, was voracious. Breakfast was half a pound of bacon, four eggs and (no word of a lie) ten pieces of toast with butter and jam, peanut butter, and honey. Lunch was the large meal my mother made for me, plus anything anybody in the lunchroom would give away. I remember quite clearly a dinner at a local restaurant with my family. After we all had the obligatory hamburgers and milk shakes, the rest of the family had ice cream for dessert. I had fish and chips.

Still, I gained no weight. Concerned, my mother took me to see the dietician at the local hospital. After perusing my skinny bod, she pushed a mimeographed sheet across the desk to me and announced, "More bread, two milk shakes a day. *Eat.*"

I was eating already! Five meals a day plus snacks, and I was still too thin. My ever-watchful mother was noticing other things, too. I was prone to bad temper. I was always too hot and leapt skyward like a frenzied ferret should someone approach me from behind and whisper my name. Mom blew into the doctor's office shaking me at arm's length and declared, "This is not a normal child."

Well, the doctor did some blood tests and came back to explain that I had a glandular imbalance called hyperthyroidism. Too much thyroid secretion and your body works too hard, like an over-worked engine. Thus the high body temperature, huge appetite, and weight loss. Too little thyroxin and the opposite occurs – sensitivity to cold, sluggishness, weight gain.

318

Eureka! After the diagnosis came a quick and painless proce-
dure – and I was cured! For the first time in my life, things slowed
down. My speech sounded to my ears like a 45 played at 33 RPM,
and my movements seemed dreamily languid, almost like I was
underwater. "Life is good," I said, as I ate a Big Mac, Fishburger,
a Chickenburger, two large fries, and a Coke.

By then I was well into my late teens and it's not too difficult
to figure out what happened to me. I simply followed the eating
pattern I had established in my life *pre-cure*, and kept the image of
myself firmly rooted in my mind. I was a *thin* person. Then, one
day, months and pounds later I caught sight of one of those awful
fat people walking down the street towards me – the double chin,
eyes like raisins afloat in a bowl of rice pudding, the rolling
flab doing 180° rotations around the thigh bone. Yes, it was me,
reflected in a storefront mirror. I was *fat*. Not cherubic, not
voluptuous, not plump. *Fat.*

I went back to my doctor. I begged. I wheedled. I cajoled. This
was unfair. I was a *thin* person. This was all a mistake. I wanted
drugs, stomach staples, my thyroid back, anything. She smiled and
slid a mimeographed sheet across the desk. "Cut back on breads,
avoid dairy products – *Don't Eat!*"

I went home and decided then and there. Me, fat? Ha! This
should be easy. I tried every diet known to man. The banana diet,
the protein diet, the diets named after doctors, the diets named
after celebrities, diets that weren't diets at all but were "eating
programs." I tried the chewing gum that numbs your mouth and
some evil-smelling horse-sized pills that when taken with copious
amounts of water were supposed to sproing into shapes rivaling a
toaster once they hit your stomach.

None of this worked. I don't know about you, but my stomach
isn't where I get hungry. I get hungry in my eyes when I watch
those steaming pieces of cheese-draped pizza being dragged backwards out of the pan on the television. I get hungry in my nose
when I pass the open door at the Colonel's, and in my ears when
I hear someone describe some incredible meal they enjoyed.

Real-and-for-true hunger rarely enters into it.

So now I go day by day. So far I have lost fifteen pounds. I zap those commercials on the television, avoid fast-food outlets like the plague, and change the subject when friends, with the same addiction I have, start going into orgasmic caloric detail about their last binge. I've stopped trying to get my poor old thirty-three-year-old body to look like those sylph-like creatures that flit through the glossy pages of the magazines I buy. They are not normal humans. I could not be that thin through the torso *and* retain my liver. I no longer "diet." Diets make me want to eat.

See? I always knew it would be easy.

Trudy Urquhart
Vancouver

✉ When I was thirteen, my mother took me and my siblings to Buffalo to buy some clothes for Easter. She didn't tell me beforehand that she was aiming to buy for me a brand called "Chubettes"!

Everything I tried on with that label was enormous, so I felt vindicated, but by then, of course, I was sensitized to the fact that my mother thought I was fat. That summer, at Lake of the Woods, I went on a smelling diet (my own invention), in which one is allowed to smell everything in the kitchen and pantry, but only allowed to eat tuna fish and rabbit food. It worked well, and I was quite a hit when I returned to school that fall.

Since then, I've been on low carbohydrates and high carbohydrates. I've used ketostix to see if I'm burning enough fat molecules. I've tried lecithin and vitamin B, herbalife, and wallpaper paste (it certainly tasted like it). I was on the Scarsdale diet (but look what happened to him), and the Dr. Abravanel's Body Type Diet, which divides body types into groups according to which endrocrine gland is underactive. They ask you a lot of embarrassing questions about your sex life, the answers to which you wouldn't want your children to read.

More expensive were the clubs I joined. Weight Watchers, in 1970, was the embarrassment of my life, because I wasn't very fat at all, and lost the most weight of anyone in the class during the first week. They made me stand up in front of people who had to sit on two chairs to "share" my success! (It's a wonder they didn't sit on me.) At Face and Figure they showed me pictures of fat people in their underwear, and threatened to photograph me in mine! I didn't spend any money on that one. Nutri System is a little more respectful, but I found it very boring. It is difficult to feed a family and not eat with them – food and nurturing are all so bound up with each other – and no one else shares my very efficient metabolism.

Once my father stood up at the dining-room table, pounded his fist on it, and loudly declared, "I have never to my knowledge committed an athletic act." Since his death, in 1966, I have joined about ten health clubs and practised serious yoga (including vegetarianism and fasting). I am sorry to confess that I have jogged. Presently I play squash, but not competitively, and swim, which everyone says is the best, but somehow it seems too easy.

I can't remember all the seven deadly sins, but gluttony, lust, and avarice are all sins of wanting more. Wanting More is also what brought the apes out of the trees and started us on the road to Homo Sapiens and the space age. It's all a vicious circle – and that brings me to my advanced smelling diet. A baker of muffins and cheesecakes has recently moved into the front of my pottery studio, and the smelling is no longer voluntary.

If I were not so neurotic about losing weight, I wouldn't have lost the 300 pounds I've gained (and lost) over the past fifteen years, and I'd weigh 449½ lbs today!

Mary Lazier
Scarborough, Ontario

✉ It occurs to me, while I stand here stirring and listening to *Morningside*, that one of the magic things about motherhood is that you can make jam. I mean *jam* – the cohesive fruity mixture, filled with minute seeds, not overly sweet, not tastelessly sour, not runny, not hard, not too dark, not too pale. It smells and looks gorgeous and makes an indisputable statement at the breakfast table: "The lady that made me is a mother."

Before you are a mother, you can't make jam. It stubbornly refuses to congeal, the seeds precipitate to the bottom of the jar, and it will develop an enthusiastic layer of green mould all over the top.

Before I had Theresa, I could stand beside my mother and repeat, berry for berry, her recipe for jam. Hers would be fabulous, mine would dribble. My husband would consolingly say, "Never mind, it'll make terrific ice-cream sauce!"

I would wait until Mother left, then sneak bottles of Certo out of the cupboard and boil it up again. Ice-cream sauce. I would let it boil for two hours! Ice-cream sauce.

The day I discovered I was pregnant was the day I discovered I could make jam. I could make raspberry jam, I could make plum jam, I could make strawberry jam, I could make gooseberry jam, I could make pomegranate jam, I could even make marmalade.

I could take outdated frozen fruit, identity unknown, which had been buried in the bottom of the freezer, and turn it into a compote that would break your heart.

Breakfasts were greeted with applause for the cook.

Then I discovered that the old tradition of waxing the top is strictly for theatrical effect – especially where it pertains to raspberry jam. Anybody who keeps raspberry jam around long enough for it to go mouldy is probably deceased. The wax is for the anticipation.

The mother unscrews the yellow metal top from a dusty old jar, and there, underneath, pristine and virginal, is the clam shell of paraffin. Gently, with a silver knife, she eases the wax carapace up the edge, slowly, slowly. "Aah," the children sigh.

You do this, of course, in front of the children. Mothers need all the admiration they can get.

Gail Mackay
North Vancouver

✉ I realized when I was a child that, willingly or not, someday I was supposed to outgrow certain things. I paid great attention to the fact that adults had no need or desire for milk, Kool-aid, or Batman. They didn't wear their mittens on a string. I presumed that peanut butter would disappear from my life accordingly. I never saw my father with a knife in the peanut-butter jar, and grandparents didn't even have peanut butter in their cupboards.

Then my father made friends with a lady whose lust for the brown stuff made my eyes bulge. When she came to visit I would rush down to the kitchen to greet her, knowing I would find her reaching in the cupboard where the jar of peanut butter stood. She would grab the jar, help herself to a spoon, and plunk herself down at the table to chat with my father. Within half an hour she could spoon down one-third of the jar of peanut butter as casually as my father smoked five cigarettes. Sometimes she would take a banana from the bowl on the kitchen table, peel it, and delicately spoon some peanut butter on top. Then she would bite off the top and proceed to spoon on some more. Wow! How could my father let her do that? I was impressed. Not only could I eat peanut butter when I grew up, but I could eat it any old way I pleased.

My brother and I called her the Peanut Butter Lady. I used to ask my friends over to witness the phenomenon. She was the next-best show to Johnny across the street. (He could throw up on request, and that was very hard to beat.)

I'm thirty now, and for all its wonderful qualities, peanut butter still gives me the odd ugly pimple. So periodically I have to go off it. I don't last long, though. This past summer I lasted three weeks. Breakfast was a letdown; toast without peanut butter was so disappointing. But I was determined to get peanut butter out of my life, for the sake of a clear complexion. Then one day, I ran into a grocery store to buy some cat food and there, down the aisle, was a magnificent display of peanut butter – on sale! I heaved a happy sigh as I bought a jar. My boyfriend shook his head as I slapped it on an English muffin. He gave me a foreboding look, as if to say, "It's got you under its lid." But two days later I caught him spreading it on his hot dog. Give me a peanut-butter-and-banana sandwich and I'm smiling for the rest of the day. I'm not the sort to spoon it into my mouth straight from the jar like the Peanut Butter Lady, but I'm indebted to her for showing me that I, too, could grow old with that smooth brown spread.

Sara McCormack
Toronto

✉ I love creamed salmon, made, of course, with frozen peas. I know, I know, it's nursery food; but surely a little nostalgia is an acceptable thing. Sometimes, creamed salmon reminds me of Mrs. McGregor's Grade Eight Home Ec. class, where, as I recall, every recipe we learned started with "Take one package of Bisquick." We made Bisquick biscuits, pie shells, tarts, and Christmas-tree decorations. Bisquick was the bulwark of the modern woman's kitchen. Bisquick was the future. Everything was made with Bisquick except creamed salmon, which was served with toast tips. It was in Mrs. McGregor's class that we learned how to make the cornerstone of creamed salmon – white sauce. We did not learn how to make white sauce as the first step toward Béchamel. Oh, no. We learned how to make white sauce so we knew how to make white sauce. An end in itself.

Most often, creamed salmon reminds me of home. It was served in our home on only two very distinct and very special occasions; first, when my father was not coming home for dinner and it was just Mum and the kids; and second, when – and even now my heart stops at the thought of it – the teacher was invited to lunch at your house.

Whether real or imaginary, there was a protocol to these lunches. Grade four to grade seven teachers were served salmon loaf. The grade eight teacher ate tuna casserole. But my favourite days were when we had teachers from kindergarten to grade three. *Those* teachers ate creamed salmon.

Lynda Weston
Stratford, Ontario

324

✉ My secret passion is snack-bread crackers and process-cheese sandwiches!

I particularly like them during Blue Jay baseball games, although the Expos or the Tigers will do! I feel dirty – especially about the process cheese – and I know I'm beyond help, but there it is – we are all alone in this life – we are born solitary and free, and we will die that way – making round pots, watching television baseball, and eating snack-bread (whole-wheat) crackers and process cheese! But one more thing, and I'm not sure I'm brave enough. Here goes: I sometimes drink cheap Scotch whisky and soda with the sand-wiches – not very much, because I need to follow the games, and snack bread is expensive!

Jack Ouellette
Arichat, Nova Scotia

✉ For me, life in Canada is divided into two seasons: winter and mango season. Once they begin arriving at my local West Indian store, my life is driven by my desire for these fruit. At a dollar fifty or more each, it is not an inexpensive passion to indulge, but indulge I do. Each day on my way home from work, I make one stop at the store – to feel, and smell, and *always* to buy these fruit that change me from a generous, open, honest woman into the most unfeeling, unconscionable, lying brute.

I sacrifice *all* relationships for these fruit: conjugal, filial, and parental. When I buy mangoes, they are mine; and only in the rarest of situations might I give a face of one – yes, they do have faces or cheeks – to someone, but only rarely. I hide them un-ashamedly; eat them when no one is around so I won't have to share and, what's worse, feel no guilt, no moral compunction about my actions. Is this a passion, or is this an affliction? Greed and gluttony, two deadly sins satisfied in one fruit.

How to tell of the sensual, secretive pleasure of eating mangoes? Partly because I hate to watch the faces of my family as they stare at me eating three or four or five mangoes – having shared maybe *one* – I like to eat mine alone. Also, there is an intensity that comes from eating this fruit alone. First you squeeze the flesh a bit to make it soft; then bite a tiny, a very tiny hole in the top of the mango; then you suck on the mango, squeezing the juice slowly up into your mouth. Is this a passion, or is this a passion?

Marlene Nourbese Philip
Toronto

✉ Roasted Red Peppers are one of the Great Tastes. They're simple to prepare. First they are broiled until blackened and blistered, then sealed tightly in a paper bag until they're cool enough to handle. Then you simply slip off the skins and remove the seeds. They're delicious with a little chopped parsley, lemon juice, and olive oil.

I always have the best of intentions for this wonderful food, planning to purée them for a bright red, slightly sweet sauce or cut them into strips for inclusion in a salad. But somehow they never make it. I nibble a few pieces, I eat a few more, then, after devouring several more bites, I see in alarm that there are hardly enough left for the intended dish, so I eat those few pieces, too. The only solution I can see to this dilemma is more peppers.

Lately, I've been growing my own. And my passion for peppers has led to drastic reshaping of limited garden space. Onions are out, beans have been banished, even tomatoes have been curtailed in favour of more room for peppers. But it's still not enough; I need *more* garden space. Maybe next year, we could do without some of those good-for-nothing flowers. . . .

Barbara Bickell
Whitby, Ontario

✉ Bananas – I love them! Sometimes I feel God created them just for me.

My earliest recollection of this attraction is of my grandmother storing hers in a white enamelled cupboard in the kitchen. I used to stand in front of it, wordless, until she reached in and gave me a banana. I remember my father coming home from the grocery store late one Saturday afternoon with a cardboard box full of ripe bananas. The box was only a dollar because the store wouldn't keep the bananas over the weekend. He laughed and said they should keep me happy for a while. I recall sliced bananas and milk, bananas on my cereal, warm banana bread, ice-cold banana popsicles (a flavour that has disappeared), banana splits, and, of course, the peanut-butter-and-banana sandwich.

When I got older I found new ways to enjoy my passion fruit. I tried flambéing bananas, barbecued bananas, and bananas dipped in semi-sweet chocolate. One winter in Cuba I drank a quantity of banana liquor at the bar on the beach for fifty cents a shot. That was a wonderful vacation. My favourite indulgence is eating bananas straight up, raw, as it were. I do not eat them daintily on a plate, or in the monkey manner, skin peeled down while I chomp. Instead, I remove the entire skin and eat the banana out of my hand. This enables me to enjoy the full flavour of my banana without the bother of the empty skin after the last bite. Of course, I'm not talking about one banana now and again. I eat bananas until they're gone – and then I buy more. I admit to greedily eyeing my two-year-old's leftovers and polishing them off with relish.

Andrea Bishop
Burlington, Ontario

✉ I have hammered into my family's brains the idea that junk food will rot your teeth, bung up your bowels, stop your bones from growing straight, produce giant zits, and cause you to fail maths.

I bake only brown bread. I make my own soups to get away from those horrible preservatives. I try to have two meatless meals a week, and when I bake cakes and cookies, I put bran, whole wheat, nuts, raisins, apples, and other healthy things into them.

Now, having said that, I wonder if I dare admit what my secret passion is. I guess it's really an addiction. It hit me again just the other day when I was standing at the check-out of my local grocery. I hadn't had any for two weeks and I was feeling pretty good about it, when someone leaned around me and grabbed something off the shelf beside me. I heard the crackle of cellophane and I knew without looking around what was in that package she was opening for the five-year-old at her side. I tried to ignore them, but then I smelled that delectable, slightly medicinal scent of my secret passion: red licorice.

Quickly and calmly, without looking at anyone in the lineup, I leaned over and stuffed a big package of red twizzlers under my Brussels sprouts and frozen cod. The clerk didn't bat an eyelash when she pushed them through. I resisted them in the car, but when I got home, I opened the packaged with palsied hands, rolled a soft perfumed twizzler into a snail coil, and stuffed the whole thing into my mouth.

After devouring five while I unpacked the groceries, I realized with a sudden surge of panic that I had to get rid of the rest before the family got home.

I'd already been humiliated once, when my daughter found a half-eaten package behind one of the pillows on the living-room couch. I had thought they were safe there. Everyone hangs around in the den watching television, and the living-room is rarely utilized. I'd used that couch as a storeroom for months. That way, when I was alone in the afternoon, I could lie on it, read a good book, and eat twizzlers. Then I could leisurely pick the gummy bits out of my teeth and revel in the after-taste for at least an hour before having to brush my teeth and tongue to remove the evidence.

Right now, I'm using my little office in the basement as a hiding place. It's where I'm writing the novel of the century. I have to be very careful, because my family thinks the office is their supply room for pens and pencils and anything else they need for school.

I've been really clever this time, though. I stashed the stuff in my empty typewriter case, beside my desk. I wish I'd thought of it sooner. This way, I can have a red beauty hanging out of my mouth while I write – like I'm doing right now. It leaves both hands free for the typewriter, and if you're an old mainliner like me, you can inch your way through about two twizzlers a page. Ah, rarely has debasement seemed so sweet.

Margaret Macfarlane
Winnipeg

✉ I cannot cook. Tales of my culinary failures are legendary: cookies the dog couldn't chew; pumpkin pie and chocolate cake that blew up; right on to the time I served strawberry jam instead of cranberry sauce with the Christmas turkey. (They *were* in identical bottles!)

My children all learned to cook at an early age. They called it survival. When they were living at home, we ate at a very late hour. The strategy behind this was that the starving will eat anything. The meal would be punctuated by, "Gravy? One lump or two?" or "What were those little black things?" In self-defence, as camouflage, or just because of a perverse curiosity, I have begun collecting kitchen items from the past. Cookbooks, utensils, or cupboards – they all find a place in my kitchen. An eighteenth-century recipe prepared in a nineteenth-century bowl and cooked on a twentieth-century stove – who can honestly say what it is supposed to taste like?

Garage sales are a treasure trove for collectors like me. Estate sales are shunned by the serious collector of fine things, because the valuable items have usually been pre-sold to dealers. That leaves the sellers with a few hundred items, mostly from Great-Aunt Clara's kitchen. I console myself by thinking, "She probably couldn't cook either," as I dive into the piles of tin cookie cutters, rusted old knives, blackened silver flatware, and the inevitable assortment of K-Tel plastics.

I have to justify every item in my collection. The meat tenderizer, while useless with its loose handle, might come in handy as a weapon. The chart of equivalents (obviously pre-metric) tells me that two wineglasses equal one gill and two gills equal one tumbler.

Miss Parloa's New 1880 Cook Book is fascinating, all of its seventy-one pages. She advises to boil fresh string beans or carrots for one to two hours, and beets from one to five hours. I like that kind of flexibility. Her main dishes include Larded Quail, Pigeons in Jelly, Saddle of Venison, Escaloped Tongue and Dropped Fish Balls. For dessert, we could try her Bird's Nest Pudding or Black Pudding. I've made vanilla pudding that could have qualified for the latter on more than one occasion.

I have a nut chopper, an onion chopper, an ice-cream maker, a hand-held potato ricer that weighs eight pounds without the potatoes, a meat grinder with one blade missing, and a three-gallon crock and lid that the owner told me is the right size for preserving eggs in waterglass. Should I ever raise chickens, it might come in handy.

I bought an old kitchen cabinet that has a handy printed grocery list on the inside of the door. Among the everyday items like bananas, kerosene, lye, and lamp wicks, there are three that have me baffled: Bulgarzoon, Sapolio, and Bath Bricks. Bulgarzoon, incidentally, comes in a bottle and has 130 calories.

Diane Armstrong
South Porcupine, Ontario

MORNINGSIDE BESTIARY

This is a sampling of some of the wildlife we've reported on over the years, which has ranged, in the words of Glen Allen, who tends to mastermind many of these items, "from Barbados black-bellied sheep through horned vipers, prolific boa constrictors, and dung beetles to birds in the back yard." They're not all here, which is okay by me, since I have, as most listeners to *Morningside* know – certainly Elizabeth Creith does – an aversion to snakes.

This opens with chickens. As I hope you noticed earlier, Stuart McLean started this. Or maybe Margaret Visser did. Anyway, someone was talking about whether chickens were smart, and later someone else was talking about whether they're carnivorous. It ends with things that fall from the sky. There's a lot of other fauna in between.

CHICKENS HAVE NEVER INVENTED A
P.C.B., OR HARPOONED A WHALE,
OR ROBBED A VARIETY STORE,
OR RUN FOR PUBLIC OFFICE, OR
MINED A HARBOUR, OR OWNED
A HULA HOOP, OR MADE A PUN,
OR SHOT A DUCK, OR OWNED
A SLAVE, OR RECITED A LIMERICK,
OR SPIT IN SOMEONES BEER, OR
DRIVEN WHILE DRUNK, OR SUNK
A SHIP, OR BROKE A PROMISE,
OR HUNG WALLPAPER, OR SUNG
"MARES EAT OATS", OR WRESTLED
ON NATIONAL T.V., OR PROMOTED
PEOPLE SOUP AS A CURE-ALL
ELIXIR, OR BET ON A SLOW HORSE,
OR BOMBED A CR... ED AIRPORT,
OR DEBATED THE ... OF CA...
PUNISHMENT, OR S... OUR ...TED
IN GINGERALE, OR B... RID,
OR EATEN A MOOSE ... ETC.

AND YOU GUYS
CALL US
STUPID?

- Transcribed from a conversation with Terry the chicken.

332

✉ Until a recent assault by a stupid fox, my wife and I were the proud neighbours of two sensible and articulate hens. They lived in the small coop beside our house.

They were sensible in that they understood that I was capable of procuring epicurian delicacies far exceeding the normal four-grain fare common to the poultry yard. As chicks, they soon learned that I was useful for scratching up earthworms and June-bug larvae with a digging fork, or revealing a moist, earthen plate of snow bugs, ants, slugs, or baby field mice simply by flipping a field stone. They learned to come arunning whenever I called.

As our relationship matured, they would follow me around the yard and would respond to my calls from the back door either by awkwardly jogging from the far reaches of our half-acre, or clucking contendedly from their dusting holes under the back porch. Regardless of whether I called them in English, French, or Japanese they would always respond. How many people do you know that can respond to three languages?

They were also sensible, in that they could discriminate between proper and improper, good and bad food. Bees, for instance, are insects. Chickens eat insects. Cats and dogs aren't known for their entomological appetites. However, I have witnessed a dog chomp down a misdirected bumble bee, and our cat has had sparring matches with the occasional hornet, trapped between the sheers and window in our living-room. Stupid dog. Stupid cat. I never once saw a chicken attack a bee. They would notice, scrutinize, and disregard even the most plump and available bee morsel. (They would perhaps eat the flower, once the bee had left.)

At a barbecue in our back yard, our chicken neighbours were congenial and friendly, mingling with the guests and sharing bits of hamburger bun. They were not afraid to broaden their palates and became quite adept at leaping, grabbing, and devouring the hot dogs from the partiers. Then they gobbled down the discarded empty buns with some degree of relish.

Chickens also have a vocabulary. Granted, it is one of squawks, clucks, coos, and intonation rather than words, but one can learn to understand them. Our hens uttered a cooing warble, which meant "we love laying here with the bright sun beating down on our black outstretched wings" or a clucking warble, which served as a lullaby "to my unhatched eggs, which I am protecting and turning and warming with my body."

Then they had a sharp, high-pitched warble, when one of them would insist, "Okay, one of you baby chicks has wandered too far from me, come back and get some food," as well as an abrupt, short cluck accompanied by a rolled head so one eye stared skyward, which meant "hawk" or "predator" or "Boeing 747," usually followed by a dog or raccoon or fox.

On reflection, though, they never did learn to roll over, or fetch a ball, or unbutton a cardigan. Stupid chickens.

Dave Cox
Glen Williams, Ontario

✉ Chickens are stupid, terribly so; but only *some* chickens. You see, there are two distinct types of chicken: egg-laying chickens and meat chickens. Egg-layers are reasonably intelligent. They have personalities, a pecking order in the flock, a definite routine for their day, and certainly an affinity for the one who feeds them. They also can be beautiful and quite sociable.

Then there are meat chickens, "meat kings" as I call them. They are bred and raised for meat. They are terribly stupid and have no redeeming qualities. They live to eat and sit. I suppose this is a divine plan so that, come slaughtering time, you hate the damn things so much that it brings a small pleasure to kill them. God knows, anything that brings any pleasure to the plucking of a seven-pound construction of bones, meat, and feathers is appreciated.

But turkeys – now turkeys are a breed unto themselves. They are marvellous. Stately, curious, of a genius level when compared to a meat king, and a high achiever when compared to an egg-layer. They are sociable, talkative, and street smart.

Kate Carmichael
Lunenberg, Nova Scotia

✉ On Christmas Day a few years ago, I went out to feed the chickens a little later than normal, because it was, after all, a holiday. On that morning, one hen in particular did not hang around to eat, but instead began following me along the well-trodden path through the snow. When I reached the porch she was still there, eight feet behind me. Amused and curious, I went into the house, leaving the inner door open a crack, wondering just how far she'd come. She marched right into the house for a Christmas visit. The cats were shocked as the hen sampled their food, and the budgie was thrilled that one of the birds he watched out the window had come in.

We thought this was just an amusing Christmas gift from the universe, so we were even more surprised when the next day, at the same time, that hen came into the porch, hopped up on a box, and knocked on the window to be let in. These daily visits continued for a couple of weeks; after a while, a second hen ventured to accompany the first. We have pictures of the hen and the budgie both eating out of the cat dishes.

We had one little rooster that was part Bantam. A tiny little guy with bright plumage, his tail was bigger than his whole body. He reminded of me one of those seventeenth-century courtiers dressed in satin and lace. Despite the fact that he had fighting spurs, his small size insured he was picked on unmercifully by the other roosters. We named him Genghis Khan and isolated him from the others for a while. He became a pet and followed my wife around as she did her gardening. She would hold her arm out, slap it, and call to him, and he would jump up on her arm and start crowing, very pleased with himself. He also responded to flattery. When friends were visiting and wanted to get a picture of him, we just talked to him. "Oh, Genghis, what a handsome guy." He would jump up on a post and start crowing.

Joe Dahn
Grand Forks, British Columbia

✉ My chickens seem to me very curious, busy little creatures, always marching around, intent on some business of their own that I know nothing about. One of my small pleasures is to let them out of their house every morning and watch them peck at the grain I have thrown on the ground for them. During the day, if I stop to watch them for a while, I will see Cogburn, the rooster, calling to the hens to come with him, as he has obviously found something good to eat, and off they run across the field to see what it is.

In the evening they all file back to their house; Cogburn waits at the bottom of the ramp until they are all inside. Sometimes he has to go and get one who is in the tall grass pecking away at something, heedless of the time. Now I suppose this is just instinct, but all the same it isn't *stupid*.

This summer a fox came and took three hens and Cogburn was chased about half a mile away from home. Friends saw him on the road chasing cars. Well, he managed to find his way back home across the fields the next day, and I think that was pretty smart.

Genevieve Berry
Williams Lake, British Columbia

✉ Chickens are such enthusiastic carnivores that cannibalism can be a major hen-house problem. Red lights are used to fool baby chicks so they don't peck each other to death; with the light on, blood is no redder than anything else in their surroundings. A solution to the problem of cannibalistic hens is to hang a dead rabbit in the hen-house.

William H. Halewood
Stirling, Ontario

✉ We used to harvest corn by hand and tie it into sheaves and store them in the barn. One day I pulled a sheaf of corn away from a pile and there, in one nest, were three generations of rats, twenty-one in all, from little pink ones about the size of my little finger to ones with fur on them yet still too young to run away. I scooped them up in both hands and took them to the hen-house, where we had about fifty leghorns.

I had seen hens eat a mouse before, once in my life, so I thought I'd see if they would eat the rats. You wouldn't believe how viciously they attacked those baby rats. They would just give a couple of smart cracks with their beaks to kill or stun the rats, then swallow them whole. I can still see the hens, with necks extended and bulging.

Thorold S. Dupré
Napanee, Ontario

✉ While chickens are not known for their smarts, on our farm they have actually been taught to read. If the same person every day wears the same clothes and at the same time of day carries out a large white pail marked FEED, the chickens will, within a relatively short period of time (for a chicken), learn to read the lettering and will flock around looking for grain to eat.

For the dumbest turkeys, chickens rate very highly on the BIQ (barnyard intelligence quotient). We have had turkeys hang themselves, drown themselves in two inches of water, starve to death in a pen with a full hopper of feed, and peck their penmates to death by mistaking a dark feather for food. Being referred to as a turkey on this farm is a well understood curse, for example, "That was a turkey thing to do."

Doug Green
Athens, Ontario

✉ I name my chickens after girlfriends of mine. I have two beautiful blue-black hens I call the Black Maria Sisters. Also there's Miss Money Penny, Rambling Rachel (a fickle hen), Miz Leopard,

Mouthy Margot, Damn Pam, and Pegleg Peggy. I have many more hens unnamed; I'm waiting for the appropriate people to come along.

The most glorious of our bunch, however, is our old rooster, whom we call Joe Cocker. Joe Cocker has been around now for three years; he's big, fat, with long spurs, and certainly does his job. He's the papa of them all. My husband has created a blues tune in praise of Joe.

The Chicken-Hawk Blues

I used to be the cock of the walk.
I used to have my chickens in twos.
But now all's I got
Is dem ol' ol'
Chicken-hawk blues.

Isabel Mosseler
Verner, Ontario

✎ The question of bats was raised by Suzanne Finlay after she heard a series of "critters" that became household pests. She's a founder of the British Columbia Brotherhood of Benign Bat Catchers.

✉ I write to offer you a foolproof method for catching bats in your house, your attic, your belfry, or wherever they may be troubling you. My method is harmless and painless for both the bat and the catcher.

Until recently I lived in a cabin in a hollow at the foot of a mountain on the banks of Vancouver Island's Cowichan River. The cabin, like most things in life, had its "firs" and its "agins." The "firs" included the tall Douglas variety that surrounded it, the river that ran in front, the sheep who kept me from needing a lawnmower for five years, the wonderful neighbours, and the cheap rent. "Agins" were a wood stove with a fire box as holey as a hair net, power outages that could last for a week, the lack of a car, and the fourteen miles to town.

But none of the "agins" compelled my attention more than the small rural creatures who had established squatters' rights in the cabin before I, a city critter, moved in. They quickly taught me that in such surroundings, I had no need of a calendar. It was easy to tell the seasons by which creatures claimed the shelter of my cabin. In March the boldest of the humming-birds appeared at my windows, and when I opened the doors for a closer look, they flew into the living-room.

An unexpected April snowstorm brought a mouse family running for the comforting cover of my kitchen. May sunshine roused the slumbrous snakes, who crept in through the cracks beneath the doors and made peaceful beds down deep in my rubber boots. June guaranteed battalions of ants following the route surveyed by the snakes. July was relatively easy, with all of us living outside; their tolerance of my invasion of their territory was so far superior to mine of theirs that I resolved to mend my ways. No more mouse traps, no more bug bombs, no more ant-stamping. It's no way to spend (or expend) a life. The wasps of August, flying through the gaps around my window frames, weakened but did not break my resolve. It was the bats of autumn that truly challenged it.

Bats are not easy to live with. They move dartingly. They are as unsettling as mice, and for the same reason: a human being knows at a glance that he hasn't got a snowball's chance in hell against their quickness. Bats are also a social hazard: lady guests shriek and cover their hair; men guests swat at them with overcoats and frying pans and other inappropriate objects, which are sure to be ineffective, or to splatter bat guts all over your walls. And the humming-birds had already taught me that trying to shoo out a fast-flying creature with an up-ended broom was as aimless as a game of Ping-Pong with canoe paddles. A new approach was needed.

Here's my method; it's efficient and cost-effective. Get a sieve. If you don't have a sieve, grab your spaghetti strainer or anything that is cup-shaped, perforated, and big enough to enclose the bat. In a pinch, use a saucepan. Now get a splatter screen. This (for the culinary uninitiated) is a flat screen-wire lid that deters grease from exploding out of the skillet all over your stove.

Locate the bat. This can be tricky, but it is vital to your success. Otherwise you will spend all night with your head under the covers and then discover that the bat is there, too. (They like the dark.) Most of the bats who invaded my cabin quickly went to roost as soon as I turned the lights on, folding their wings and clinging vertically against a wall, just like Batman. When you have located the bat, do not hesitate: clap the sieve firmly over it and hold it hard against the wall. When the bat is secured, slide the splatter screen gently up the wall beneath the rim of the sieve.

Now that you have the living, unharmed bat in a cage, you need only open a door or window. This can be unhandy if you are holding a cookie sheet with one hand and the sieve with the other, but it is possible. Once the other door or window is open, you need only release Batman into his natural habitat, where he will work diligently to rid the world of Evil in the form of mosquitoes, houseflies, and a wide range of pesky bugs.

Suzanne Finlay
Sidney, British Columbia

✉ I grew up in a tourist camp in northern Ontario. There was a big barn of a lodge that was visited regularly by bats. Either the bright lights would confuse the bats, or the screaming visitors (and my mother) would interfere with their radar, but they would never alight. If someone is confronted with that situation, here is what we found worked best.

First, open a door or window to the outdoors. Chances are good the bat will find its own way out. If not, use something soft, like a pillow, towel, or straw broom to swat it out of the air. The important thing to keep in mind is that their radar and reflexes are so good you'll never hit them from the front. Stand quietly until they pass by and then get them from behind. Gently, please – just stun them enough for you to deal with them. A towel or container can be used to pick them up.

Angie Brammer
Kingston, Ontario

✉ I once lived with my brother and his family for the summer in Sheffield, Massachusetts, at their summer place. My two nieces and my daughter, all under six, were sleeping in one room. From the middle of the ceiling hung some flypaper tape. One night, the screams of the three girls woke us. One very agitated – and, I might add, sticky – bat hung on the flypaper. My brother, certainly an unknowing member of the Benevolent Bat Catchers' Society, ran to the kitchen for a pair of very large kitchen mitts (the long-arm, well-padded variety for barbecueing). He carefully removed the sticky, furry, hissing bat from the flypaper. I remember watching him wash the bat with soapy water, painstakingly removing the glue from her wings, which were stuck together. It was a warm evening and we decided the bat should have a chance to dry out first before any further adventures. My brother put the bat in the screened-in gazebo. In the morning the bat was gone, surely with stories to tell.

Carol Gaskin
Owen Sound, Ontario

✎ This is a small but representative miscellany on animals that are – and are not – man's friend.

✉ In Powell River, which hasn't bothered tooting its flute about the biggest of this or the most of that, we have bald eagles we haven't even counted yet. We have bald eagles sitting in trees

341

watching the tourists get sunburnt on the beach in the main part of town. We have eagles flying overhead looking down on sunburnt bald heads from places whose names we can't pronounce or spell. We have eagles sitting on crags, we have eagles sitting in snags, we have eagles limping in to the bird sanctuary so they can be fixed up and set loose. We have eagles sitting on the banks of streams waiting for the salmon to come up and spawn. We have so many eagles that there are places the ground is stained white with eagle "guano."

Familiarity breeds contempt, they say, and it's true. I guess some place with a few eagles would make a big deal about it, but when eagles are more common than swans, poodles, shar-pi dogs or even bureaucrats, you stop feeling excited. You stop looking on them as symbols of free, wild, glorious, et cetera, and take another look at them. Smeared with grease and oil from spawn and dead fish, poking around on the beach picking up dead crabs, waiting impatiently for stuff you can't even identify any more . . . they start to look like feathered Smithwrights.

Anne Cameron
Powell River, British Columbia

✉ I keep both chickens and cattle, and both are very adept at getting out of enclosures. Cattle, mine at least, seem more capable of finding their way back into an enclosure if motivated and left to themselves.

A few months ago a small group of cattle took a cross-country jaunt. They were sighted five miles, as the crow flies, away from home base across hilly, swampy, forested terrain, and returned to their home in spite of meeting other cattle en route, by themselves, via a diametrically opposite direction from the one in which they set out. Not once in their going or coming did they encounter a road.

Gordon M. Scott
Warsaw, Ontario

✉ About the horned viper and its reputed ability to leap up to seven feet and strike with its deadly venom at a height of one foot off the ground: you may visit Egypt in peace. First, the horned viper (*Cerastes cerastes* or *Cerastes cornutus*) only reaches a length of two to two-and-one-half feet. Nothing that small in the way of snakes preys on farm livestock, the supposed rationale for the seven-foot-forward-one-foot-up striking range. Second, it is not *that* venomous a snake. I quote John Compton's "Snake Lore" on the legend that *C. cerastes* is the "asp" that Cleopatra used to commit suicide: "If Cleopatra had encouraged it to pump all its venom into her it might well have killed her, though it is not a particularly venomous reptile." In other words, not instantly fatal.

However, there are a couple of interesting bits of behaviour that could contribute to the "leaping snake" myth. The "horns" of the viper are two little scaly excrescences above the eyes. The snake buries itself in the sand with only the eyes and "horns" exposed (it can manage this in ten to twenty seconds). When a bird or small rodent happens by, having either failed to notice the horns or mistaken them for an edible insect, the snake makes a grab at it. I'd put my money on the snake – those little beggars are fast!

Furthermore, I once watched a ball python run from one end of a bathtub, in about three inches of water, to leap out eighteen inches at the other end and hook his head over the rim of the tub, so I have no trouble with the idea of a foot-high leap. There would also be some forward momentum, and as people tend to be terrified of snakes out of all proportion to their danger, I can see the exaggeration progressing until the snake had covered not the probable one or two feet, but a dazzling seven feet.

Elizabeth Creith
Toronto

✉ We live in an old frame shingle-sided farmhouse, the sort of dwelling ideally suited to sheltering what we call "shingle-flies." There are your summer flies (they are small, fast, and occasionally bite) and your winter flies (they come in a variety of sizes but are generally largish, dessicated bumblers). Both are a plague and a nuisance. I have counted more than five hundred on one choice window. We have perfected the art of "de-houseflying" – we use the vacuum cleaner. In fact, we now have a small battery-operated number we use exclusively for "fly-busting." We may vacuum the same window four or five times in a day without any obvious effect on their numbers. The only time there are very few is when it's extremely cold outside and we haven't overstoked the furnace. The spring is the worst, when the outside temperature goes up during the day, activating the teaming hordes in the walls, and the furnace is running at night. We tried one of those electronic ultra-violet capital-punishment-type fly-zapper units designed for luring mosquitoes to your garden barbecue. We installed it in the bathroom, but the eerie blue light and the zzzt of frying flies were too much.

We've looked for fly-eating pets. Dog and cats will have the odd snack, but they lack dedication. Budgies and other common bird-type pets are seed eaters and aren't interested in house flies. We have scores of well-fed spiders. Some get as big as quarters, but the spider big enough to handle our problem wouldn't stop with the flies. We have a friend who swears her aunt collected the dead flies and cooked them into little biscuits for her cat.

We took the front off our house one summer to make repairs and found the uninsulated wall cavities filled two and a half feet deep in fly bodies. In another two hundred years, the house will be completely insulated.

Peter Powning
Sussex, New Brunswick

✎ Things that fall from the sky. This started with an item from Nova Scotia, when people reported that toads were falling from the sky. It led to several items from others (Jay Ingram was one guest) with explanations for this and other instances of the phenomenon.

344

✉ About toads and tornadoes: experiences I have had at different times and places suggest to me that toads can appear to sprout from the sand *and* that they can fall from the sky.

While working as a reporter on a daily paper in St. Joseph, Missouri, a hundred or so years ago, I served one afternoon and evening as "debris editor," a title I assumed after taking the fifth or sixth in a rash of calls from hysterical residents who were being showered with everything from financial documents to green apples. While the apples bore no return address or other indication of their point of origin or departure, the papers told us they were from miles away, around Topeka, Kansas, where earlier in the day a number of tornadoes had struck. Meteorologists explained to us that a tornado can suck all sorts of debris (and why not toads?) into the upper atmosphere, where the stuff can then be carried along in the jet stream for great distances before it falls.

As for toads sprouting, it seems plausible that little toads sheltering beneath the top surface of sand on a sunny day – which I have seen them do – would erupt in a summer shower, and seem to be tumbling from the sky.

Dirk van Loon
Liverpool, Nova Scotia

✉ This event happened just south of the city limits of Medicine Hat, Alberta. The exact date escapes me now, but I believe it was in late July, perhaps early August, of the year 1961. I was twelve years old at the time, and on that particular day I was pursuing my favourite pastime: fishing.

That day the warmth of the wind and the rapidly forming clouds promised one of those terrific prairie thunderstorms that always seem to make the fish bite better. The wind was picking up speed and the gusts made it necessary to scramble in search of a rock to hold my jacket and packsack down. I recall that I had removed my shirt and, as usual, had nothing on my feet. The swirling winds could be compared to blasts of air from a huge hair dryer, and when the rain started, it would alternate with the wind. First the sheets of warm water would literally soak you to the bone. Then, within seconds, the force of the drying winds would make you stagger to keep your foothold.

It was during one of these wind-and-rain baths that I stood, eyes closed, head up into the gale, and realized that I was being hit with small objects.

I opened my eyes and stared in disbelief as the ground, and myself, continued to be pelted with little fish and frogs. Holding my hands out in front of me, I was actually able to intercept these little critters before they hit the ground. Although the fish and frogs were all small, I was able to fill my cap in three or four scoops along the top of the marsh grass. The little pail I usually tried to fill was running over in no time and I spread both my jacket and my shirt on the ground, and heaped the bounty on top. Tying them as well as I could to prevent the loss of my good fortune, I danced around in childish glee.

Although I was scared stiff to use the word "miracle," something *had* happened. I'd been there lots of times before, but I'd never seen anything like this. It had to be some sort of divine intervention. That was almost twenty-six years ago. I'll never stop thinking about it. I was one of the happiest kids you ever saw.

Dick Sommerville
Calgary

✉ I am a native of Galt, and I spent a lot of time at Dickson Park, playing ball in summer and skating on the outdoor rink in winter. I recall quite clearly playing ball one day and the game being called because of a torrential summer rain. I lived near the park, and I made a dash for home, getting thoroughly soaked in the process. I have never been rained on by cats and dogs, but that day I was pelted by hundreds of tiny toads. After the rain stopped, the ground was covered with what appeared to be new-born toads. They weren't pretty, but they certainly were *there*.

Victor Wilson
Midland, Ontario

✉ We have a cabin high above the road leading to Silver Star Ski Village, and we are surrounded by extremely greedy whisky jacks and Steller's jays. It has become a habit to place any meal out on our little deck for them, and we always watch in amazement as they attempt to cram as much in their beaks as possible before flying off.

A few weeks ago there was one remaining pancake left from breakfast. Of course it should have been cut up, but out it went in one piece. It wasn't long before a jay came to inspect it, arranged the whole thing in its beak, and literally waddled to the edge of the deck. With great effort it launched itself into the air, heading across the road. But the load must have been too heavy, and it started losing height. Lower and lower it went, until it must have realized the mission was suicidal. It dropped the pancake into the traffic, and soared to the safety of the trees on the other side of the road. What I would have given to have been at the village two minutes later, to see the puzzled expressions of the skiers, reaching to unload their ski rack, and discovering a pancake cemented to the roof of their Chevy!

Penny Baughen
Winfield, British Columbia

✉ While in the east the rain is crammed
With worms or toads or frogs,
We in the west are fending off
A rain of cats and dogs.
The end will come to warts and slime
Precipitating pets –
They'll shrink in spring to fragment fall;
A rain of violets.

Catharine Hay
Ganges, British Columbia

THE
MAKING
OF WAR
AND
PEACE

In the spring of 1987, Richard Handler wrote an article for the *Canadian Institute for International Peace and Security Magazine* that did such a splendid job of explaining not only the background and methodology of one of the regular departments of which *Morningside* is especially proud that I asked him if I could reproduce it here. This is, indeed, how it came to be and how it works, and what it can come to mean to a thoughtful and careful producer.

For two years now I have produced *Morningside*'s War and Peace column, the segment of the program we devote to nuclear, defence, peace, and security issues. The column airs on Thursdays, usually in the third hour (at 11:05, half an hour later in Newfoundland). When we started we may have been the only mainstream radio program in the country, and perhaps the only media outlet, to give nuclear war and peace issues a weekly slot. Why we started the column, and how I fashion it, might interest people who follow the emerging security debates in this country, and the way journalists cover them.

Morningside is talk radio with a personal touch (what in CBC parlance is called "companion radio"). We are on the air fifteen hours a week, from 9:05 to noon (half an hour later in Newfoundland). Peter Gzowski is the host. About a million people listen during the week, with each quarter-hour segment gathering up to a quarter of our total audience, depending on the time (about 180,000 for the War and Peace slot).

Our listeners have a place on the show; they feel at home here. They write thousands of letters to Peter Gzowski, short and very long, filled with commentary, suggestions, confessions, recipes, and poems. Gzowski attends to these letters with an editorial passion. He believes his letters (more than he believes his producers, to our everlasting despair!). And so it was that Gzowski began to notice, sometimes in response to items we had aired, that some of his listeners were getting nervous about the prospects of a nuclear war.

As a producer, it's my job to put people on the air. I come up with ideas, interview potential guests, research the story, and write what we call a "green" – an introduction, a set of questions, and a background essay or notes. I have always produced items on nuclear issues – on arms talks, on nuclear tensions and superpower fears, on deterrence, on nuclear winter, and on what it's like to live, as a parent and child, in a nuclear world. On *Morningside* we never rely on news pegs for our items, unlike other "chase" shows (although we chase breaking stories, too). But in spite of how much I'd done, I'd always been perplexed about how much to "do" on the issue of nuclear war. And though we weren't subject to the tyranny of the headline, I still felt many of the same rules applied that apply elsewhere: somebody's got to come up with something "new" about nuclear war, a new wrinkle on nuclear winter or a breakthrough in the arms talks, before I'd put him on air.

But the rules of news – of novelty – didn't apply to our listeners. They are not current-affairs producers. They had witnessed the breakdown of *détente* and the increased tensions of the 1980s. They were nervous – and some of them were scared.

So the letters started arriving, including one from a listener who suggested we devote a part of our program to the nuclear threat. Gzowski, at one of our story meetings, forwarded this listener's suggestion and proposed we create a War and Peace column. (Another listener later suggested we call it our Peace and War column, and upon reflection we think he may have been right.)

I jumped at the idea of the new column, arguing that it was the least we could do for the most important story in the world.

But of course what is "important" can be deadly radio, especially when the subject is the end of the world. How much doom and gloom could our listeners take? Is this what they wanted to hear? I had to figure out what we would talk about every week, without paralyzing our listeners, Gzowski, my colleagues, and myself.

So here are the *Morningside* rules, about all stories, from the most important to the incidental (these rules are broken more than we wish, but these are our rules nonetheless). Here's rule number one: a *Morningside* guest has to "think" on air.

That means no shtick artists, no travelling thought salesmen, no guests who are pushing a line they have pushed a thousand times before. We don't want people who turn on a tape machine when they open their mouths (though I must confess, a few of these have appeared on *Morningside*).

Our guests have to talk *with* Peter, not at him, which brings up the problem of the "expert." Other programs thrive on experts – all that arcane and disinterested talk from men (generally) who inhabit the capitals of the world.

But for our purposes, experts can be boring. They're often like neutron bombs: they kill people but leave the furniture standing!

I knew if I populated the column with experts, the War and Peace segment would not survive.

So I went back to the root of the problem, the fact that our listeners – homemakers, professionals, business people, those who drive and those who listen to us at home – were worried about nuclear war.

I decided that, along with the occasional expert, I would invite people to come on *Morningside* who had begun to think about nuclear war and the whole concept of security – and this is crucial – even it if wasn't their business to do so.

These people would have an unusual "take" on our dilemma. A schoolteacher like Susan Hargraves might look at the attitudes of children to nuclear war, and a psychologist and logician like Anatol Rapoport would use games theory as his nuclear prism.

Our guests would have to work at it. No casual thoughts were allowed. There's nothing like catastrophe to bring out banality. Our guests would have to expand our awareness of the dilemmas involved.

Censoring the banal may make us undemocratic, but it's essential to our understanding of how the program and the column work. Each week I get press releases from nuclear enthusiasts who jog, walk, run, meditate, chant, or ring bells for peace. I can't put these people on air. Most of them are well-meaning, but they fail what we call the test of the second question.

The test simply asks: after these people tell you why they are doing what they're doing, have you exhausted their knowledge and the range of their response?

(I am not judging these people, dedicated and fine as they are. I am talking format – sixteen minutes! – and intellectual breadth. People who fail the test of the second question may get to heaven before I do, but they will not be invited on air.)

What we need are people with an argument. Because *Morningside* is one of the last places where you can hear the spoken essay, disguised as an interview.

I say essay, because the best *Morningside* guests speak from a personal position that advances the line of their argument (which

351

is what the best essay writers do). The essay is always about discovery, the structures of inquiry, and its personal intent. These are the features that make not only the best essays (or mystery stories) but the best radio interviews.

And what is more compelling than to seek out intelligent people who – in spite of "official positions," the fog of jargon, and the inhuman doublespeak – come upon what they believe to be the truth of an impending catastrophe, or its opposite, the prospects for hope?

And what about balance? You may think the War and Peace column is simply a conduit for smart peace activist-thinkers, members of the professional guilds for social responsibility that are flourishing in Canada.

I do try to strike some sort of balance.

True, I have never put anybody on who was *for* nuclear war, though I have heard guests say they would prefer it to the capitulation of the West.

One of the times balance comes in is when we deal with superpower conflict. Many of our guests have been critical of both sides. I have heard few apologies for the Soviet Union, though many guests feel the initiative for arms control has swung to the Soviets. But I also go out of my way to feature items on the independent peace movement in Eastern Europe and the Soviet Union, as well as interviews on Soviet life, its military-industrial complex, and its own colonial war, Afghanistan.

A range of "conservative" opinion does appear on *Morningside*. I try to feature it in two ways.

First, by using the same criteria, I try to select those who feel passionately and know a lot about the problems of our adversaries. This is, to some extent, an American phenomenon. Neo-conservatism is, after all, renegade liberalism, and a form of self-discovery. We have featured long interviews with Norman Podhoretz, editor of *Commentary* magazine, and with Cold Warrior and national security consultant Michael Ledeen, among others.

But most of our guests are Canadian. So, though they are less abundant and not as well organized, our Cold Warriors do make it to air. Also, we have featured Canadians from Eastern Europe and their allies – those who despise the Soviet Union and desperately want us to despise it, too.

Secondly, War and Peace adversaries do appear on our debates, a regular feature of the column. Debates on Stars Wars, NATO and neutrality, nuclear-weapons-free zones, and peace studies add some heat to *Morningside*'s obsession with light.

(I once put on what I consider the war and peace equivalent of the abortion debate: two Eastern European mothers now living in Canada, one afraid of nuclear war, the other traumatized by Stalinism. I wanted to see if these women could speak to each other, find some common ground. But all they did was invalidate each other's position, talk past the other, like those who argue for or against abortion; an instructive insight in itself.)

Not all the items are about peace or the fear of war. Like all people immersed in the subject, I am interested in the military: how they do their job and how they think. Soldiers and former soldiers have appeared on the column, including an especially good piece with three cadets from the Royal Military College in Kingston, who gave our listeners an insight into why they are choosing a military career.

One of our best items was a week-long series with the American military analyst Richard Gabriel, an ex-career officer and a Vietnam vet. Though a critic of his country's military, Gabriel has few quarrels with its foreign-policy goals. He saves his anger for his country's military failings, its bloated command, and its incompetence. His insights into how armies are motivated to fight – and how they fail – was one of the highlights of the war and peace column last year.

Still, and here's my confession: there are no doubt more "pro-peace" people on *Morningside* than those who don't like them. And for this I offer two reasons. One has to do with the satisfactions of novelty, and the other with the notion of conservative thinking in this country.

I have already said that the column began with the listeners' concerns, with the fact that the global arms race was getting out of hand. The central assumption here is a critical one. Those who are *rethinking* war and peace in new and interesting ways are those who don't like what they've found.

I also said that journalism lives – thrives – under the rule of novelty; and novelty is interest, above all. There's a built-in bias, then, for critical thinking, even if the intention of the column or the program is neutral or "non-aligned."

Secondly, what does it mean to be a *conservative* in Canada on the issue of nuclear arms? (Remember, Canada gave up its nuclear weapons in the sixties!) It may mean watching out for the Russians and supporting America – but a whole host of conservatives are breaking down the categories of their thinking, even if they are anti-Soviet and pro-NATO.

Many of the peace people who appear on *Morningside* are not radicals. They do not call for revolution. They are people with a real stake in this society. (I have heard it said that Doctors for the Prevention of Nuclear War just want a world safe enough to preserve their privilege – and so be it, if that's what motivates some of them.) But lots of "conservative" people in this country, our listeners included, feel they are conservative when it comes to conserving the planet.

Retired military officers and business executives are now worried about American and Soviet plans to fight and win a nuclear war. Are they liberals? Misguided conservatives? I find it hard to label them.

Even the most pro-American Canadians are disturbed by the cavalier attitudes displayed by the United States on the issue of Arctic sovereignty and the American militarization of Canadian air space.

It is estimated that ninety-five per cent of the peace groups in the country are five years old or less.

There is an amazing flowering of activity on a local level. "Peace" is becoming mainstream. The Liberals passed a resolution, at their last convention, calling for a nuclear-weapons-free zone in Canada. Even if this is never implemented, its passage is significant.

I have a favourite question I like to ask the experts I pre-interview (that's our scouting term for the interview that takes place before the on-air interview). The question is this: can you tell me why there are fifty thousand nuclear weapons in the world? Do these weapons make any military sense?

The experts rarely have a good answer for me. They suggest that lots of weapons are needed to do lots of jobs. (You wouldn't want big bombs to do little jobs and little bombs to do big jobs, would you?)

But mostly their answers come down to fear: you need these weapons, irrational as they are, because if the other side can neutralize a lot or some of them, then you need more weapons to overcome the threat.

So in the end it comes down to this: nuclear weapons are the world's biggest Rorschach ink-blot test. They are the perfect projection screen for the fears and illusions of nations, corporations, armies, and the employees of the world's industrial-military complex. What an incredible admission – all these weapons exist as a *psychological ploy*, a figment of our imagination, dispensing money, power, prestige, and dominance.

But people are worried – about the numbers, about the chance of an accident, a mistake.

No wonder people – and not just *Morningside* listeners – are beginning to rethink what it means to exist in a world where fifty thousand nuclear weapons are "normal," a world where any reduction of even a few of these weapons panics those whose business is "national security." Who wouldn't be nervous under these circumstances? What does "balance" in journalism mean here? I find it hard to believe that balance means just another rehash of the same old Cold War arguments.

That's why the people I talk to want to examine how they fit into this collective suicide arrangement. And that means re-examining Canada's relationship to the superpowers and the nuclear arms race.

It just may be that the new nationalism of the 1980s – after the demise of the nationalizations of the seventies and the glimmer of free trade – will be in the area of what it means to be nationally secure.

And that may mean a new rethinking of the legitimacy of a global system that insists that being *normal* is living with the threat of nuclear war.

Richard Handler
Toronto

SHORT SHORT STORIES: PART THREE

A final selection for our anthology-within-an-anthology: self-contained works of fiction, each written, as the rules dictated, on a single manuscript page.

✉ A particular lady caretaker at a school where I used to teach was so intimidated by my name that she never attempted to pronounce it. Instead she mumbled an incoherent sound that faded away.

Mrs. Harris was a big woman. Everybody called her "Mrs. Arse." She use to sweep the corridors with a four-foot-wide broom. She had an enormous bosom counterbalanced by a huge behind. She was like a walking S without the grace of that letter. She used to put the broom under her bosom and push along as if the broom were a part of her.

Quite often I would meet her charging forward with her broom as I was leaving school for the day.

"Good afternoon, Mrs. Harris."

"Good afternoon, Mr. Aaaaaa."

This went on for a few months. I felt I had to do something about it. The first thought was to confront her and say: "Look, my name is Calleja!" That, however, seemed rather pompous.

After a lot of thinking I hit on a brilliant idea. When she started saying, "Good afternoon Mr. Aaaa . . ." I would drop Calleja in the right place and that would solve the problem once and for all.

So all I had to do was wait for the opportune moment.

One day the corridor was empty except for Mrs. Harris. She was walking towards me. We were a yard away from each other.

"Good afternoon, Mrs. Harris."

"Good afternoon, Mr. A – "

"Calleja!" I said.

"Oh, *did* you?" she exclaimed.

"Yes, I did" was my reply.

"Thank you very much" she said as she swept past me.

I still wonder what she thought I said.

Joseph Calleja
Willowdale, Ontario

✉ When I was a child, my parents seldom spoke Italian at home, but occasionally they would help each other refresh their knowledge of the language they'd learned to speak from their respective families.

One evening at the supper table, my mother announced that the new priest had arrived at our church. "His name," she said, "is Fittuchi."

My father nodded approvingly, and then asked, "Jean, what's *fittuchi?*

"String," my mother replied.

"No, string is *fibrio*," Daddy countered.

"Carl," Mother chided, "string is *fila*."

"*Fila* is thread!"

"Thread is *filamento!*"

"You don't know what you're talking about! *Filamento* is ribbon!"

"Ribbon is *funicella!*"

"*Funicella* is twine!"

"Twine is *spage!*"

"*Spage* is rope!"

"Rope is *corda!*"

"You know better than that! *Corda* is cord!"

"Cord is *cordone!*"

"*Cordone* is the fibre the cord is made from!"

"No, it's not. Fibre is *fibrio!*"

"*Fibrio* is string!"

"String is *fittuchi!*"

There was an ominous silence as my mother dismissed the subject by clearing the dishes from the table.

The next night, my mother apologized. "The new priest's name isn't Fittuchi after all. His name is Rittuchi."

There was a pause as my father took this in. Then, he put his fork down, turned to her, and asked, "Jean, what's *rittuchi?*"

Barbara Florio Graham
Gatineau, Quebec

✉ God lives next door to me. That is to say, the man who lives next door to me *thinks* he's God. His wife seems to think he's

God, too. She doesn't speak to me often, but when she does, she always begins the conversation with: "Cecil says . . ." or, "Cecil thinks . . ." Perhaps the man next door doesn't allow his wife to speak or think for herself. Cecil has never spoken one word to me.

Cecil used to work for someone who paved driveways. Cecil is a great big man. He's two times the size of me. His wife's rather large, too. Cecil watches me a lot.

Cecil watches me shovel snow. Cecil watches me cut grass. Cecil watches me saw down branches off my trees.

Cecil has lots of things to ride on. He goes for a ride when he cuts the grass. He goes for a ride when he clears the snow. Cecil has a snowmobile, a tractor, a boat, a truck, a car, and a scooter. He even has a small house on wheels. Cecil has a roto-tiller, a chain-saw, and also a gun. Cecil doesn't like squirrels, rabbits, or birds. Cecil doesn't like me, either.

I till my flower beds with a spade, a hoe, and a rake. My drive-way is cleared with a bright red shovel, except when a heavy snow falls and the wind blows it into drifts. Then I hire someone to plough it out. Then the big yellow grader comes down the road again. Then my bright red shovel and I go outside again. And Cecil watches me shovel snow, again.

Cecil saw my clothes-line fall down when I was hanging out sheets. Cecil saw my clothes-line fall down and went inside his house. I'm glad Cecil is married . . . to the lady next door.

Barbara M. Duncan
Stouffville, Ontario

✉ I'm a reasonable sort of guy. As long as everything goes right, I seldom give in to outbursts of temper, but this morning was the start of one hell of a day: it was minus fourteen, east wind blowing sixty kilometres per. But I'd promised the boys I'd take them hunt-ing, so I heaved myself out of bed. The ribs I cracked last week hurt like hell. I gave a yelp. (My wife likes to know when something hurts me.) I ate porridge. (I prefer bacon and eggs.) I hurried outside to off-load the camper. The new pick-up was stuck. The damned hitch had stuck in the bank last week when I'd backed the truck into the open shed, and now it was frozen tight. The hitch was frozen. The ground was frozen. And by now my ears and hands were frozen.

I went to get the tractor. It wouldn't start. Wouldn't start! After the way I've looked after it, oiled and greased it, added anti-freeze, and even kept it in a shed. I know, I know, it's hard to believe, but that's how things go sometimes. I started up the old wood and garbage truck and with the tow line tight and my wife in the new truck, I pulled it loose.

It's important to understand how I feel about this new truck: it's got a diesel engine, power windows, power steering, AM-FM stereo, and cruise control. I mean it's got everything a man needs and wants in a pick-up. She's a real beauty. God, how I hated to yank her out of the frozen ground like that.

The kid at the Husky said, "Sorry, sir, we only got summer diesel."

I'm two hours late. The porridge has worn off. I'd sell my soul for a cup of coffee.

"Ready to go?" I say. "Put your things in the truck while I grab a coffee with your dad."

"Grandpa," they say, "the pick-up doors are locked and the keys are on the seat."

Diane Salmon
Sardis, British Columbia

✉ Bedelia Bewdley, a poor but honest governess, trudged towards Brooding Castle, which glowered on a wind-swept cliff. How she wished her heavy portmanteau had wheels. To her right, in the shadows, a hooded figure glided. To her left, a black panther slunk. Before she reached the castle, she was run down and trampled by Eleazar, a black stallion ridden by the irascible Baronet, Sir Tybalt English-Twitte.

Nevertheless, at nine sharp the next morning, she began teaching immersion French to little Farley. Between classes, to avoid the piercing eyes of Sir Tybalt, the crossbow of his evil nephew,

Crispin, the paring knife of Zurlina, the witch-like vegetable cook, and the slingshot of little Farley, she explored the castle in her bare feet, nightie, and a candle. She saw a ghost in the Minstrel's Gallery, swam an underground river in the castle cellars, and was locked in the jam closet by the wicked Zurlina, who left her to perish in the flames when the evil Crispin torched the castle. The jam-closet door was clawed open by Sir Tybalt's faithful panther, Diablo, and she fell out into the arms of the baronet just as the castle roof fell in. (The village bucket brigade could not quench the blazing stones.)

Bedelia confronted Crispin and Zurlina, who shrieked vile verbal abuse into the wind and flames, then flung themselves off the cliff, and were dashed to death on the foaming rocks below.

Sir Tybalt and Bedelia were married a week later, and joined the other Barr Colonists on the S.S. *Lake Manitoba*. They steamed away to a life of ease and riches in Lloydminster, on the border of Alberta and Saskatchewan, in Canada.

The black stallion, Eleazar, learned to pull a stone boat and Sir Tybalt picked enough rocks off his 160-acre homestead to build three castles. While she waited for next year, when the baronet had promised he would get around to putting up another brooding castle, and also a broody house for the chickens, Bedelia happily tended the flowers that grew on the roof of her sod house, and raised chickens and goats to feed the faithful panther, Diablo.

Then, one day, a chill wind stirred the hair on the back of her neck, and she stared in disbelief at the vegetables she had just dug up. They were already peeled, and ready for the pot! Diablo dropped the goat's hoof he had been gnawing on, and stared at the sod belfry, uttering low growls. Little Farley had always said she would end up with bats in her belfry and there they were, two of them, hanging side by side. Had the evil Crispin and Zurlina come back from the dead to haunt them? Did they need an exorcist, or an exterminator? Does this story need an ending or a paper shredder?

Laura Cunningham
Marsden, Saskatchewan

THE CARE AND LANGUAGE OF TREES

Well, maybe not quite the last of our fiction – although I'm not sure if what Anne Mullens wrote from Vancouver was a story she'd made up or a true memoir of her childhood in Toronto. Anne is a reporter at the *Vancouver Sun*, I happen to know. She'd been writing what appears second here in the spring of 1987 with an eye to sending it in to join the flow Pat Wolfe had started. She decided it was too long, and as she says, "I couldn't bear to cut it." Then I did the piece that appears here first, and she decided to send her story in anyway. I thought the two pieces worked together, and that it was appropriate that I began my radio essay by citing a much earlier letter.

There's a postscript to all of this. I'll leave it till after Anne's story.

✎ Sandra Leckie, who lives in Duchess, Alberta, wrote to me about a year and a half ago about trees. Sandra's letter was inspired by a report she had heard here about logging on Lyell Island, in British Columbia, but I remembered it the other day because of something that happened to me, here in Ontario, and I dug it out this morning.

Here is my story.

The lady in my life and I have been, as you may have heard me say last week, fixing up a little cottage we bought near Lake Simcoe. More accurately, we have been having other, more skilled people, fix it up *for* us. But one of our most pleasant pastimes of this spring has been to drive up each weekend and watch our dream house take shape as we had imagined it: the perky clerestory to let in the summer sun; the ambling verandah, for playing bridge and reading old novels while the rain spatters on the roof. A couple of weeks ago, one of the several friends and relatives who have shared our fantasies suggested that, since we were doing all this work anyway, and the front yard was scarred with roofers' tar and the tracks of dumpsters, this would be a good time to bury the power line that runs in from the road. We agreed. The line was unsightly. It detracted from the loveliest features of our small retreat: the towering old evergreens that shade the lawns. And the part that would have to go underground involved only about thirty feet, from the road allowance to the new verandah.

Last weekend, when we arrived for our regular check of progress, the ditch had been dug. They might as well have cut it through my arm. It was four feet deep and two feet wide. With the mud piled on either side and brown water filling its depths, it looked like part of the Maginot Line. Worst of all, the trench began right at the base of a spreading, triple-trunked pine, and as we stood in the cold, cruel April rain we could only stare at the naked roots, some as thick as our legs, ripped in two by the back hoe, their bark splintered, their nerve ends exposed.

The tree will live, I suppose. According to a forester friend who came to join us in lamenting the ugly slash, it has stood there for a hundred and fifty years, and while the roots the hydro's machinery tore asunder *are* part of its system, there are more under the ground, more and bigger, reaching down for the moisture that has sustained it for six generations of human delight.

But that, surely, is not the point. The point is what we did to it, or might have done: how easily I said to dig a ditch, how thoughtlessly some workers showed up and ripped their gash in the earth. A hundred and fifty years – and, so one power line, plugged into our washing machine, would not sully our priceless view, we might have killed it. And what could I have done? Sued the hydro, I suppose, though maybe not. And planted a sapling for my great-great-grandchildren's shade.

I'm sorry, tree.

Here is what Sandra Leckie wrote from Alberta, after coming in from a November walk with her dog, during which, as she said, she had managed to reach her windbreak of willows just before the frost on her eyelashes blinded her.

This is dry-land country, where it is difficult to grow anything but sagebrush and tumbleweed, and yet people continue to lavish care and attention on pine, spruce, poplar, and Russian olive trees. In fact, many of the farmers would handle the death of a cow better than the loss of an old spreading poplar, which brings me, in a roundabout way, to my feelings of horror and frustration over the logging on Lyell Island.

I spent three years on the west coast, and make yearly pilgrimages to breathe the mist-clenched air and wander through the mossy cathedrals of giant cedars. Quietly born again, I return to the prairies, ready to do battle with winter winds and summer heat. It is little wonder that the Haida are willing to sacrifice themselves for these forests. I think of these people every time I look out my window and see the poplars lying on the fields like bleached whale bones. I lost my tree to old age and wind. The Haida could lose theirs to greed. I wonder which is more difficult to combat.

✉ The summer I was six, when the warm evenings turned our Moore Park street noisy with children playing hide-and-seek and kick-the-can until the street lights came on, there was a maple tree that talked.

It was an ordinary-looking maple tree in the Camerons' lot, three houses down from ours. It had the usual round scars from branches sawed off and tarred over by city workers who seemed to cut only the limbs a child would want to climb on. Since its first branches were too high for any one of us to shinny up and grab, it wasn't a tree we particularly noticed.

That is, until it began to talk.

It happened one balmy June evening after dinner. My parents had excused us from the table early, letting us eat our ice-cream cones on the street, where games were already in progress. Ours was a dead-end street and, after the fathers parked their cars in the driveways at the end of the day, it belonged to us. There were sixty-three children in the one-block portion between the school and the corner (one mother had counted).

I was an ender in a game of skipping that night, holding my cone in one hand and turning the rope in the other, catching the butter-scotch-ripple drips with my tongue while chanting "Peas in a pod, peas in a pod." My two older sisters had joined the bigger girls in a game of double-dutch close by, when Janet Cameron strolled down the street announcing that the tree on her front lawn was about to talk.

Now Janet, age thirteen, was older than most of us. And she was bigger, too. My cousin Billy had called her fat. Janet punched him, starting a scrap between them that a parent had to pull apart. We thought she was wonderful. She directed us all in plays of her own creation, put on puppet shows, and told us stories full of princesses and magic. Her brother Jimmy was old – in grade ten at least. He had black horned-rimmed glasses. He wore a tie to school and carried a briefcase. Some evenings he would knock on our screen door and ask Dad if it would be all right if he used our Encyclopaedia Britannica for a while. Dad would show him to the study and say to our mother, "Now there's a nice, bright boy."

"Ladies and gentlemen, come this way for the show of the century," Janet yelled, strolling down the street with her hands cupped like a megaphone around her mouth. "Come hear the talking tree."

Soon there were twenty of us or more sitting cross-legged on the grass around the base of the maple. The older boys were on the perimeter, still straddling their bikes, looking just slightly disinterested, so that none of us thought they really cared if the tree talked. Janet put her hands in the air for silence.

"This is indeed a momentous occasion, ladies and gentlemen. After more than two hundred years of silence, this ordinary maple tree before us has decided to talk. Hello, Mr. Tree."

There was a crackle from the branches and from within the leafy foliage a slow comfortable voice began to speak.

"Hello there, Janet, hello boys and girls. How nice of you all to come to see me," the tree said. "Is that Mary I see in the pretty red dress? And there's Anne. Have you been eating ice cream?"

The tree seemed to know us all. He knew what we'd been up to. "What's this I hear about you refusing to be an ender in skipping, Suzie? That's not being a good sport, is it? Everybody has to take their turn."

All that summer, whenever Janet announced that the tree was about to talk, we'd stop our games, and run to the tree.

Sometimes parents would bring the younger kids, bathed and ready for bed, allowing them to sit at the tree's feet in their pyjamas while they stood on the sidewalk. The tree would tell us stories and Aesop's fables and, like a wise King Solomon, decide street justice.

The tree's reputation grew beyond our street, and kids from the next street over would come by on their bicycles to see if it were true.

It was one of the older boys from the other street who yelled out, one day near the end of August, "Look, there's a speaker in the tree. And you can see a guy in the window. He's making it talk."

Parents and the older kids scowled at him. But we all turned to look to the second-floor window, where Jimmy was sitting at his desk. We could see a wire leading from the window to the tree. We looked to Janet for an explanation.

"Nonsense," said Janet. "He's just studying." Jimmy kept his head buried in his book.

That was the last time the tree talked; the next week we returned to school.

When we asked Janet when the tree would talk again, she would shrug her shoulders. "Maybe never."

Anne Mullens
Vancouver

✎ As I said, my own adventures had a resolution, though it's at best an ironic one. After my original complaint on the air, I grew more and more concerned about the triple-trunked pine at my cottage. I called a specialist. He agreed the tree was threatened. He put some mysterious elixir around its exposed roots and covered them with rich top soil. Then, with my neighbour's agreement – I have understanding neighbours, to say the least – he ran guy-wires from the upper reaches of the pine to the ground. If all goes well, they'll only have to be there three or four years.

If *my* tree could talk, it would probably have something to say about people who, in order to have a few aerial wires buried, spend hundreds of dollars on landscaping and post-landscaping care, then hundreds of dollars more to put – what? – wires in the air.

STAYING SOBER

This chapter, or at least the second part of it, really picks up, as I suggested in the introduction, where the chapter of the original *Morningside Papers* called "Getting Sober" left off. That part is, as that chapter was, by Glen Allen, who has contributed to this collection in so many ways. The first time round, as you may recall, he wrote about days 3, 10, 20, 21, and 29 of his long climb back from the bad times. In this book, he's much further along the road.

First, though, a story by a friend of Glen's who's been through similar times. His name is Herb Nabigon. Glen knew he'd written this account of one native man's struggles with alcohol and his triumph over it. He asked Herb to appear on the radio and talk about it. When I'd heard about his experiences, and about the spiritual strength that lay behind them, I wanted to read it, too. Here it is.

I was born on the Mobert Indian Reserve, near Thunder Bay, on July 16, 1942. My father was a trapper, close to nature; he lived off the land. My mother saw to it that her three children had good clothes, enough to eat, and lots of affection. There was love in that home.

I was always interested in learning how to set beaver traps and rabbit snares. I wanted to copy my dad. But when we were kids he spent the winters trapping away from the reserve; he was always very busy on his trap line. I started to build a fantasy world for myself. When I was about eleven years old I wanted to be a hero, do good, and save other people's lives, like the Lone Ranger in the radio series. I never wanted to be Tonto.

I had my first drink of wine when I was still just a kid. All I can remember is that I got really sick and I had a blackout – that is, I couldn't remember afterwards what had happened or what I had done when I was drinking. Although this was a sign that alcohol was no good for me, the drink made me feel good. It gave me courage. When I wasn't drinking, I had a feeling of fear, like a hole in my chest. After I had a couple of drinks the hole disappeared. I didn't drink again until my mother's death in the spring of 1957 when I was fourteen. I drank myself into a blackout the night after they buried her.

A little later I quit school and went to work for the railway as a station agent. It was an inside job, and since most of my friends had jobs in construction or around Mobert, it gave me special status. All of a sudden, in my mind, I was a big shot. Anybody who wanted to travel on the train had to buy a train ticket from me. I was in control of movement itself.

But I had no control over myself and my drinking progressed: my hangovers were getting worse, and so were my nerves. I couldn't see how it was destroying my life and my mind. For example, I got fired for lending my railway pass to my uncle. They caught him in Sudbury. My father was very angry with me but I really didn't care – easy come, easy go.

After that I partied and planted trees for a year and then was hired by the Canadian National Railway in Hornepayne, Ontario.

My first assignment was as an operator and station agent at Long-lac. One night I was working the graveyard shift and a friend brought over a twenty-sixer of rye. We had a couple of drinks in the station and around two in the morning I decided to lock up the station and party at my bunk house. An hour later a freight showed up but had to stop because the operator – me – wasn't there to give him clearance to go further. He waited for three hours and I lost another job. As I look back on things today I know my boss was a kind man who was concerned, but I thought the whole world was against me. I thought, "He is only firing me because I am an Indian." I didn't even bother to go home and pack my clothes. I had to leave, but where to go? I tossed a coin. That was how I made decisions in those days. Heads, I go to Toronto, tails, I go to Winnipeg. The coin came up heads. I caught a train for Toronto but stayed only six weeks, loading and unloading freight from trucks and boxcars to make money for beer. Then I headed back to Mobert. I was only twenty.

My dad told me that aside from murder and rape the worst crime a human being can commit is to destroy his mind with alcohol and destroy the natural cycle of life. But I was mindless and careless: I didn't listen to him. I didn't have the vaguest idea of what he meant. The cure for me was more whisky.

Then came a date I'll never forget. On August 3, 1962, I spent the night drinking with friends in White River. The next morning, still drinking, I went over to visit my grandfather. About noon of that day I was hit by a train. I was in another blackout so I don't remember the details, only talking to people around me, my res-cuers; I don't remember what was said. Anyway, on August fifth, I woke up in Marathon Hospital minus my right arm. It had been cut off at the shoulder.

Alcohol had complete and absolute power over me. I learned nothing at all from my accident: a year later, my father found me passed out again on the railway tracks. He told me to sober up or leave home. I did not want to quit drinking so I left, first to work as a mailboy with the provincial government in Toronto, then with the Company of Young Canadians in Thunder Bay.

There I met bright and articulate young Ojibways who were interested in helping their communities achieve some degree of self-sufficiency without the aid of government handouts. I shared their aspirations. I knew the reserves were poor and I had seen the enormous wealth around them and asked myself, "How come?" Being a problem drinker, I was already angry, and in a way, the poverty of the reserves justified my anger, hence my alcoholism.

In the CYC I was assigned to start a radio program for the local reserves and I was sent to Edmonton to interview Indian leaders. Though I was there for three weeks I didn't even try to arrange interviews; instead, I found any excuse I could to drink. The day came, however, when I had to come home and the only tape I had to give my boss was of some Hank Williams songs. Shortly afterwards I became the only Indian ever to be fired by the CYC.

Then I met the woman I would marry. She encouraged me to go back to school and I got a diploma in Social Services at Centennial College in Toronto and enrolled in the Native Studies program at Trent University in Peterborough. But I continued to drink and I made life difficult for my wife. I thank the Great Spirit for the two beautiful children we had together but I created great anxiety and stress for her. I didn't know how to love her because I didn't know how to love myself. Our marriage ended, and once again I found myself on the road, tossing a coin to determine if I should go east or west. The coin turned up heads – east – so I went to Ottawa. I continued to drink heavily, and, though I was often irrational, paranoid, suicidal, an embarrassment to my professors and peers, I managed to complete a master's degree in social work at Carleton University.

In my final semester I was assigned to write a proposal for a hostel for homeless men. Most of these men had broken dreams and very little hope and when I met them and looked them in the eye I thought, "These men are me." I drank with them and lived on Skid Row for six months. I was one of them and they are part of me.

When I graduated, I was hired by the Department of Indian Affairs as a policy analyst and though I tried to restrict my drinking to weekends, I slipped back to my old patterns. I began to miss work, I was unreliable, my analysis of various issues was weak, and because of alcohol, I had little or no comprehension of what I read. My only defence was to become offensive: my favourite line with my boss was to say, "You guys don't understand because you're not Indian. How can you write policies on Indians if you don't understand them?" I was supposed to be part of finding a solution and I was part of the problem. And I drank to forget about my problems, to forget about the problems of the Indian people in the cities. I drank because I felt inadequate as a father and as a male, because I felt like a useless human being. I felt as if I had big hole in my chest, as if I was a hollow tree.

I finally wanted to change, and with the help of a friend the change began. I stopped drinking but when I had been sober only a couple of months I realized I was filled with both old anger and new anger. My feelings were twisted and they disturbed my vision. It was as if I was the fourteen-year-old child who had begun drinking twenty-five years before.

At that time I got a new job in the department: I was responsible for improving human relations between my Indian and white co-workers. Through this job I met some Indian elders, or spiritual leaders. I asked them to come into the department to use native philosophy to improve the work-place climate. In the process they helped me to learn to stay sober and to learn that I, and no one else, was responsible for my own life. They helped me to become a useful human being. They also taught me how to pray, something I hadn't done in years.

For the white man, who has other traditions, our spiritual customs, principles, rituals, and tools may seem deeply symbolic, but perhaps *his* traditions are remote to many of us.

One of the life-giving tools I made use of in finding myself again and rebuilding my life was the sweetgrass. With my sobriety came guilt, anger, and fear. They were to control me. I felt guilty about losing my family, losing my arm, losing so much time and so many opportunities. But the elders gave me the sweetgrass, a wild grass found on the prairies, on Manitoulin Island and near Curve Lake, Ontario, for my anger and my guilt. It is braided as hair is braided, then it is burned by an elder. It gives off a sweet odour, cleaning mind, body, and spirit. It represents honesty and kindness, the simple honesty and kindness of young children. I used the sweet-grass to heal myself.

The elders also gave me what is known as "the hub," or the central principle of our spiritual life. Life without the influence of the hub can be one of not caring – about appearance, job, children, or self. Such a life is full of fear, jealousy, envy, and resentment. The positive side of the hub is the opposite of these things, just as the opposite of caring is not caring. It is possible to learn to respect both self and others, to trust, to be at peace. In my drinking days I was very impatient. I did not even have the patience to sit still and be with another human being. I didn't feel I was equal to anyone. I could not see the beauty and the grace of the simple things in life – the voice of a child or the soft sound of the wind blowing in the summer-time.

Now I have learned to care and show others that I care: I don't have to play games. I can be just plain old Herb, I can build up my fire, my affections. But it is as slow as carving a statue – it takes many days and months of chipping away at the edges to produce grace and beauty. I look at the word "respect." Its literal meaning is "to look twice." If I look twice at myself I see that I am a good person, but I am capable of fear and violence. I think this is true of everybody who walks the earth. But it is through my weaknesses that I learn to teach myself to be strong.

The four directions of the compass are also important to us. It is our belief that caring is symbolized by the north. When the strong north wind blows in, its clean air is a life-giver: it is a master of movement and it moves everything on our planet, Mother Earth.

When the east wind comes our way the earth begins to get warmer. Everything is healed and all life is reborn in the season of spring that it brings. One of creatures reborn then is the moose, the symbol for food in the Ojibway culture. The moose provides us with clothes, tools from her bones, meat, snowshoes. The moose is a life-giver, too. A long time ago my grandmother told me that the earth was our garden, made for us by our Creator. It was up to us to live in harmony in our garden. When we took from Mother Earth to feed ourselves, we should always put something back.

Late in the spring, the soft south wind comes. The sun teaches me patience when it is at high noon because I must seek out the shade of a tree and wait. Patience teaches me to respect the people I resent. The sun reminds me of our Creator. But I must remember that the sun doesn't only shine for Indians. It shines for everybody. This is what my grandmother told me a long time ago.

When the west wind comes, fall is near, and with it, winter. Water is also a symbol of the west and also a symbol of the power to see. I use my two eyes to look twice at things, to reason.

The sweetgrass, the hub, and the four directions were passed on to me by the elders. They kept this knowledge so that I might find a way to live today. They taught me how to pray, to live with the Spirit, and how to get close to nature. In my first year of sobriety I was invited by the elders to come into the mountains near Calgary to pray the traditional native way. We fasted for four days and four nights – no food or water. I prayed for honest and simple caring while I was on the fast. Afterwards I felt clean, as if something had been washed away. On my second fast, I was alone near Ottawa. I was always afraid to be alone in the bush: this time I wanted to meet my fear face to face. I realized that I was nothing without the Great Spirit. On my third fast I was with a friend. It was then I fasted for a good relationship with myself. I shared my feelings with my friend. We made a sacred fire and we talked. I still hadn't found the plateau I was reaching for but I felt even cleaner.

I fasted a fourth time, this time for respect. Respect for myself to look twice at myself and to look twice at all human beings on earth. I fasted for three days and three nights without food or water. It was a good fast. I felt very close to myself. I was at peace.

As I understand it now I fasted for the four directions – for the north, or movement and caring; for the east, for feelings and vision; for the south and relationships and for time itself; for the west for respect and reason. I thank the Great Spirit for the four directions.

I was powerless when I was drinking and my life fell apart. I had no control when it came to taking a drink. The elders told me that if I wanted my power back I must reflect on my past and examine my weaknesses and strengths thoroughly. My first act of honesty was to admit that I was powerless over alcohol. When I admitted my weaknesses I started to grow in strength. If you walk into the bush there are different shapes of trees, different sizes of trees. Some are tall and straight, some are crooked and misshapen. When I walk the sweetgrass road I like to be tall and straight like a tree. But if I'm living dishonestly, I will be a crooked tree and that tree will represent me.

My father passed away on July 1, 1982. His gift to me was his honesty. His strength was his honesty and his kindness, a tough kindness. When he asked me to leave after I lost my arm he didn't want me to become dependent on his kindness. If I went fishing every day and I gave my neighbour a fish as an expression of my kindness, after a period of time he would come to expect the kindness. But if I took him to the lake and showed him how to fish this would be a different, more productive expression of my kindness. And my father once told me, "Whatever you do in life, do not compromise your honesty." I forgot about his gift for many years; now I have recaptured it.

The four virtues of honesty, kindness, sharing, and building on my spiritual strength are part of my values today. When I was drinking my values were greed, hate, revenge, and personal ambition. Now I do things not out of fear but out of goodness. I try not to judge other people and I try to give unconditionally. The moment I attach conditions to my caring and to my giving, it is no longer giving and sharing. The best sacrifices are the small ones.

You shouldn't speak about helping another. If it works quietly, it works better.

I'm grateful for this life today and I feel I have been reborn with the help of the elders and traditional native culture. It has been painful, but it has been good. I'm grateful for the hub, the four directions, Mother Earth, and the grandfathers. Thank you, Great Spirit.

Herb Nabigon
Toronto

I am driving around the bleak, far edge of Toronto in the ancient Mazda wondering, among other things, what I'll tell the listeners of *Morningside* about my life since the day seventeen months ago when – a sick and frankly deranged alcoholic – I crawled into a Montreal hospital to dry out and get straight.

I am no longer wild about being a nationally known drunk and I've lost all appetite for the confessional. And I wonder if the people I heard from – Wally in the Yukon, Lise in Laval, Ray in Cape Breton, and all the others trying to break one kind of bad habit or another – wouldn't be better off without the latest chapter in the soap opera.

Then, on a bridge over the Don Valley Parkway, I see her looming out of the damp and grey Saturday afternoon. She's wearing a flowing white robe with a home-made look and a kind of tiara spangled with tinfoil stars. Nestled in the angle of her right arm is a long staff and she's staring down into the teeming, whizzing highway blessing the traffic – a dip of her splendid shepherd's crook for every Chevrolet, a queenly wave for every Volvo, a little benediction for each passing Dodge. She seems happy and comfortable in her mission and for some reason she makes me think of the truth. Why not just tell Wally and Lise and Ray the truth?

The idea seems novel. But the truth is simple enough and might as well be told. Since I had my last drink on October 4, 1984, I had two more drinks. No just two drinks but two *evenings* of drinks, once at Christmas, two Christmases ago, and another time in an airport shut in by fog and a long way from town. It tasted bad and it didn't even work. So since then I have avoided Christmas and airports – those twin museums of lonely hearts. And when those moments come again – and they still do – I set out on forced marches of twenty miles, phone somebody who knows the territory, and cruise from one meeting of Alcoholics Anonymous to another.

I won't say anything about AA now: I've come to see all these hours of intense and amazing grace in church basements and club-house back rooms as something like cell meetings, ones where the only revolution being contemplated is the revolution of the self. The anonymity of AA goes far beyond simple discretion. But it works. You can't do it alone. And since you only live twice you had better not even try.

No, the hard part is learning how to live again. If you have been a stealthy, solitary boozer for a quarter of a century, you come to with the emotional equipment of an adolescent who hasn't yet discovered beer. Quick frozen, on hold.

I am down from the hills but still in hiding. And it's going to take years. But for the first time I'm someone I don't recognize, someone different.

So here is my other truth. It is, like all these stories, deeply maudlin and maybe self-serving, but since it is my only real accomplishment I'll tell it. Even soap opera has its own integrity.

Every one of the thousand or so fellow addicts I've met since 1984 tells a story that may be different in texture but the same in substance. It has to do with parents and children, one generation following the other and always repeating the same mistakes. My own father and I never spoke more than ten words to each other at a time. And these conversations were grim – they had all the flavour and fun of the Geneva arms talks. I catch myself doing the same with my own kids. I don't know why it happens that way, it just does.

Anyway, I remember him now, many years later, in only one setting, waist deep in the middle of the Beaver River north of Toronto, fishing for speckled trout. I am watching him from the dark forest behind – this beautiful and mysterious man who always competed in everything, even fishing. He always had to have the first fish, the biggest fish, the most fish. And here, in this moment I have in my mind's eye, I see him easing the trout towards him, cradling them in his hands, and then, contrary to everything I had ever thought possible, letting them slip back into the stream in a way that seemed to me, that far-off day, to awaken all nature.

That cool and quiet image led to something better. The day before he died, choking on the plastic tube that had replaced his throat, he began to write me a letter. All he was able to write was the date – December 1, 1966, and my name. For almost twenty years I carried that little morsel of paper next to me, wondering what the rest of it would have said. Then, not long ago, sober, and somehow less afraid than I have ever been, I put that piece of paper away with all the other little bits and pieces – because I finally figured out what it said. It was, of course, a benediction. "Goodbye," it said. "God Bless. Peace. Pass it on."

Glen Allen

SNOW ANGELS AND BLACK ICE

The collection of letters *Morningside* has received about winter over the years has a beginning that's just as clear as the various stories about dukes and forks. David Nadeau, a school teacher from Swan River, Manitoba (I've deduced that from what he's written; I've never met him), wrote the first of the two I've retained here in January of 1986, and on the margin of his original you can still see my scribbled note, wondering if other people might have other things to say about our most characteristic season. I wondered aloud, too, on the radio, and for each of the next two winters people have written about their memories and sensations. There's no real pattern to the responses I've chosen to publish; in subject matter they range from the colours of snow shadows to memories of a boy's cold behind in Newfoundland, and in their points of origin from Victoria to the Arctic. As with so many subjects that appear in these pages, these are just the pieces – or, in some cases, the parts of pieces – I've particularly liked. And, with the same criterion, I've put in some poems.

⊠ It was nearly forty below today, January sixth, and I wanted to share something of our winter in a small northern Manitoba community. I live in Swan River, a town of about five thousand, with my family. It is about three hundred miles north and west of Winnipeg, and, believe me, that is a long seven-hour drive in December.

As I stepped outside to go to school this morning (I am an elementary-school teacher) the first thing that struck me was how *deep* a cold it was. It reminded me of a bus trip I took with my family to Toronto from Saskatchewan in 1981. The bus would pull into some snowbound little gas station in the middle of Northern Ontario and we would pile off the bus despite the intense cold for a chance to stretch our legs and buy some confections. Surrounded by huge snowbanks and trees, the stillness dominated, even over the rumble of the big bus engine. It was like that here this morning in Swan River. Dead quiet and so peacefully calm and still. As I unplugged the car, the CP yard engine two blocks away at the Cargil elevator blew its horn as it shuttled across Main Street. The horn carried so clearly with such a hollow resonance that it sounded as if the train was right next door.

One other thing about living here that might interest your listeners: Mother lives ten miles east of Swan River in Minitonas, a very small farming village. The weather this past week was certainly too cold for her to go out; she is nearly eighty. So when we visited for dinner after church on Sunday, she asked if we would check her house. We agreed. Mother lives in a seniors' chalet and has kept her old frame house, so she has a garden and a measure of independence in summer. The snow around the vacant two-bedroom house was very deep and had not been marred by foot-steps. But in the days when she lived there, neatly chiselled paths would cut from the door of the house to the woodshed and the outdoor washroom. But now, the drifts on the porch had to be kicked through just to get the door open and ice had to be carefully chipped out of the lock with a penknife.

Inside the house, it was very quiet and very cold. No wind rattled the loose windows and none of her grandchildren (my little ones) raced from room to room. On the round table Dad had made many years before his death lay the shreds of forgotten dill and two very yellow and very frozen cucumbers. As I looked around the kitchen, I noted that the big wood range was loaded and ready to be fired. Even the wooden matches were still in the right place on the wall.

Then to the basement. The furnace looked fine, lots of oil in the tank. Carrots, poorly covered, frozen solid. Potatoes, poor scabby things, were well blanketed and had survived.

The basement tour of duty is quickly accomplished and I go back upstairs, turning off the lights. I take a last hurried look around and am glad to be leaving. And I am glad to be outside where my young family waits in the warm car. I lock up carefully, kick some more snow off the porch. Why? I don't know. Then I wade through the drifts again, past the white lawn and its buried peonies, back to the street. My winter duty is done, and I gratefully slip the key back into my pocket as I reach for the car door.

David Nadeau
Swan River, Manitoba

✉ We are wintering over at the eastern end of Lake Athabasca, en route across Canada by canoe. When I wake during the long blackness of night, I hear the cabin creak and snap and pop like a wooden ship on a rough passage. Cold seeps through the walls insidiously. We burrow naked and pale as new-born bear cubs under a pile of blankets.

If there is a time during the day when despair creeps easily through my defences, it is in the gauzy light of pre-dawn. The clock ticks loudly on the corner window sill. Wide awake, the cold pressing on my face, self-doubts skate on the thin ice of my assurance.

But the rigours of rising are cathartic. My blood surges to combat the cold, clearing leaden thoughts away. I coax red embers to flame. They consume first the kindling, then the dry, split jack pine. Jack pine felled and cut and dragged out of the woods in the colourful days of fall, when the blackflies still clouded your face. Jack pine cut on a home-made saw-horse and split with the three-pound axe, an axe wielded with increasing accuracy as the cordwood stack grew against the cabin.

The first cup of coffee fits in my hand. The clock ticks. Out the window the blue-white ice on the bay runs hard into the black-green line of spruce on the far shore. The quiet northern day begins slowly.

Our chores are simple and minimal, but we have time and spread out the little tasks so that they are major landmarks on the daily vista. In the age of space shuttles, microchips, and video entertainment centres, our concerns are fundamental. Little has changed when you peel back the encrustations of technology. Water, shelter, warmth, food. Our daily concerns.

Leaving the cabin is no light matter. Heavy socks, mukluks, long underwear, wool pants, shirts, sweater, coat, mitts, a heavy hat; a dressing challenge worthy of an attendant. In time, we waddle outside, our breath marking our progress. We follow pathways beaten through the snow, trails as unimaginative as cattle ploddings to the water-hole. Paths made hard as marble by the cold.

Even if we don't need water immediately, we chop through the lake ice each day. In two days' time, the crust becomes thick and hard. We stand on the lake, big dark animals away from cover, and pound on the ice. When we break through, the water bubbles up as if expelling breath. The pool of water makes clearing the rest of the hole a messy job and we risk splashing ourselves, turning our pant cuffs into icy ankle bracelets. We fill our buckets and tote them home, only the plastic containers and the bright red child's sled distinguishing us from the peasantry of the Middle Ages.

The chores are our ritual, the skeleton on which we hang the day. Moving and splitting wood, filling lanterns with fuel, preparing meals, feeding the dog. Around them we flesh out the hours by following our own mysterious urgings: scratchings on paper, letters to friends, reading, or gazing through the falling snow, thinking.

Each day we go for a walk. The cold moving air acts like a cleanser, Comet for the soul. Sometimes we slide along on the frozen lake, peering into the holes the muskrats make in the ice. On other days we follow trails through the softened forest and find wonderful open knolls of rock, or take guided tours laid out by weasels, their tracks erratic and broken by leaps. Our feet crunch as we walk. The air feels antiseptic in our throats. Our eyes water. By the time we return, our cheeks are brittle as a china doll's. It's dark enough to light the lantern.

With the stove going in the cabin, the heat gets fierce. We peel off layers until we're doing dishes bare-chested. Outside the wall it's thirty-eight below. We open the door for relief and a fog of cold swoops in like a wintery ghost.

On the radio, announcers remind us of our other life – theatre, sports, politics, and the strangely severed news of famine and Dow Jones closing prices. It is as if we have been amputated, separated from the larger body. How will it be when we are attached again?

Our lamp light is rationed, a self-imposed austerity, and after the hiss of the lamp is gone, we hunch around the candlelight to read. The little clock ticks. Outside the cold tightens its grip. The cabin glows.

Alan Kesselheim
Fond-du-Lac, Saskatchewan

✉ I've weathered the storms and Chinooks
    Of Alberta
  And slogged my way through Manitoba's
    blustery cities.

I have skidded and slithered
  Through the slush and freeze
Of Quebec and Ontario,
  New York State and Ohio.

And plodded through the sleet and snow
  Of Illinois and Minnesota,
Missouri and South Dakota.

But nowhere in the world
  Does snow dryly crackle and crunch
And sparkle underfoot
  As in Saskatchewan

And nowhere in the world
  Have I enjoyed making
Angels in the snow
  As I have in the hushed
Blue-black, velvety cold
  Winter nights in Regina.

I was young then
  And in love.
I could reach out
And almost touch the sky
  In that clear, crisp moonlight,

And almost pluck
  A handful of stars
To sprinkle in my hair.
Oh! to be in love again
  And make angels in the snow.

Florence E. Brodie
Toronto

✉ Thirty-five years ago, when I was a lad growing up on the
north-east coast of Newfoundland, winter was a matter of survival.

Especially for the adults, it was a time of hardship and isolation. We were cut off from medical services, regular supplies, and other members of the human race. Those of us who were younger had our own little problems, of course, but the greatest hardship of them all is still printed indelibly on my mind.

The outdoor toilet.

At home it wasn't too bad. Somewhere in a closet there might be a slop pail, and under the bed a nice warm chamber pot. When the blizzards roared in from the sea and nature felt constrained to call in the wee small hours, the pot and the pail were alternatives. But there were hazards. With the ground frozen solid, we some-times emptied the slop pail off the head of the wharf so that the tides could do what the flush toilet now emulates. Imagine giving the contents of said pail a mighty heave out over the water just as a strong gust of wind sees fit to strike you square in the face.

At school it was another matter. The school board erected a fine two-compartment outhouse – a two-holer, we called it. This edifice had been built in our grandparents' day and bore sad witness to the ravages of time. But what was left of it was always given a fresh coat of whitewash every fall, and the catalogues from Eaton's and Simpson's were never allowed to run out completely.

The knots in the boards separating the boys' half from the girls' had long ago loosened from the grip of the surrounding wood, but to the credit of several generations of young scholars, not one of these knots had been lost. They were the key to our sex education.

Outhouses weren't all that unpopular in early fall and late spring. Apart from a certain pervasive thickness in the air, one could cheer-fully spend considerable time scanning the pages of our toilet paper or making full use of the knots.

In the dead of winter, however, the school outhouse was another story. The basement was not protected by R-12 pink insulation. In fact, just enough of the original foundation remained to keep the structure precariously off the ground and remind it of past glories. The wind constantly whistled through under the seats. In summer, this breeze had a welcome hygienic effect, but in the frosty days of February, a strong draft of polar air swept up from the frozen wastes and poured through the opening in the seat.

We young innocents had to lower our bare buttocks over this hole, exposing them to a wind-chill factor of minus God-knows-what. If nature directed that you remain in this position for longer than thirty seconds, a certain numbing sensation began to creep into your external organs. When you got to the point of no sensation at all, even with one of the larger knotholes in use, you knew that it was time to depart. The pain came later while you were sitting at your desk and things started to warm up and "come back to life." Boys who had been forced to go to the outhouse on cold days could easily be identified later in class by their anguished expressions, the groans that sometimes escaped tightly compressed lips, and the constant squirming in the seat. Even the strictest teacher said nothing. He had to use the outhouse, too.

When we grew old enough to understand such things, we did formulate a hypothesis that most of us were able to prove in our adult years. Exposure to perishing cold does nothing to inhibit the begetting capacity of the male reproductive system.

Edward A. Smith
Springdale, Newfoundland

✉ Some childish winter pleasures survive into adulthood. Like sucking on an icicle. Stuffing snow down someone's neck. Or standing over a heat register on a cold morning feeling your nightgown balloon around you, trapping the warm air.

Maureen McCandless
Toronto

✉ Winter is like a piece of fresh white paper awaiting the vibrant brush-strokes of spring.

Yvonne Whelan
Toronto

✉ Snow lends a different kind of definition to what we usually take for granted.

Sian Warwick
Toronto

✉ Winter is the chrysalis of the soul.

Norm Esdon
Wolfe Island, Ontario

✉ It's fun watching nature kick the hell out of our technologically civilized world by . . . just snowing.

Gerald MacDonald
Halifax

✉ I wonder if we, with our fragile technologies, will ever learn to deal with winter as simply or as elegantly as the wild animals.

David Allan Galbraith
Guelph, Ontario

✉ Winter gives us polite conversation in elevators.

Laurie Blanchard
Winnipeg

✉ Snow covers all the warts.

Dawn Crabtree
Portage La Prairie, Manitoba

✉ First snow is one of the most magical moments of the year for me. You awake one morning to find a world transformed; sharp corners softened, harsh noises muted.

I grew up in Stratford, in the heart of Ontario's snow belt. We were studying colour in our grade-seven art class when the teacher asked, "What colour are the shadows in the snow?" The man had little time for anyone who could now even draw a respectable stick figure and I had nothing to lose. I raised my hand. "Blue," I said.

Snow should never be dismissed as merely white. Look across a farmer's field. Observe the subtleties of a shadow coloured from slate grey to mauve. Sunlight through a single flake sparkling in a snow bank or caught in a window screen can reveal the spectrum of a rainbow. On a late winter afternoon, the sun can set the snow on fire.

I love snow best in a storm. Countless winter nights, I have lain in bed willing the wind to blow and the snow to keep falling, praying that they would have to close the schools. My sister and I would take turns throwing back the warm covers to run to the window and make a progress report. On stormy mornings, we'd wake up early just to listen to the cancellations, dressing slowly, hoping that the appropriate authorities would come to their senses and let us stay home.

Older now, I am more guarded in my love affair with winter, but there is still something special about a storm. There is a magic rekindling of the Christmas spirit. Perfect strangers greet each other, commenting on the weather as they trudge through drifts on the way to buy milk or a paper. People gather to push cars with spinning wheels and many open their homes to the stranded. In the aftermath, neighbours with snow blowers become gallant balaclavaed knights rushing to the rescue of the less well-equipped. There is a community pride in having made it through a crisis, the bond of a common experience.

In case you find my enthusiasm something close to nauseating, let me assure you there is justice. I was married this winter on one of the stormiest days of the year and a number of guests weren't able to make it through the blizzard. I caught a cold, too, tiptoeing through the snow banks in my high heels, which I insisted on wearing in spite of parental protests. Still, I would not wish away our Canadian winter. We may not have heroes or an aggressive self-confidence in this country, but we are survivors.

Julie Misener
Stratford, Ontario

✉ The first stage of winter in Pond Inlet, a small Inuit settlement on the north end of Baffin Island, where my husband and infant son and I moved in 1975, began in September. This is a time when snow is permanently on the land again, but the sea ice has not yet formed. It can be a time of wind and storms, of fog emanating from open water. It can also be a time of special beauty, with magnificent sunsets over the distant mountains curving around to the north-west.

The onset of real winter came with the freezing up of the sea ice, and a steady decrease in daylight. In early November, the sun rose briefly at noon one day, and then failed to show at all the following day, even though the sky brightened hopefully. That first winter, I was obsessed with the absence of the sun, and as the days marched on towards Christmas, there ceased to be daylight of any kind at all. Things were never right with me during the dark season. At the very core of my psyche, I was out of sync. Depression came easily. The winter solstice became an important occasion in my life, and I would await its arrival as though it were my birthday. At that point we had finished heading *into* the dark season. The earth was on its inevitable roll towards summer, and I never failed to celebrate the occasion.

In spite of the perpetual dark doldrums, I discovered that in the waning twilight of November, and again as it slowly grew towards sunrise in February, there were moments of wonderful, ethereal beauty. When the weather was clear, the little spell of twilight that came around noon was a moment I would look forward to for the boost of spirit it always gave me. My husband would be on his way back to work after lunch, the baby tucked in for his nap, and I would slip out into the back porch, facing south-west. The bitter air would wash over me and I would breathe it in slowly and deeply. The sky would be filled with every subtle variation of lavender and mauve, and the ghostly mountains on Bylot seemed to glow with the absorbed light and colour of the sky. The beauty was timeless and austere, perfection almost too pure to hear. I would stand there until the cold became too painful, usually only a few minutes, then I would slip back into the house.

Dodie Eyer
Clinton, British Columbia

✉ It's the sweet smug feeling of victory I enjoy every spring that makes winter appealing to me.

Each November, all my natural instincts cry out for a warm, safe place to hide for the next three or four months. Our furry friends the bears have the right idea, because they know what's coming and they behave as any sane mammal should.

But come April, when I have once again survived the terror of black ice, not just survived but wrestled it to the ground by reaching my desired destination safely and in a car that refused to be mortally wounded by the minus forty degrees of the previous night, I feel great.

I regard winter as a substitute for an aerobics class at the Y. When it tries to suffocate me with mountains of snow, I laugh in its face: *Haw!* and move that snow out of my way. When I've shovelled it into submission I feel strong. I feel invincible!

In a culture that affords us few opportunities for physical victory, I look forward each year to the challenge of our winter, and every spring I celebrate and carve another notch on my shovel. This one will make the score: Janet 49; Winter, 0!

Janet Bruce
Ottawa

✉ As a boy I went out every morning to give myself a thorough wash with cold water in a trough, even when I first had to smash the ice with a hammer. Since 1972, I have been living on a small island in Newfoundland. I resumed the old habit here, washing every morning naked in a brook that runs through my property. Two years ago, when I was forty-eight, my wife persuaded me to wash thenceforth in the house. Within half a year, I had trouble with my eyes, developing spots in them that blurred my vision.

It took me a while to discover that the only thing that seemed to improve my eyes was lots of cold water on my head and neck. I am washing outside again now, every morning. I did so today, a mid-winter's day with a temperature of eight degrees Fahrenheit and westerly winds of about thirty knots. Wearing only socks and rubber boots, an old parka and my towel, I made my way to the bottom of the frozen brook, where the rising and falling of the salt water breaks up the ice and allows me access to a bit of fresh water between the rocks.

I threw my parka off and splashed a lot of cold water over myself. And when I dried myself I took notice that the sky was of a beautiful Mediterranean blue, and that, in the wads of seaweed the last storm had driven in the cove, there were strands of coral: red and gold and eggshell blue and chick yellow. Where I stood, out of the wind, in the sun, it was actually quite warm. It seemed to me that there were an unusual number of birds around, and that they all had an air of cheerful bustle.

When I came into the kitchen, I declared, "I can feel spring in the air!"

My wife laughed: "On the seventh of February? With all that bitter cold? And the radio forecasting another snowstorm for Tuesday!"

I don't care. I tell you, I can feel spring in the air!

Randy Lieb
Swift Current, Newfoundland

✉ Surrounded by open meadow, hills, and mountains instead of grey, slushy cityscapes, I love winter. Gone are the green frills and furbelows of summer; the bones of this elegant world are there to see. I never tire of the lean poplar limbs; each twig is unique. Pines surprise me every year by taking on, in their blackness, a resemblance to the finest Japanese paintings. A dead elegance? Not at all. Chickadees and whisky jacks boldly risk the dozing cat for a bit of grain. At its darkest hour, winter solitude brings my favourite winter visitor: a cow moose who comes to browse off the red willow and to bum hay at the barn. I find myself doing dusk chores, like getting in heater wood, at four in the afternoon, but the siege of cold and darkness has its special consolations: I sleep in the mornings and get to have coffee with Peter Gzowski! Winter is my season to be most in touch with the rest of the world; I make the acquaintance of Chris Czajkowski via Toronto. It is too far to go fifty miles down the road to meet her! I feel close to her anyway, when I hear that the storm that stopped her supply plane was the same one that isolated me. It ripped out my radio-antenna tree and left me without the CBC for weeks. Only when that sort of thing happens do I feel the ills of winter, and even in a storm comes hope: the storm was a chinook, the first herald of spring weather.

The Chinese are right to make the depths of February their New Year, their spring festival. By then, it isn't just a declaration of hope. Poplar branches have lost their slim elegance; they look old, knobby and gnarled, but it is because new young buds are swelling on them. Pines are green again; the woods look like young seedlings in the morning sun. Even romance comes back. Whisky jacks come close to melody in their courtship. My rabbits pursue each other in their yard, huddling no longer in sheltered corners. Even the cat stirs at last from beside the heater, and hauls in his first mouse of the season. The second chinook brings a first spring ritual, cleaning up after the dog, his fell deeds exposed in the shrinking snow back around the house. I am amazed by the smoked-up windows, and scrub them clear. Morning begins a whole two hours earlier!

Everything is stirring now. The great crescendo of spring is building up, accelerating. I love our winter. It has the inexorable force and drama of Handel's *Messiah*. December is the still "Shepherds lying in their fields," February is a rousing "Hallelujah Chorus." Winter gives the time to watch the world changing and to become quite mystical.

Penny Simpson
Tatla Lake, British Columbia

✉ Others can boast about the joys of winter – freezing their butts ice fishing, breaking legs on the ski hills, the terror of hearing the furnace make a strange noise when the weather is twenty below, and all those other peculiar habits of the true Canadian. But I have a visual problem and find the winter gives me the freedom to enjoy the nights I lose when the dark wet evenings of early spring and late fall arrive.

For those who suffer from night blindness, tunnel vision, a cataract, or some other visual impairment (and I have most of them), the snow serves us very well.

When there's snow on the ground I can walk safely to the bus station at night, or even to the Miner's Home Hotel, and stagger back. The snow provides a clear division between garden fences and sidewalks. It provides contrast on steps, and it acts as a reflector for street lights.

Fresh snow can be a nuisance on a bright and sunny day, when you walk into a snow bank because you can't tell where the flat ground ends; but it is a minor problem, once kids, dogs, and cars provide a few tracks.

Yes, I love the beauty of a northern Ontario winter, and I enjoy boasting to my southern friends and English relatives about the cold and the storms, none of which are as bad as I like to pretend. But for me, the advent of spring means carrying a powerful flashlight, walking into telephone posts, stumbling on curbs, or not going out at night without my wife.

Snow provides a measure of security and liberty for me. One of those fringe benefits of winter that few understand or appreciate.

John R. Hunt
Cobalt, Ontario

✉ When I was young, winter did not really arrive until our lake froze solid enough for skating. If we were lucky, the first sub-zero temperatures came on a still night, with no wind. Then the ice froze so clear you could see straight through it. We call it black ice and skating on it is an experience you never forget.

Skating on black ice is like skating on calm water. You can actually see sticks and clam shells in the sand beneath you. Weeds, frozen into twisted mats, reach upwards like turrets in a science-fiction city.

My dad would go out first, with a hatchet, to test the thickness of the ice. His words of wisdom on the subject of safe ice were these:

> One inch – no way
> Two inches – one may
> Three inches – small groups
> Four inches – okay

When he was satisfied the ice was safe, my sister and I squeaked across the beach in our skate guards. Our first steps offshore were tippy-toe movements on the points of our figure skates, then a cautious slide, then full gliding steps as our confidence in the ice increased.

On black ice, the more you skate the more you feel like skating. You want to fly over the preserved water world like dancing wood sprites: the kind with lithe figures and skirts made of multicoloured scarves. So you unleash yourself from the firm knot of your muffler and let the fresh air flood your cheeks till your nostrils squeak in protest.

All day, people come from basement doors on skates they haven't used for years. When the lake freezes black, the entire community stretches across the lake like a flock of birds, dipping and gliding together. A wiggling hound bounds behind the crowd, losing distance each time his back legs slip out from underneath him.

And in some kitchen along the shore there's a pot of chocolate on the stove and enough hot dogs to feed the whole group.

It's the kind of day you can't plan: it just happens. But not enough, I think.

Susan Pryke
Gravenhurst, Ontario

✉ I love winter clothes, I love the comfort of a lined wool skirt; the warmth of a fine wool turtleneck, and the elegance of a wool jacket.

I love black and navy and camel, colours that only work well in wool, in winter.

I love high leather boots and kid gloves. I love the lines of a tailored winter coat. I love hats and scarves and shawls.

Winter clothes fit and hang better. They are more classic. They last for several years and still look good. I like having winter clothes professionally cleaned and pressed. It cuts down on the laundry and ironing.

Patricia Cavill
Strathmore, Alberta

✉ In winter, one of the drawbacks of having no running water is the difficulty of bathing. It takes ten four-gallon buckets of water and about a half hour of steady pumping to fill the old bathtub, which is set up on cement blocks conveniently near the pump, and at least an hour of stoking a hot fire under it to bring the water up to a comfortable temperature. Ah, but once it's ready, what a splendid way to bathe, surrounded by the forest in snow, and immersed to the neck in hot water! The air is still very cold, so the fire has to be well-banked and fed before you get in, or it dies down and the water begins to cool. One sits on a piece of board in the tub, to protect one's lower regions from the hot cast iron. And you mustn't wash your hair first; otherwise your head freezes. But bearing these things in mind, there is nothing like a bath outside in winter.

Muriel K. Sibley
Victoria, British Columbia

✉ Winter made me first person, present tense, active voice.

For three years I travelled a bush road in northern Alberta as a nurse. I could write a chapter on the different ways smoke came out of the chimneys, and how to tell the weather from the way it hung close to the roofs or drifted in thin, white streams into a pale sky. I loved the ritual of dressing: putting longjohns on first, smoothing socks so there were no lumps to catch in boots, dressing in layers – having to do everything in exactly the right order. I took pride that this woman from Louisiana could travel alone in the bush when the temperature was minus thirty-eight. I wore a spare set of car keys on a shoestring around my neck so I couldn't accidentally drop them in the snow. Each morning I bounced on the frozen car seat, warmed the car, scraped the windshield. Snow blew in fine cold powder through the open window as I checked the survival kit and sleeping bag in the back.

Once, I spun out on black ice, blowing two tires and ending up in a ditch. I called on the mobile for help, but it was two hours of minus forty before the tow truck could reach me. I took out the stove and made tea and later chicken soup, and knew I could stay there all night if I had to.

Winter became familiar to me. I learned what it was like to come home to houses with warm yellow squares against the night. I knew the people living in the houses, knew their children and dogs and sometimes their secrets. We bound ourselves together, intertwining our lives and our gossip as protection against the cold.

Once, over beers in a skid camp, as I sat exchanging stories with three truckers, I realized I'd become a northerner.

Sharon Grant
Edmonton

✉ Winter Haiku

Deciduous trees
upturned egg whips
stored for spring

Two cats sit
back to back like bookends inside
the frost-trimmed window

Sun-polished snow
the black crow circles
a shadow moves

Driving all night
our headlights part the darkness
not the falling snow

Winona Baker
Nanaimo, British Columbia

✉ Winter: From a Train Window

Blue shadows from a copse slant icily
Across the afternoon's wind-drifted snow;
Champagne-glass elms, now bare, or dead perhaps,
Stand tall, alone, above the brittle reeds.
A train with mournful sound pursues the sun,
With every mile deserting some bright glimpse

Of winter, or dry relics of fall,
Or thoughts of coming spring, all newly green.
Do we, like trains, moan one-track-mindedly,
Through glorious winter moments of our lives?
Winter has dignity and needs more time
To love than April's passion, or Autumn gold.
  Winter's brilliance is, as well, a peace.
  Allowing memories and hope to ease.

Julia Ross Campbell
Ottawa

✉ I have a memory of a rare reflective moment I experienced as a twelve-year-old one winter's afternoon. A friend and I had been working our way home from school by way of flying leaps into every large snow bank, and I suddenly thought – "I'm not going to be able to do this much longer." In another year or so, I realized, such activity would not only be considered beneath me, but would be *practically* impossible as I made my way sedately home from high school with my legs clad in silk stockings and my arms full of books. I yearned as much as any twelve-year-old does to be part of that world, but there was a fleeting moment of misgiving – and what triggered it was the thought of losing even a little bit of the enjoyment of winter!

Lois Lawrence
Ottawa

✉ In Saskatchewan during the depression, the farm families on relief were given salt cod from Newfoundland. The fillets were a good size – big enough for a boy's behind. The kids took them, flat and frozen, complete with tail for grip, and tobogganed down the hills.

Leslie Javorski
Vancouver

399

✉ Sanctuary

I am treasure hunting today
With my dog –
We've found a rope, a fishing float, a piece of argilite.
He's found a large mammalian bone.

We are seeking
The prized Japanese fishing float.
Hand-blown, green-blue bubbled glass.
With a bit of net, perhaps;
Having floated for years
On Pacific seas.

The beach lies frozen beneath my feet,
Miles and miles of untouched, untrammeled white,

Fragments of a thousand clams
Litter the shore
And glistening in the frost
Lie agates, carnelian, and jades.
Like a jeweller's bench in disarray.

The bitter howling wind
Takes my smoking breath away.
The spray is frozen on my cheeks.
No green glass balls for us today.

R. Gregory
Masset, Queen Charlotte Islands, British Columbia

✉ I am a school-bus driver in rural Saskatchewan. I've had my
share of sliding and shovelling, of three-hundred-metre visibility in
driving snow, of fighting though drifts. I've gone out into pitch-
black mornings at forty below with sixty kilometre winds, shivering
in long underwear, sweaters, snowmobile suit, and boots with two
pairs of socks.

But I've watched the soft glow of dawn slowly unfold to a jubi-lant blaze. I've seen bright, white fields, unmarred by humans, tell the secrets of rabbits and deer in their early scampers, while hawks stand sentinel on fence posts. The valiant sun with rainbow sun-dogs beams from a sky of a deeper blue than summer knows. The wind ripples the snow and fills the valleys with mighty waves. Sometimes fog coats the trees in lace and feathers.

Winter is part of our land – free, untamed, and exuberant. It breeds toughness and the determination to endure and overcome. Winter humbles us, teaching us to keep courage and caution in vital balance. And it urges us to enjoy *all* of life; to find purpose and pleasure in every challenge, to make ourselves a vital part of our environment and to open our spirits to divine beauty.

Ruth Lovelace
Rockglen, Saskatchewan

✉ This year, my winter ended on the second day of February. I was glad to see it go.

There had been signs of its coming departure, but they were no more than hints and poorly made promises. Like the man sharing the gas pumps at the Co-op, who declared he hardly needed to make a trip to Florida this year because we have been having such nice weather. Yes, we listen to the news and hear what kind of winter parts of Europe and Eastern Canada have been suffering. Our winter has been positively balmy by comparison.

Even my wife has been passing hints that our winter is on the wane. She has said it is noticeably brighter when she walks home from the store in the evening. Encouraging comments.

There have been other signs to give the suggestion that winter was fighting a losing cause.

The students at my school want to wear running shoes at recess, not big clumsy boots. Water has been running off the roof and puddling on the highway. People seem to be more talkative in the post-office foyer. It could only be that they, too, have sensed we are in the home stretch.

But my winter officially ended when the seed catalogue arrived on Tuesday.

All other tasks were laid aside for my thirty minutes of spring dreams. Of course, the pictures, large, glossy, and tempting, did not indicate that weeds, slugs, mosquitoes, and grimy sweat were written between each and every line of copy. Ah, that copy. Enticing descriptions and glowing accounts of "super sweet, very early northern varieties." But at this time of winter, who thinks of the warts and the sore backs and the rototiller, which bucks like a Bramah bull and roars like the Indy 500?

My reverie with the seed catalogue is always bigger than the order I will place and is certainly far larger than what actually goes into the soft, spring-warm soil.

David Nadeau
Swan River, Manitoba

✉ I am alone at the end of a mile-long lane, four feet deep in drifted snow, while a seemingly endless blizzard makes an opaque window to the world.

Where is the joy of winter?

I have time to write!

Margaret Fraser
Cambridge, Ontario

The people who did the work

In the five seasons I have been its host, *Morningside* has been produced by:

Glen Allen, Grace Anobile, Gino Apponi, Michael Crampton, James Cullingham, Doug Earl, Havoc Franklin, David Graham, Richard Handler, Jim Handman, Jim Littleton, Tom MacDonnell, Marjorie Nichol, Charlotte Odele, Peter Puxley, Susan Rogers, Beatrice Schriever, Tina Srebotnjak, Talin Vartanian, Hal Wake, and Nancy Watson, with occasional assistance from Ed Reed in Winnipeg, Jill Spelliscy in Regina, and Keith Watt in Edmonton.

They have been assisted by Lynda Hanrahan, Marlene Kane, Susan Kilburn, Eve McBride, Sandy McMurray, and Victoria Wilcox.

Production assistance has been by Janet Russell, Deborah Smith, and Carol Wells.

Technical production has been by Carol Ito, Jane Paterson, and Jim Summerfield.

Morningside's music has been produced by David Amer, Alan Guettel, and Carole Warren.

The senior producers have been Graham Hall, Patsy Pehleman, Renée Pellerin, Robert Prowse, and Beverley Reed.

The studio directors have been Gary Katz, Heather Matheson, Susan Perly, and Bruce Steele.

The executive producers have been Nicole Bélanger and Gloria Bishop.

Index of Authors